THE LITTLE IMMIGRANTS

THE LITTLE IMMIGRANTS

The Orphans
Who Came to Canada

New Edition

Kenneth Bagnell

THE DUNDURN GROUP
TORONTO · OXFORD

Design: Jennifer Scott
Printer: AGMV Marquis

National Library of Canada Cataloguing in Publication Data

Bagnell, Kenneth, 1934-
    The little immigrants : the orphans who came to Canada

New ed.
Includes bibliographical references and index.
ISBN 1-55022-370-5

1. Orphans--Canada--History. 2. Immigrant children--Canada--History. 3. Home children (Canadian immigrants) 4. Canada--Emigration and immigration--History. 5. Great Britain-- Emigration and immigration--History. 6. British--Canada--History. I. Title.

FC548.I4B33 2001   305.23'086'9450971   C2001-903395-8   F1034.B33 2001

1   2   3   4   5   05   04   03   02   01

THE CANADA COUNCIL | LE CONSEIL DES ARTS
FOR THE ARTS | DU CANADA
SINCE 1957 | DEPUIS 1957

Canadä

ONTARIO ARTS COUNCIL
CONSEIL DES ARTS DE L'ONTARIO

We acknowledge the support of the **Canada Council for the Arts** and the **Ontario Arts Council** for our publishing program. We also acknowledge the financial support of the **Government of Canada** through the **Book Publishing Industry Development Program** and **The Association for the Export of Canadian Books**, and the **Government of Ontario** through the **Ontario Book Publishers Tax Credit** program.

Care has been taken to trace the ownership of copyright material used in this book. The author and the publisher welcome any information enabling them to rectify any references or credit in subsequent editions.

J. Kirk Howard, President

Printed and bound in Canada.
Printed on recycled paper.
www.dundurn.com

Dundurn Press	Dundurn Press	Dundurn Press
8 Market Street	73 Lime Walk	2250 Military Road
Suite 200	Headington, Oxford,	Tonawanda NY
Toronto, Ontario, Canada	England	U.S.A. 14150
M5E 1M6	OX3 7AD	

THE LITTLE IMMIGRANTS

Table of Contents

Preface
by Roy MacLaren*

In 1980 Kenneth Bagnell wrote a remarkable book. *The Little Immigrants* was both a lively and a reliable account of the history of the migration of British children to Canada and elsewhere in the Empire. Child migration, promoted by the pioneering Dr. Barnardo and by a variety of church groups, was in the 1920s discouraged and finally terminated by the British Government, following mounting misgivings about the reported abuse and exploitation of children on the farms and in the workshops of the Empire. As recently as the year 2000, a committee of the British House of Commons attempted to assess the impact on the children of their forced migration as "surplus population". In part, they uncovered and recorded, as Kenneth Bagnell had done already, a not very pretty story.

Yet for some "little immigrants", possibly a majority, their childhood experiences were no worse and in many instances better than in the loveless and brutal slums of London, Liverpool or Glasgow from whence they came. Some eventually achieved prosperity and distinction in Canada, in turn raising themselves families in which the loving home life that they themselves had seldom or never experienced made possible the contributions of their descendants to the development of Canada. That is the story that Kenneth Bagnell tells so well, making real and moving the experiences of individuals who otherwise are recorded only in government documents as mere statistics. His account of the "home children" is an important element in our social history, leaving us all in his debt.

*The Hon. Roy MacLaren, P.C., served as a federal cabinet minister in the governments of prime ministers Pierre Trudeau and Jean Chretien and in 1996, was appointed Canada's High Commissioner to Great Britain. He is the author of several books including *Canadians Behind Enemy Lines, 1935—1945*.

*To the men and women
who were once the children.*

Introduction to the New Edition

Now and then over the past twenty years and more I've been asked why I chose to write the book now reissued between the covers you hold in your hands. My answer is the same as one a celebrated artist once gave me about why he paints this or that subject: "Because it spoke to me." As with a painter so with a writer — at least sometimes. I have no personal connection to child emigration; I am not a descendant of anyone who was part of this long, painful chapter of Canada's past. But, in the late sixties, it spoke to me. The subject formed a landscape that appealed deeply — its people, its events. I mentioned the idea of doing a book to a friend, a respected journalist and an astute man, but his reply was only mildly encouraging. It would be a worthwhile contribution, he said, but he couldn't see much public appeal. I still remember him as astute but he showed that astute men can be wrong.

The Little Immigrants was a surprising success. It was, as this new book jacket attests, greeted by almost universally favorable reviews. This brought personal pleasure — a pleasure I see no harm in. A writer requires encouragement. As John Kenneth Galbraith, a more accomplished writer than I, wrote a few years ago: "Any author who tells you that he doesn't pay attention to his reviews is either James Joyce or a consumate and unconvincing liar." In any case, the reviews, and some other facts I refer to shortly, had more important benefit. They assisted the book to various bestseller lists where it remained for roughly a year. Between autumn 1980 and spring 1981, it was reprinted eight times.

I want to say early in this introduction how grateful I am for the generous words of a distinguished Canadian, The Hon. Roy MacLaren, which accompany this new introduction. Mr. MacLaren is himself the author of several books, and after a notable career served with distinction as Canada's High Commissioner to the land in which the child immigrants were born. I'm honored by his good opinion of *The Little Immigrants*.

A book is never all one person's doing. Especially this one. Hundreds of people help a book to life and even more in the case of The Little Immigrants. The most obvious people are the many men and women, from almost every province, most of whom have since died, who spent many hours with me in the late 1970s when I was doing my research, sharing their experiences as child immigrants. Further, the body of literature by scholars on the subject of both child emigration and child development, in which I read widely, and gratefully attest to in the original foreword, informed much of my perspective. Mary Rutherford, who was my researcher on the book, as she has been on many of my later projects, is one of Canada's finest editorial researchers; she was fundamental to any success the book has had. My editors of those years, Douglas Gibson and Jan Walter, then of Macmillan Canada, were taken with the idea and were a strong and supporting presence throughout. Now, over 20 years later, I owe a debt to Beth Bruder and Tony Hawke of Dundurn Press for their gracious approach to me and their decision to release this new edition.

The actual writing went on over two years, mostly in 1978 and 1979, and I take responsibility for the book's structure and style. These are mine alone — as much as anything one ever does can be so described. It was a lonely sojourn and when I look back I recall a reference from a late *New Yorker* writer, who described the difference between writing an article and writing a book as the difference between rowing across a pond and rowing across an ocean. There's a bit more to it than that, but the comparison is still apt. In the early chapters, there were times when, out of sight of land, I wondered if I could manage the waves, to give the vast sea I was on a coherent form and readable style. The reader can judge.

Many books, and many authors, are launched at glamorous events, attended by glamorous people at glamorous suites in glamorous hotels. *The Little Immigrants'* launch was much less auspicious. I can't recall who dreamt it up but it was a family idea and took place on a Sunday afternoon, Thanksgiving Sunday, early October, 1980. It was one of those fall days in which summer seems to linger without regard to the calendar. The event was planned as a reunion of home children to which all were invited. My wife Barbara and my mother Mary between them made 1,000 cookies; it was held in the hall of Deer Park United Church on St. Clair Ave. West, Toronto. It received sympathetic prepublicity by various media people who, quite early, sensed the subject was of wide public interest. Horace Lapp, a widely known pianist and organist — he was Kate Aiken's organist on the CBC for almost 30 years — was happy to entertain, his only fee a donation to the small church where he was then organist. A nearby funeral home, A.W. Miles Ltd., also part of Toronto history, was happy to enliven the room with colorful floral pieces.

It was widely attended, not just by the public, but journalists and most of all, by large numbers of those called home children: the men and women, then well on in years, who had come to Canada as child immigrants in the early 1900s. Since my publisher, Macmillan of Canada, thought it a good idea to have the very first books on hand at the close of the day, they were available at the door. A bookstore couldn't send a representative but instead supplied its credit card machine which was dutifully attended by my sons David and Paul as their sister Andrea served tea.

One radio journalist who was there, Andy Barrie, then the gifted host of a late afternoon program on Toronto's highly popular CFRB, asked if I might walk to the station afterward — it was about five minutes on foot — with a few of the men and women at the event whose stories were part of the book. We did. The audience was especially large: it was drive home time from the cottage on Thanksgiving Sunday. We were on the air, answering callers questions, for an hour. Thus *The Little Immigrants* was launched.

As I mention earlier, a book's success is determined not just by the content but the interest in the community and country when it comes out. Does it meet a current of public interest? In this case the answer seems to be yes. There were several such currents running, each growing ever stronger by 1980. To them I now turn.

Around the 1960s, especially the late sixties and Expo 67, there were signs that Canadians were seeking answers to the question: what is our past? For years our historians, men like Donald Creighton and James Careless explored our beginnings. But broad popular interest seemed tepid. Placing a book under the Canadiana sign in a bookstore was almost to announce before anybody saw it that it was an also ran. But by the 1970s, the tide picked up, on the way to becoming a running river. At the opening of the decade, Pierre Berton's *The National Dream* appeared, to be followed by *The Last Spike*. They told the story of the creation of a coast to coast railway but, as we know, they were about more than that — the vision and the visionaries of the nation. Over subsequent years, Berton's many books helped bring Canadian social history off dusty back shelves. The appeal of his books did more than mirror widening interest in Canada's past. They widened it still. So have numerous books of others, popular academic historians such as Michael Bliss, Ramsay Cook, and Desmond Morton.

With this growing interest, the public of 1980 seemed receptive to a book on child emigration. It had been overlooked, in part because it was deemed of little interest, but something else was involved: the reticence of those who experienced it. They were people, mainly British, from a reserved culture, not given to revealing their personal lives, especially the painful aspects, to a writer. Moreover, they'd felt the lash of public disdain in Canada — scorned as orphans, waifs, the offspring of a lower class. For decades a great many were so reluctant to speak of the experience, they refused to discuss it in detail with their own children.

This reticence had begun to wane when I began my research just past the middle 1970s. By then multiculturalism was well underway, encouraging newcomers of various ethno-cultural groups to tell their stories. It was time for child immigrants to tell theirs. I placed a note in most of the county's rural papers, inviting replies; an avalanche of letters resulted. Had it not been for the goodwill of my employer at the time — I was then editor of *Imperial Oil Review* — and the kindness of many of its support staff, I could not have coped. I replied to all, then went across Canada to interview many. While it's never possible to include the story of every person in any narrative, all were deeply instrumental in shaping my reportage and my perspective. (The tapes of these interviews were later placed in the Public Archives of Canada in Ottawa.) The willingness of men and women, then well on in their years, to reply and to be interviewed later at length, was itself a revelation: Canada's child emigrants were ready to speak up. Our history was becoming truly inclusive.

There was something else also at work. I've been told by Kenneth Bird, President of the Ontario Genealogical Society that in the early sixties when the society was founded, it had one chapter and 80 members. Today it has 30 chapters and 6,000 members. There are, he says, roughly six million people in Canada actively involved in pursuing their family past — "their roots" as it's popularly known. This is another reason why the book seemed welcome. For years after it appeared, I heard from hundreds of men, women, even teenagers, compiling family histories, trying to find out what had happened to a mother, a father, a grandparent, an aunt or uncle. All they knew was that he or she had come to Canada as a child long ago. They had read The Little Immigrants and wondered if I could help in their specific search. To some degree I could. Several of the organizations which sent children, in particular Barnardo's of England, (through which most were sent to Canada), had kept meticulous records.

When the book appeared, Barnardo's — today doing highly regarded work with all sorts of vulnerable children — was most helpful to inquiries seeking information about a parent or grandparent. They had the original records. The replies took time because of the number of queries, and there were sometimes legal or other limitations on information they could provide. But through Barnardo's hundreds of Canadians received basic backgrounds, sometimes with actual photographs of mother or father when they became children of Dr. Barnardo's Homes.

Today, the internet has greatly propelled interest in genealogy and enhanced the ease of acquiring or sharing available records. Some websites are specific to child emigration. One of the best know has been created by David Lorente, a teacher, in Renfrew, Ontario who has devoted many hours to helping descendants of child emigrants trace their family past. His own father, Joseph, came to Canada as a teenager in 1914. (Mr. Lorente is pleased to help with any inquiry on child emigration and can be reached by Email at lorente@sympatico.ca.) You can find a variety of sites simply by entering "British child emigration," on your internet server.

With all of this — our widened interest in our country's past, our longing to know our own family history — there was the ageless, ever deepening concern about children. That precedes all else and accompanies all else. It is as old as scripture, as current as the newspaper. By 1980 it was a major matter and is even more today. It's a point salutary and sobering that over 2,000 years ago Jesus gave his sternest rebukes to those who mistreated a child. That's the salutary aspect. The sobering aspect is that in the many centuries since, mistreatment has been so common, including mistreatment by many who claim to work in the name of Jesus. I don't mean just the forms of abuse that are now so well publicized — physical or sexual abuse. These are real and horrifying. I mean also the less tangible abuse of emotional deprivation.

Child emigration was born in an age that did not know and could not heed the emotional life of a child: the need of all children for words that are kind, deeds that are compassionate, homes that are secure. It was not until the 1920s, when the child emigration movement was beginning to end, that the earlier writings of men such as Freud, Adler and Jung, persuaded much of the western world that humans, especially children, had not just physical lives but emotional lives. The latter must be nurtured.

Consider the ritual of emotional deprivation these children endured: the child is first taken from a family, sometimes troubled by illness, poverty or other circumstance, then placed in an institution of spartan condition and rigorous discipline. Then, a year or so later he or she is placed aboard a ship bound for a distant country and a foreign culture. Finally, once in Canada the child is swiftly placed with absolute strangers in a family not selected with true care. Even in good situations, most of these children felt no familial affection. They were treated, often by the best families, not as children, but as workers. They were denied a normal childhood. This was the common tragedy of child emigration.

Was it, some have asked me, at least better than what they left behind? Perhaps at times. But at other times, as in the case of some I tell about here, most certainly not. More probably Britain itself should have confronted the problems that gave birth to child emigration — grave, widespread poverty and social destitution. Had it found a way to deal with these problems, it would not have fallen into the false solution of exporting children to farmers in Canada most of whom wanted cheap help in fields and kitchens.

All of this is being said in hindsight. Years ago the child emigration movement was deemed to be good for all parties, the children, Canada, Great Britain itself. I recognize that. I have, as best I could, tried to convey a sense of the attitude of men and women of the time in which the events occurred. I acknowledge that the basic intent of most of the homes — not all — was decent in intent.

The reception the book received brought natural pleasure, but its true worth is that it has, along with other books, helped assure that the place of countless children, many nameless, has been secured in the story of Canada's past. That is the satisfaction that matters and may endure. It is also the reason for the words you'll find on the dedicatory page of the first edition and this edition.

Kenneth Bagnell.
East Moore Lake,
Haliburton County,
Ontario.
May, 2001.

Author's Note

This is the story of a special group of children, over eighty thousand of them. Some became our mothers and fathers; all became the parents of much of our history. It is about their journey to this land.

Their presence in Canadian life was first known to me while I was still a boy growing up in Nova Scotia. For the most part they were at the margin of my life then, people I would see on Sunday afternoons on the farms of distant relatives, or at the edges of the crowd at summer fairs. They were, I was told, "from away". In the mind of a child they seemed touched by mystery.

In the early sixties, when I came to Toronto and to my work in journalism, I began to meet in my travels—especially in small towns in Ontario—men and women who, it would turn out, came to Canada by the same route when they were very young and when they had virtually nothing. The story of their coming, about which so many of us know so little, struck me then as a deep, moving part of Canadian life. I began to gather material. Then, over a period of three years I corresponded with and met several hundred of them, in every part of Canada, who quite willingly discussed their experiences with me. I shall remember them all my life.

My research has taken me to numerous archival collections in Canada and given me a fresh appreciation of the scholarship and diligence of the men and women who work in them, in all the provinces and in the Public Archives of Canada in Ottawa. Much of my work, for reasons that will be clear, has been done in Britain, and I must record here my deep gratitude to the members of the staff of Barnardo's, the child care organization in London whose founder, Thomas John Barnardo, is so close to the heart of this book. They have provided me with innumerable forms of assistance.

In my treatment of Dr. Barnardo I am especially indebted to Dr. Gillian Wagner, whose biography *Barnardo* (London: Weidenfeld and

Nicolson, 1979) is warmly recommended to any reader seeking further information on this extraordinary nineteenth-century figure. I have made wide use of that book here, and I am especially grateful to Dr. Wagner for her pioneering research into the famous arbitration case of 1877. That research, which was the subject of her thesis at the University of London, has informed much of my own description of the case.

I must also thank, for their help during my visits with them in Britain, people at the Family Welfare Association, the National Institute of Social Work, the Goldsmith Library of the University of London, the Public Records Office, and the British Library. All of them have made available for my study numerous letters, records, and documents.

My research assistant, Mary Rutherford, has been more than diligent, and I can only record here my recognition of the intelligence and thoroughness that accompanied her efforts. My colleague, Daniel Mothersill, my editor, Jan Walter, and my typist, Eileen Greer, have all been generous with their gifts and their support. As in all that I have done, my wife, Barbara Bagnell—who also assisted greatly in the research in Canada and in Britain—has borne in her calm and patient way much of the strain that has attended the work.

Beyond all of this, I owe more than I can say to the men and women who have opened their lives to my questions and my scrutiny. For many of them it has not been easy. If there is in this sometimes grim and painful story, anything of courage and anything of compassion, it is indeed a reflection of them.

Kenneth Bagnell
Whitby, Ontario
June, 1980

Prologue

O n a grey and chilly day in June some years ago, very early in the
morning, a boy named Horace Weir—eleven years old, with
eyes that were quick and dark—stood on the deck of an old steamer, the *Franconia*, and watched the coast of Nova Scotia rise beyond
a curtain of fog.

He was silent. He had been that way for almost all of the voyage,
ever since the ship had left Liverpool in England ten days earlier. Now,
as she came into the harbour of Halifax, the boy, staring at the wharves
and sheds and spires that stood beyond the harbour, felt again the
worry that had hovered like a cloud over his life, ever since that night,
over a year earlier, when the police came to the door of his parents'
home in Birmingham. They said that in the interests of all concerned
they were going to remove the Weir children—seven of them—and see
that they were placed in better surroundings, in an institution where
they could be fed and clothed and given the upbringing their parents
were not able to provide.

Horace Weir, the oldest boy in the family, knew why the police
came that evening. His father had been terribly wounded in the war, so
badly that he could never work again, and his family struggled to survive on the pittance of pension given to injured veterans. His mother,
driven to despair, sought solace in the bottle, becoming such a severe
alcoholic that she began pawning furniture in an attempt to slake her
thirst. Then one night—the police station was just across the street
and the authorities could see the way things were going—a couple of
officers came and told his mother that they would take care of everything. A few days later all seven children were removed.

They were placed in the Middlemore Home in Birmingham, a
large, dark building surrounded by lawns and playgrounds, a place set
aside for children like themselves who, the founders felt, could only
benefit from being removed from their bad situations. They would live

in the home for a year, perhaps two, and then they would be sent out to Canada, to farms where, as everyone knew, life was better and the future would be theirs.

All of this the boy recalled as he stood on the deck of the *Pranconia* that day in early June, 1924, in Halifax harbour. He was, after all, the oldest brother, the one to whom the others looked. But he did not know where he was going, other than to Canada; he did not know with whom he would be placed, other than with a farmer. He worried, for he had never seen a farm. And he worried for the others, especially for Beatrice, the youngest, who was only three.

It was dusk when they were taken down the gangplank—Horace; Kathleen, who was fourteen; Violet, who was twelve; Alfred, ten; Gladys, seven; and finally, in the arms of someone he did not know, Beatrice. (Another brother,. Lewis, had been found to have ringworm and was left behind in Birmingham, to come to Canada the following year.)

Perhaps it was because of the gathering darkness or the rush and confusion, or perhaps it was planned that way to avoid the sadness of it all, but Horace Weir did not see any of his brothers or sisters to say goodbye. That same evening, someone put him on a train, with his trunk and his suitcase and a ticket to a town called Kingston in the Annapolis Valley of Nova Scotia. There, he was told, he would be met by a farmer who would take him to his home, where he would work and live.

His brothers and sisters were put on other trains headed for other places, the names of which he would never be told. He peered out the train window at a new, strange land, field after field, and felt again the old fears rising and the tears behind his eyes.

It was very late when he arrived at Kingston. The farmer met him—with a horse and buggy and a lantern—and together they set out over the mountain, along roads so narrow they were brushing the alders as they passed, for a place called Margaretsville. There Horace Weir was to stay until he became a young man, doing chores, milking cows, making hay, and receiving, in return, his room and board and a dollar a month to spend. He was, as he told someone many years afterward, one of the lucky ones, for he was not whipped or beaten and the food was good.

Once, after he had been there a year, he was sitting on the couch in the kitchen after supper when suddenly—he could not understand why it came upon him so quickly—he began thinking of his brothers and sisters, especially Beatrice. He burst into sobbing and could not stop. The farmer's wife asked if he was sick or in pain. He said no, it was not that, he was thinking of his brothers and sisters and wondering where they were and if he would ever see them again. She told him that she did not know where they were, that the main thing to remember was that he had a new home and must put the past behind him. He must try to forget.

In 1931 when he was eighteen years old and on his own as a farm worker in the Annapolis Valley, Horace Weir, still in search of his brothers and sisters, got word somehow that one of his brothers, Alfred, and one of his sisters, Gladys, had been sent to a distant part of Nova Scotia, in the highlands of Cape Breton, where they were placed with Scottish farmers. Alfred lived near Whycocomagh, and Gladys in the mountains around the lonely community of Tarbot.

He decided that he would go in search of them. Perhaps, if and when he found his brother and his sister, he could settle down near them. The farmer he was then working for—he had been there for nine months at ten dollars a month—would not pay him. A man from Halifax who represented the Middlemore Home in Canada tried to get his pay for him, but he could not. "You can't," he told Horace, "get blood from a stone." The best thing, he said, was to forget it.

And so, hoping to find his brother and sister, Horace put all that he had in his old steel suitcase, the one he had brought to Canada, and, scraping together a few dollars he had hidden away, bought a train ticket to the farthest destination he could afford, which was barely across the Strait of Canso on the island of Cape Breton. The rest of the way he would go on foot.

It was many days before he reached Whycocomagh, his toes bleeding and his palms raw from the weight of his suitcase. But he found the farm where his brother was living. He went to the house and asked for Alfred. The farmer's wife told him to come in; she said that Alfred was in the field and that she would call him. He should, she said, wait in the kitchen.

All his life he would remember waiting there for Alfred. In time, his brother came. But, as Horace Weir would explain it years afterward, it was not as he had hoped it would be. "For brothers," he said, "it was not like brothers." He noticed that Alfred had a bicycle and, since he had a long distance ahead of him to try to find Gladys in Tarbot, he asked Alfred if he might borrow it. For reasons he would never really understand, his brother said no.

In time, on foot, he reached Tarbot, a quiet and gloomy place set back among hills strewn with rock, where the farms were small and poor and often empty. Gladys lived on a patch of a farm owned by a man and a woman who spoke mostly Gaelic and who made it clear that he was not welcome. He did see Gladys. Many years later she would confide in her brother something of the terror of her childhood in Tarbot, a story so filled with pain that her brother would never divulge it, but for now she simply took him outside the house and told him that it would be better if he went away and did not come again.

Horace Weir had found his brother and sister. But in finding them he found also that he no longer had a family, that on that first night in Halifax, in the summer of 1924, his family life was lost forever.

He went back to the land to which he had been sent, the Annapolis Valley, where, in time, he made for himself a new life as a carpenter and bricklayer. He married and, in the green and peaceful countryside near the town of Annapolis Royal, raised a son and a daughter. Over the forty years of his life in that area he met, here and there, almost all of his brothers and sisters, all except Beatrice, about whom he had worried so much. Since she had been hardly more than a baby when brought to Canada, Horace eventually concluded that she had been adopted. Her fate would be forever unknown to him.

One day in the middle of June, 1974, fifty years after he came to Canada, Horace Weir, who was working on a house in the town of Middleton in the Annapolis Valley of Nova Scotia, placed his tools in the back of his car and headed home. As he drove along the highway, he wondered idly if that evening he and his wife might go to the local ballgame, and then perhaps drop in at his son's house down the road to see the grandchildren.

When he got home—it was just about 5:30 in the evening—he saw, beneath the maples that spread near his house, a man and a woman, standing as if waiting for him. He got out of the car. The man, impressive in his appearance, spoke softly and a bit formally. His name, he said, was Ralph Roberts, now retired from the service and living in another part of Canada. Then, turning to the woman beside him, he asked Horace Weir if, by chance, he had ever met her. Horace Weir looked and smiled but said no, he had not.

"Mr. Weir," the man said, "this is your sister. This is Beatrice."

They stood there, he remembers, a long time. No one said anything. Then she reached out and she shook his hand.

One
The Ladies of London

Annie Macpherson, according to the memories that pass among her descendants, was above all else a woman with a sense of destiny. Her eyes, peering out from beneath a high forehead, were large and strong, and her mouth, which was straight and correct, was set among features that spoke of a will of iron. Her parents—James, a school-teacher in Glasgow, and Helen, a gentle woman of Scandinavian background—saw to it that after she finished her schooling in Glasgow she went to London, there to study the methods of Friedrich Froebel, the German scholar who was the founder of the kindergarten movement. The Macphersons had seven children and also raised two foster children, a task that was to impress their eldest daughter, Annie, and through her affect the lives of countless thousands of other children throughout Britain in that century and the one to come.

When she was twenty-three years old, in 1865, Annie Macpherson — like many in her time a convert to evangelical Christianity—decided that her life work would be among the poor in London, in the East End, where, for an entire population, life was a burden of unending desperation, disease, and crime from which the only release was death itself. The area known as the East End, so named during the middle of the 1700s, was a vast neighbourhood stretching as far east as the River Lea. From 1800 it was filled with factories, tenements, and chronic poverty. Most people died before reaching the age of twenty. The causes of this agony would occupy the minds of scholars far into the next century—the impact of the Industrial Revolution, the doubling of the city's population in only thirty years, the departure from the East End of the middle and upper classes who might have given stability—but it was for Annie Macpherson, as for numerous other reformers, a sea of desolation. "The poor East of London," lamented the preacher who influenced Annie Macpherson's conversion in a note to her in 1860. "Do not let the West neglect it. It does not so much want more buildings—of these there are enough deserted, some shut—but more living, loving labourers."

During her first summer of work in 1866, an epidemic of cholera swept the entire East End, killing 1,407 in a single week. "We can but be deeply grateful," Annie Macpherson wrote at the time, "that in parts of the East End four out of five infants die before they reach their fifth year, because the other side of the picture among the living ones is so black, so awful, so crushing in its dreadful realities.

She was by then twenty-four years old, a woman of medium height, with a full figure and light-brown hair. Almost daily, people saw her in the courts and dim alleyways of the East End, her hair swept straight, her intentions as firm as her step: to do something, anything, about the appalling conditions of the poor. She visited the sick and distributed food, and in the evenings, in her room that was as spare as the cell of a convent, she held meetings for mothers, talking with them of ways in which they might stave off the tragedies that stood at their doors.

Then, one day in the late autumn of 1867, in the company of another woman—she was working in an area of the East End known as Bethnal Green—Annie Macpherson entered a dark, smelly house and heard voices on an upper floor. She climbed the gloomy stairway and opened a hatch upon a sweltering attic. Inside was a sight that would move her to direct the rest of her life, not to the miseries of poverty in general, but to the suffering of children. Everywhere in the attic, beneath the rafters and in the dusty corners where shafts of light fell through cracks in the roof, crouched more than thirty small girls, their arms thin as broomsticks, at work making matchboxes.

"They were hired," Annie Macpherson said later, "by the woman who rented the room." Each child received three farthings, less than one penny, for making a gross of boxes, each gross requiring the child to handle two hundred and eighty-eight pieces of wood. The girls, she estimated, were mostly between the ages of eight and ten, though there were a few who were younger. On a table was a loaf of bread. When the children were so hungry they could not go on, they were given a slice. They paid for it out of their earnings.

Annie Macpherson came back down the stairs, her solemn face more serious than ever, convinced that she must begin that day to try ending the misery of the matchbox-makers. She was certain that part of the answer was only a short distance from the garret she had discovered. It was an abandoned building on nearby Commercial Street. The street, like many others in the East End, was a place of factories and warehouses, and one of them—an abandoned warehouse known as

Number Sixty Commercial Street—had been used as an emergency hospital during the cholera epidemic. Now empty, it had about it a stern and forbidding look, but it was large, with four storeys, accommodation for one hundred and twenty on every floor, and spacious rooms, which, in her active imagination, she could see as kitchens, workshops, and schoolrooms.

She turned for help to a newspaper editor of the day, R. C. Morgan of *The Revival*, a paper of evangelical Protestantism, who, from his own pocket and those of his readers, raised enough money to assure the rent at Number Sixty Commercial Street. Thus, at the end of 1868 she was able to transform the empty warehouse into what she called the Home of Industry, in which the children—by this time she and her workers had located hundreds of matchbox-makers in garrets and cellars—were able to work at their menial tasks, but in certain free hours receive a bit of food and education. Parents, desperate for help, were only too willing to send their children. Even some employers, recognizing hardships they felt powerless to correct, sent the children in their time off, hoping that somehow this would provide the youngsters with relief from the monotony of their work.

"Tonight," Annie Macpherson wrote to some friends early in 1869, "how your hearts would have rejoiced to have seen me and my happy hundreds of little toiling children in our new schoolroom at the Home of Industry. Their joy knew no bounds when told to ask their mothers to come one afternoon a week to sew and earn sixpence. My object was twofold; to secure an opportunity of telling them the gospel, and to endeavour to help them in the management of their homes and their little ones." And then, in a comment which was an afterthought, but which was to be a revelation of the attitude she brought to all that was to come after in her life, she added: "The children are no idlers themselves; tailoring, shoemaking, matchbox-making, are all being pursued on different floors of the building."

Many of the children who came under her influence in those early years came not just to work in the Home of Industry but to live there. They and thousands of others—there were, some said, more than thirty thousand destitute children in the East End in those years—had been abandoned by parents who themselves had been destroyed by the poverty that broke the spirit of an entire population.

Within a year, Annie Macpherson, whose influence no one could have foreseen, would extend her rescue work even further. With the assistance of her two sisters, Rachel and Louisa, and a number of volunteers, she would open four other homes for London's orphans, waifs, and strays, taking into her care thousands of children, both boys and girls. But it was Annie Macpherson alone who went to the government and the philanthropists and the press of the day, raising the money to house, feed, and clothe her children, but above all else to bring them up in the love of God, whose children she believed them to be and who, according to Annie Macpherson's faith, cared for each one of them as if He had no other. There is no way of knowing if Annie Macpherson had ever heard of Robert Chambers, an obscure police magistrate in London who, almost forty years before she began to rescue children, appeared before a government inquiry and put forward the idea that the children who cluttered the streets of that city be gathered up and shipped to Canada. It was in 1826, on the fourteenth of April, and Chambers was appearing as a witness before a select committee of the British Parliament, called to deal with the whole question of emigration from the United Kingdom. "I conceive," he said early in his brisk testimony, "that London has got too full of children." They were, he pointed out with a sense of complaint as well as concern, begging in the streets and sleeping in the gutters, and turning whole neighbourhoods into dens of thievery. For Chambers, a man in whose courtroom this tide was always running, there was a clear solution, one in which he could see a way of improving the life of London, the poor, and even the children them-selves. He would send the street waifs to Canada.

"I am of the opinion," he said, "such a system of emigration would be productive of great benefit. There has been a great increase, as I can show by returns now in my hand, of juvenile offences, which I attrib-ute, first, to the increase of the population, secondly, to the want of employment for children, thirdly, to the discharge of children from ships in docks" (in the main cabin-boys who joined the ranks of the unemployed after their ships returned to England). He went further, reading aloud letters he had received from officials of various munici-palities, each one encouraging him in his view that children who were down and out, those twelve years of age and upward, should be sent to Canada, where they were badly needed, to be apprenticed to persons who, Chambers predicted, would be glad to receive them as workers on the land. He felt this way, not merely about abandoned children— street arabs as history would name them—but about the many thou-sands of children who lived with their parents in the misery of the workhouses. "I think," he said, "that if the parents saw that govern-ment were going to take the children under its protection, and that there was a prospect of their future welfare, they would be glad to offer their children for that purpose."

A month after Chambers testified, a man named William Henry Bodkin—a philanthropist of sorts and secretary of a charity group called the Mendicity Society—said much the same thing. "There is one class of vagrant," he replied in answer to a casual question, "if they could be made objects of such a plan as this, that I think it would be extremely desirable to send out of the country; I allude to boys. A great many sleep in the market places and situations of that kind in London; and I have observed that even though there were receptacles open for the reception of the homeless, many of these boys preferred herding together in the way I have described. I think that if any judicious scheme could be devised for the sending away of these boys, it would be a great public benefit; and I have several times suggested it to persons of influence."

Four decades later, in the winter of 1869, Annie Macpherson—with the help of one of her volunteers, a woman named Ellen Logan—wrote an article to distribute to the public in London in which she said, "We who labour here are tired of relieving misery from hand to mouth, and also heartsick of seeing hundreds of families pining away for want of work, when over on the shores of Ontario the cry is heard, 'Come over and we will help you.'" She announced that she was opening a fund to which the public could contribute, to help send, not children only, but families, to Canada. "We are waiting to seek out the worthy," she wrote, "not yet on the parish list, but who soon must be; we will see to their being properly started on the Canadian shores if you will give us the power to make a golden bridge across the Atlantic."

That summer, five hundred people were sent to Canada by Annie Macpherson. They were met at the port of Montreal, inspected by immigration officers, and sent to farms where the parents had already been hired, some in Quebec but most in Ontario around the town of Belleville. Then, once she received word that they had been settled, she made plans to go herself the following year—in the spring of 1870—with one hundred boys. Some were already living in her rescue homes, some she would take from the workhouses, some from reformatories, and some, in the weeks just before the trip out, would be gathered from the streets of London. It was, in every way an undertaking that was to be not just formidable, but frightening. The ship on which she sailed that May offered only the barest accommodation for the children. It did not provide bedding, so Macpherson and her band of volunteers had to round up blankets. It did not even provide soap, and while she and her helpers did what they could to encourage cleanliness among the youngsters, the charge that she sent vermin-infested urchins to Canada was one that would haunt her work for years to come. Moreover, though she was leaving England with the firm idea of setting up a permanent institution in Canada—a home where the children could be received and a system by which they could be settled on farms—she had no place in mind and no person to meet her, only Canada's permission to come and bring her children.

In the last week of May they landed in Montreal, and were cleared through immigration, housed overnight in an orphanage, and then put on a train—all except twenty-three who were farmed out immediately in Quebec—bound for the bright promise of the Ontario farmland. Early next day the train led into the station in the lovely and quiet town of Belleville, Ontario. On that soft morning, with the lilacs just in bloom, the Warden of Hastings County, A. F. Wood, presented Annie Macpherson with a letter inviting her to establish her distributing home in his town and assuring her on behalf of the council of Hastings and himself as warden that, if she accepted, the rent would be looked after and she would be left free to run the home as she saw fit. She quickly agreed.

The house given to her by the town of Belleville was set among large, vaulting trees on a residential street not far from the heart of the town. It was called Marchmont. A woman who came with her on the ship that spring, Ellen Agnes Bilbrough, a woman who would later be praised, even by the critics of child immigration, for her limitless devotion, was placed in charge.

That spring and summer, Annie Macpherson spent eight weeks in Ontario, travelling throughout the province, her stout, strong figure rising at council meetings, outdoor rallies, and church services as she told the story of her children, appealing not entirely to the charitable instincts of her audience, but to their more practical inclinations—their need for help that was reliable yet at the same time affordable. Many in her audiences came up to her when she finished speaking, not just to shake her hand and offer support, but to ask for children. So many made requests that she sent word back to London, to her sister Rachel, that more children were needed. Rachel dispatched her husband with a load of seventy. Then, her speaking tour ended, Annie Macpherson went back to England and quickly returned with another party of children, the third group she had brought to Canada in four months. Within two years she opened a second home, in the town of Galt, Ontario. In 1877, convinced that Quebec should not be overlooked as a place for children, she persuaded her sister Louisa to open a third, in the village of Knowlton, seventy miles from Montreal, from where she distributed children for many years to the farmers of the Eastern Townships.

The farms on which the children were to make their new lives, mostly in Ontario, were sparse, small places. Usually there was a man, himself new to Canada, a wife, and a child, perhaps two. Together they struggled against the odds of nature to earn the barest living. The land they worked was hard, the life they led was lonely. In winter the only pastime was work, and the only sounds that broke the silence were the blowing of the wind at night and the barking of a dog on a faraway farm. In a nation barely established, with a population so small and so scattered, they had nowhere to turn for help. So, seeing the advertisements in their newspapers inviting them to send for a boy or a girl just arrived from England, they would sit at their tables beside the kerosene lamps and write a letter, hoping that in this way even they could afford an extra hand to help in the field, to milk a cow, to light a fire in the dead of winter.

It was this world into which Annie Macpherson sent children from the tenements of England. Almost alone she set up a system in Canada through which she, along with, the support of her sisters Rachel and Louisa and their families, would transfer from the streets of London to the farms of Canada fourteen thousand children. Most were in their teens, many were younger, and a few were hardly, out of their infancy. Her work—which would receive great support and great criticism—would provide the example for scores of similar workers in England in her time who would set up similar programs in Canada until, by the middle of the 1930s, when the immigration of children ended, it was said that more than eighty thousand of them had come to this country under the auspices of fifty organizations that shared the vision of Annie Macpherson.

It was her sister Louisa, the youngest of the three Macpherson daughters, a woman of delicate features and uncertain health, who first sent children to Nova Scotia. She had been approached by a group of citizens in Liverpool—men who had heard her sister Annie speak—where, if anything, conditions were worse than those of East London. Louisa Birt had seen the children of such misery herself when she, had gone to Liverpool with Annie and groups of children to board the ship to Canada. And so, in the spring of 1873, four years after her sister began her work in East London, Louisa opened a home for the waifs and strays of Liverpool. In the first year, six hundred sought admission, and when she was asked to describe them she did so vividly. "They came," she said, "with the old story of widows' children left to their own devices, while the poor mother goes forth to toil over the wash tub or the needle for their daily bread; poor stepchildren, who are felt to be burdens, and are knocked about and ill-used accordingly, as though to make them run away; drunkards' children going through the education which will fit them for the reformatory, prison, or penitentiary, as the case may be; illegitimate children, on whom the sins of their parents are weighing with crushing power; all these were in the ranks of those whom we have learned to call 'street arabs', 'waifs and strays'—named lightly and smilingly spoken, yet overlying thoughts too deep for tears."

It was a whim of history that decided that these children of Louisa Birt would go, not to Ontario, but to the often small and poor farms of Scottish settlers in Nova Scotia. Just a few weeks after she opened her home, Mrs. Birt received a letter from a man in Halifax, John Wimburn Laurie, inviting her to come to Nova Scotia with a party of children and offering to take full responsibility for placing them and overseeing them. Laurie, who had been born in England himself (where he had enlisted when he was eighteen, serving in India), was, when he wrote Louisa Birt, a major and the newly appointed inspector of the militia for Nova Scotia. At thirty-eight years of age, with large, penetrating eyes and a full beard, Laurie was a commanding and influential presence in the life of Halifax. He would serve, in time, as second in command during the Riel Rebellion of 1885, then as a member of Parliament, and, on his retirement in the country of his birth, as the mayor of one of the boroughs of London.

In those early years in Nova Scotia, Laurie was living at Oakfield, an estate of some three hundred acres on the shores of Grand Lake, about fifteen miles from Halifax. He had ten cottages for his staff, mostly British immigrants, his own church, a manse for his minister, and three barns. He travelled a good deal throughout Nova Scotia—among his innumerable activities he was a member of the board of agriculture—and he was certain beyond any doubt that he would have no trouble placing hundreds of children on the farms of the province. So he wrote to Louisa Birt, telling her two persuasive things: he would take personal responsibility for every child, including costs, once the child reached Nova Scotia; moreover, he had been to the officials of immigration in the province and they I had assured him that Nova Scotia would help pay the passage of the children from Liverpool to Halifax. After all, he pointed out to his government friends, Nova Scotia had been pleading for many years for Britain to send immigrants to that province; the journey was shorter and hence less expensive, and the cost of living generally was lower. Indeed, as Laurie well knew, the province's attorney general back in 1826, Richard John Uniacke. had gone to London to appear before a committee of Parliament studying immigration and said that farmers in Nova Scotia would be ready to take children as young as five if they could get them. "In fact," he said, in a reference filled with meaning, "the want of labour is so great they will take anything; but a boy of five years old is able to do something for his living, and he soon begins to earn his clothes and his maintenance.

It was May 1873 when Louisa Birt first heard from Wimburn Laurie. She had already swept from the streets and alleyways of Liverpool almost a hundred girls and boys, each one of whom had but one thing in common, a destitution that left them at the doorway of depravity or death. Naturally, she thought she would send them to Ontario, to the Marchmont Home in Belleville, but there was about Laurie's letter something authoritative and promising, and so she quickly changed her plans. She would go to Halifax.

It was in the last week of August, on a day when the first scent of fall was in the air, that Louisa Birt sailed into Halifax harbour, bringing with her seventy-one children. Laurie, who already had a deskful of applications for them, met her at the ship, and together they took the children to two Halifax orphanages, where they would stay a few days until each was sent to the farmer expecting them. "I was careful to distribute these children to all parts of the province," Laurie was to say later, "so that the working of the scheme might be better tested; if they did well, homes would be opened up for a large number, and if they turned out badly, it might as well be generally known at once that the scheme had failed, and that we could not prosecute it further." That October he wrote a letter to the local paper saying he had told Mrs. Birt to send two hundred children in the spring of the following year. "I shall be happy," he added, "to receive applications from Nova Scotia or the neighbouring provinces for these children in March or April."

As soon as they landed in Halifax. Laurie bought a ledger book, a plain cloth-bound volume, in which he inscribed each child's name, and beside it the name of the farmer to whom the boy or girl was sent: Anne Hawkins, twenty-five, sent with her child, E. Hawkins, seven, to Hugh Fraser near Hopewell; Georgie Duckworth, who was three, sent to Joseph Weston of Wolfville. Here and there, in a right-hand column, written at a later date, were the words "returned" or "removed" or else, "returned to England". The register did not reveal what lay behind these brief references, but from all that was to known later about the experience of such children, it was probable that they were rejected as being too small or too shy or too bold or too lazy.

Either that or they were so badly beaten that someone, usually a minister or a teacher, sent word to Laurie to have them removed.

During the years between 1813 and 1876, Louisa Birt made many trips to Halifax, bringing in total almost six hundred children and delivering them to the supervision of J. Wimburn Laurie, who, like most other people who worked in child immigration, had a program which, in its theory, had the best interests of everyone at heart. "On arrival," he told the provincial immigration agent in 1875, "they come at once under my charge, the legislature by enactment confirming the action of their parents or nearest relatives and appointing me the legal guardian. Regular applications distinctly prescribing the conditions under which the children are allotted are received by me, and these in all cases must be recommended by a clergyman. I make the best selection that careful enquiry and local knowledge will admit of and, whilst looking on the allotment as a permanent arrangement, I require quarterly reports, giving full particulars of the child's health, conduct, progress in and out of school, and this in every case certified by the local minister." Obviously there were imperfections in this system of placement and inspection. Farmers were unlikely to report on their own mistreatment of the children, and the local minister, given the attitude of the day, could have only a passing acquaintance with the shy, lonely children who were placed so casually on those distant farms.

After only three years in the work, Wimburn Laurie abruptly withdrew, owing, according to his descendants, to illness. His decision was mysterious, since a few years later he embarked on some of his most strenuous years, as a soldier, a parliamentarian, a Grand Mason, and a citizen of both Britain and Canada. He died in London in the spring of 1912 and his body was brought back to Canada and buried on his old estate near Halifax, in the province to which he had brought so many children whose lives, like their gifts, would remain unrealized and unsung.

In the middle of the winter of 1875, the Provincial Secretary of Nova Scotia received a letter forwarded from the Ottawa office of the Secretary of Agriculture, whose department coordinated immigration, and signed with a name that was vaguely familiar to him, Maria Rye. He had not met Miss Rye, but he knew that a few years earlier she had arrived in Halifax with a group of children from England and with the help of some local people had distributed them throughout the Maritimes. In fact, Maria Rye was, in the strictest sense, the first person to bring British children to Canada, arriving a few months ahead of Annie Macpherson, in the autumn of 1869, in the fruit lands of Ontario at Niagara-on-the-Lake, with sixty-eight children and the widely publicized blessing of the Archbishop of Canterbury and *The Times* of London. She was in every sense a strong, even strident, woman with a personality that was determined and domineering. Raised in London in good circumstances, she became, like many other women of her time and position, a zealous worker among the poor. She was—so she always claimed—a friend of the great reformer Lord Shaftesbury, who, as early as 1860, told her she should direct her efforts to children, trying to find homes for them in Canada. Then, during 1867 (the year when she actually began her work by placing women in Canada), it became obvious to her that there was indeed a great demand among Canadians for such youngsters. So, with her own money—raised, she always said, by her writings for the popular press of London—she was able to buy, in early 1868, the old jail on the outskirts of Niagara-on-the-Lake. She had it refurbished, named it Our Western Home, and in October of 1869 arrived with her first group of children, fifty of them, taken from the workhouses of Liverpool. She said later that she had some trouble placing them, for, as she put it, people were a little afraid of them. But in time she settled them all.

Over the years, from that early Canadian autumn to the turn of the century when Our Western Home was taken over others, Maria Rye crossed the Atlantic time after time, bringing, in all, some five thousand children, mostly girls, who were settled in Ontario. Her work would never equal the efforts of Annie Macpherson in either numbers or organization, but her home, set amid the gentle atmosphere of Niagara, would be for over twenty-five years the centre of fierce controversy and condemnation. Near the turn of the century, J.J. Kelso, Ontario's famous architect of child care, would say of Maria Rye's Our Western Home: "Without going into detail concerning past defects, it is only fair to say, in justice to agencies, that I consider this home responsible for a good of the odium that now attaches to child immigration in this country."

The problems that always seemed to engulf her work were already apparent that day in the winter of 1875 when her letter was opened in Halifax by the Provincial Secretary of Nova Scotia. He knew of Maria Rye, and his impression, like those of so many others, was of a domineering, freewheeling woman who brooked no interference but who had no hesitation in appealing for support. She had no distributing home in Nova Scotia, only a couple of casual friends—a Miss Cogswell and a Reverend Mr. Hill—who were willing to look in on the children she sent there. Within a year or two, however, she was hearing from both of them with problems. Some of the girls were not working out;

they were too young and could not take the long hours or they were too small and could not do the work. Or, in the case of some that had lived for years on the streets of London, they were too rough. For whatever reason, they were being rejected and had nowhere to go. So, Maria Rye asked, would the Nova Scotia government provide a home for them, those who were returned as unfit? "Actual experience has shown during the past six years," she wrote, "that fifty in one thousand children are so returned and on the average each child stays thirty days in the home; the remainder—that is to say the great bulk of these children— prove to be very desirable immigrants and the demand for them is always in excess of the supply."

The Nova Scotia government did not grant Maria Rye's request. But Ottawa helped her in other ways—a grant of a thousand dollars that year, and in the following years a bonus for each child she brought into the country, set in the beginning at two dollars for each. In addition, she was also given a bonus by the government of Ontario, six dollars for every child over twelve. Then there were several concessions, such as reduced fares for passage across the Atlantic and free travel on the train from Quebec to Niagara-on-the-Lake. All of this—put beside the fact that Miss Rye, like Annie Macpherson and Louisa Birt, was receiving help from local government in London and contributions from benefactors in both England and Canada—led to the inevitable suspicion that Miss Rye in particular was turning her benevolence into profit. In fact, breaking down her figures, it was apparent to some that she was making, on the average, just over twelve dollars a child. Nevertheless, she and the others insisted that all money received was put back into the work.

The most worrying thing—the thing that haunted the imaginations of some of the London politicians— was the welfare of the children themselves. About two thousand had been shipped out between 1868 and 1874, scattered upon the farms of Nova Scotia, New Brunswick, Quebec, and Ontario, and little was ever heard of them thereafter. There were, however, dark, fleeting rumours—often set off when a girl who got in trouble was returned to England or a boy was sent home after being in jail—that for many of the children life in Canada was not charmed, and that for a few it was filled with brutalities of which no one dared to speak.

The men most bothered by these rumblings were members of a London group called the Local Government Board. In essence, the board had taken over the work of the Poor Law Board and, as such, was responsible for encouraging the emigration of children, especially those who lived with their parents in the workhouses that came under the board's jurisdiction. The workhouses—cold, crowded, and festering with disease—were nonetheless home to over half the children whom the board in its wisdom (with or without the consent of their parents) had signed over to Maria Rye, Annie Macpherson, or Louisa Birt for a new life in Canada. In the face of the rumours, therefore, it felt a sense of responsibility and unease. It knew certain things, of course, for Maria Rye, the most; aggressive of the three, had made them utterly clear when she spoke to the members between her trips to Canada. She had shown them the circular she distributed in Canada, mostly through friends and the clergy but also in the press, outlining the work of her home. "The children vary in age from nine to twelve years," the circular said, "all are Protestants, and nearly all are absolute orphans, are bound (when not adopted), till they are eighteen years old, on the following terms: up to fifteen years old they are to be fed, clothed, and sent to Sunday school. From fifteen to seventeen they are not clothed but paid three dollars a month wages and four dollars a month from seventeen to eighteen. If, through any unforeseen circumstances, it is necessary for a child to be returned to the Home, due notice of the same must be given, in writing, a full fortnight before the child is removed; and if the child has been away from the Home six months, her clothes must be returned new and whole and in same number as they left the Home..."

The board members also knew, in vague and sketchy ways, that all three women had agreements drawn up that were to be signed by any farmer taking a child, promising that he would see to it that the child, first of all, got to Sunday school and then, as work permitted, was sent to day school. These agreements, known as Forms of Indenture, were intended not only to set out the farmers' responsibility, but to bind the children until they reached the age of eighteen. They could not leave.

In the case of the children from Our Western Home, Maria Rye had drawn up a variety of forms, depending on whether the child was to be adopted or, in the case of the boys, put out as a farm worker. For the girls who became maids, the indenture was clear and specific, stating that the girl would "well, truly, and faithfully serve the said party hereto of the third part, as help or servant and shall obey all his lawful and reasonable commands, and that she will do no damage to her said master in his goods, estates, or otherwise...and that she will not absent herself at any time from the service of the said master without his consent first obtained; but in all things as good and faithful servant and apprentice shall well demean herself and conduct herself to her said master." For his part, the master agreed to provide the basic necessities for her survival—food, shelter, and clothing. He would also see that she received an elementary education, a Protestant upbringing, and instruction in "the arts and duties of housewifery and the use of the needle". Then, when she reached fifteen, the girl was given, not clothing, but wages, a few dollars a month until she reached eighteen and was finally on her own, free from the contract which had been drawn up by others and would have such a decisive influence on all of her life.

There was, of course, nothing in Maria Rye's letters of indenture to indicate that she understood that the children she shipped to Canada were often heartbroken. Nor was there any sign that she believed that each of them deserved a kindly home. As for the farmers who received the children, they were not, in most cases, callous or indecent men. But when they answered the advertisements of Maria Rye and Annie Macpherson and Louisa Birt, they did so because they were in search of help—for the farm or for the house—for which they had great need and little money.

Thus the children came to a new life in a new land a long way from home. Often they were frightened of what lay ahead. For too many it was a fear that was all too ominous.

It was early in 1874 when the members of the Local Government Board in London, their sense of responsibility nudged by certain rumours, decided that since children had now been sent out to Canada for five years under their auspices, it would only be right for them to examine how things were going. "These children," the board would say later, "were partly such as had been entrusted to Miss Rye and Miss Macpherson by the Guardians of various Unions, and partly as such as had been collected by them among the destitute poor from the streets and alleys of the large towns, and after being placed in Homes established in this country, were subsequently sent out to Canada. As the expenditure incurred by the Guardians in the emigration of the children required the sanction of the Board, the proceeding imposed a serious responsibility as regards the arrangements for the passage of the children to Canada, the reception of them on landing there, and their subsequent distribution among the farmers or other persons resident in Canada."

And so, that spring they sent a man to Canada who would visit hundreds of the children and judge how they were faring. His report would contain evidence and conclusions that would appall the men who sent him. In Canada it would shock governments and excite public opinion for years to come. His name was Andrew Doyle.

Two
The Verdict of Andrew Doyle

The air on that June afternoon around the port of Liverpool was heavy with sweat as men, working hand-to-hand, finished loading the hold of the steamer *Sarmatian*, the 3,600-ton pride of the Allan Line, the steamship company that hundreds of thousands of men and women took from England and Scotland to the new land. She was set to sail the following day, the fourth of June, 1874, for Quebec.

Her accommodation, outside of cabin and intermediate passage, was steerage, which was cheap and communal, though the company now provided supervision by stewardesses for the welfare of women and children. The *Sarmatian's* food was plain. But for many of her passengers it was better than anything they were used to—fresh bread, potatoes, meat, and tea. On Sundays there was pudding. Still, life aboard was often rough. She rolled a lot, and in steerage the air was foul.

From a landing stage just beyond one of the sheds along the waterfront, there appeared a line of children, mostly small, walking in single file toward the gangway. All of them, even the smallest who were six years old, carried over the shoulder a grey cloth bag. At the head of the line strode a tall, elegant woman in her mid-thirties, her thick brown hair protruding from beneath a fashionable bonnet. At the foot of the gangway she stopped and shook hands with a man obviously waiting for her, a rather stout man with a smile that was easy and generous and tended to soften the official nature of his job that day. They stood there together, chatting and watching as the long line of children, mostly silent and solemn, walked up the gangway and aboard the *Sarmatian*. There were one hundred and fifty.

The woman was Maria Rye, now in her sixth year as head of Our Western Home in Niagara-on-the-Lake, ready to leave Liverpool once again on one of her many trips with more children for distribution among the people of Canada, mostly in Ontario. The man beside her, nodding and talking, was Andrew Doyle, a lawyer, born and raised in

Dublin. He was sixty-five. He was by then a man of long experience as an inspector of the conditions under which the poor lived. He had been an inspector with the Poor Law Board for almost twenty-five years, and when its work was taken over by the Local Government Board in 1871 he stayed on. In the spring of 1874, when he was near retirement but still active and robust, the board chose him to go to Canada to see first-hand how the child immigrants were working out and how they were being treated in the homes of Maria Rye and Annie Macpherson, and also in the homes of the Canadian men and women with whom they were placed.

He went on board the *Sarmatian* that day and spoke with the captain and several of the officers. Then he strolled through the ship, talking with some of the children, taking note of their clothing, their appearance, and, so far as an inspector could tell, their general health. They were, he knew, of two distinct types, a fact in itself that he would ponder for the next several months. First, there were the pauper children, about a hundred of them, brought to the *Sarmatian* from workhouses in the cities and the country, where they had lived, usually with their parents, and where they had been given a basic education, albeit skimpy, by the board for which Doyle worked. Then there was the second group smaller in number—about fifty— and altogether different in background and attitude. These were the street children, who have been etched forever in the imagination through the description by Charles Dickens of the little thieves of Mr. Fagin. Some of them had lived on the streets for several years, stealing food, sleeping under railway arches, and surviving only by their wits. They were known as street arabs: "One hundred and twenty-seven children have during the past year been received into the home from the streets and gutters and back slums of London and other big cities," Maria Rye said the year before. "Of these, ten have been removed by friends or proved unsuitable to emigrate for various reasons, but the remainder were sent to Canada." It was such children, mingling with all the others, that Andrew Doyle speculated on as he strode back and forth along the deck of the *Sarmatian* on that hot June day. He spent several hours on board, taking note of the arrangements for supervising the children, for feeding and sleeping them, and also the attitude toward them of the captain and crew. Then, after a few words with Miss Rye, he left, returning the next morning to see them off.

Almost one month later, in the early days of July, Andrew Doyle arrived, quietly and alone, at the port of Montreal. He spent a couple of days around the immigration shed, talking with the agent and his officers, until he satisfied himself that he had an accurate picture of the way in which the children were received upon their arrival. Then he set out for Knowlton, the little community seventy miles south and east of Montreal where Annie Macpherson had one of her homes. His plan, already drawn up with the thoroughness for which he was so well known, was to spend several days in and around Knowlton and then take the train to Ontario, where he would put in several weeks visiting Macpherson homes in Belleville and Galt, Maria Rye's home in Niagara-on-the-Lake, and four hundred children placed among the settlers on the farms and in the villages.

At each of the distributing homes he met first with the ladies themselves—Annie Macpherson, Maria Rye, or one of their assistants—and did his best to get things off on a friendly basis. He was by nature an affable man—though several people he met in Canada came to regard him as a bit officious and talkative—but he also knew from long years as an inspector that going about his job in a courteous manner was the most effective way. He sat down with the women, had a chat about the weather in London, the trip over, and then, gracefully but deliberately, he began his work. First, he would tour the building, investigating it, floor by floor, room by room, for its structure, its size, its suitability, and its cleanliness. How many children could it accommodate at one time? How was the food chosen and prepared? What were the arrangements for the sleeping of the children? What were the provisions for those who might take sick? Sometimes in the evenings he would sit in the living room—often past dark, for he never seemed to tire—asking Annie Macpherson, and later Maria Rye, question after question about the arrangements for financing the work, supervising the children, selecting the homes, and seeing to they later welfare of the children. He wondered, for example, what care they took to see that the children they placed in homes were kept track of, were not passed from settler to settler, until they ended up lost in the cities of Canada or the United States. Then, when he was convinced that he had an understanding of their system—at least as they saw it and explained it—Andrew Doyle began the most crucial part of his investigation: his visits to the children themselves.

He studied the register in each home and, after noting the areas in which there seemed to be a concentration of the children, he would spend most of his time there, going later on to the far and remote places, where often a lone child lived in the cabin of a homesteader, In the beginning he went from each home in the company of a worker or a volunteer—in Quebec it was an able man named Christopher

Dunkin, at former federal agriculture minister and one of Annie Macpherson's most loyal supporters—but, once he had gained a sense of the area, he went alone. He could be seen throughout much of that summer, a brisk, aging man, leaving small and silent hotels early in the morning, climbing into his buggy and racing along dusty roads to see as many children as he could most of them welcoming the sound of his voice as a sound from home. Years later, when he was well on in years, he would still remember how some of them, eight and nine years old, were so overjoyed at his visit that they mistook him for a beloved friend or teacher back in England.

For the most part he kept his impressions to himself, though once, when he was invited out for the evening at the home of Senator Billa Flint in Belleville, he so dominated the conversation that Flint, a businessman in Belleville and one of the original backers of Annie Macpherson's home there, told friends later that he couldn't get a word in, that Doyle was a know-it-all. Generally, however, he kept his feelings in check, even after he was told by a girl he took to be intelligent and believable that once, after some minor problem at Maria Rye's home in Niagara-on-the-Lake, she had been banished to a cold upstairs room, to stay there for eleven days on bread and water. Once, in September, he was invited by Miss Rye to visit home for a special evening, to be attended by more than three hundred of her girls, gathered from near and far, and by he Anglican Bishop of Toronto. But though he was given two weeks' notice and told the evening was being arranged so that he could see hundreds of the girls, Andrew Doyle did not appear.

Then, in October, he said a friendly farewell to Maria Rye, Annie Macpherson, who felt, in general, that he looked kindly on their work, and went home to England. Once there, he started to organize his findings and his opinions; within a couple of weeks he began to write his report. He worked steadily much of that winter, until by the end of January it was complete. Then, one week later, on February 8, 1875, it was made public. In Britain and in Canada it hit like thunder.

Doyle was generous enough—and also shrewd enough—to say several times in his report that the women, especially Annie Macpherson, were inspired by the highest motives and accomplished much that was good. He realized the hardships they faced. And he cautioned anyone who might review their work to avoid damning it simply on the basis of a few cases in which particular children had had bad experiences. This was especially true, he argued, in the case of the children who were taken directly from the streets to the homes in London and then, sometimes only a few days later, brought to Canada. "Of what these ladies have done and are endeavouring to do," he wrote, "for that class of children, it is impossible to speak too highly." He went on to praise, in the fulsome way, the devotion of the men and women who worked for the homes in Canada, mostly as volunteers, especially Ellen Bilbrough, who came with Annie Macpherson in 1870 and stayed to supervise the Marchmont Home in Belleville. "The liberal and unostentatious way in which that lady devotes the rare gifts with which she is endowed," he said, "the fulfillment of very onerous duties is beyond all praise."

The presence of those passing comments, however, only served to make the full report seem more balanced and fair and—as Doyle well knew—more forceful. He said near the beginning that he would make no statement or claim that he was not prepared to back up with full evidence. Then he went on to condemn almost everything about the entire enterprise, from the methods by which the children were taken into the organizations in London, to the ways in which they were sent to Canada, established in the homes, distributed among Canadians, treated by the settlers, and inspected while in their care.

He was troubled first of all by the fact that the children the board was entrusting to Annie Macpherson and Maria Rye—children from the workhouses—were being thrown together without discretion with the children from the streets: the waifs and strays, the notorious street arabs. In Doyle's mind, the children of the workhouses were destitute but not depraved. Many of them, forced into their circumstances, still lived in families and received a degree of moral teaching and a token education. The workhouses, in which tens of thousands people lived at the time, were shelters of despair but they were not schools of vice. The streets, however, were another world.

He knew that the women, like other rescue workers, looked upon the street arabs through eyes of religious compassion. He referred to one such worker who, when asked where the street children came from, replied that they came from "the night asylum, the police office, cold stairs, haylofts, and barrels and boxes along the harbor." He said he understood their idealism, but their attitude to such children was naive and caused nothing but trouble in Canada. To Doyle, drawing upon his years as an inspector, such children were out of the gutter. He called them semi-criminals. "It appears to be thought," he wrote caustically, "that within a few weeks, in some cases, indeed, within a few days, these children who have grown up with the habits and associations that Miss Macpherson and others describe, can be brought under such moral and religious influence as to make it safe to place them out in service in a new country and under conditions that are certainly not favourable to their future success."

The street children and the problems they brought made their first impression on Doyle when, while visiting the Belleville area, he heard a rumour that one of the children was in the local jail. He visited the boy and quickly learned that he was not a workhouse child but a street arab. Doyle was distressed, not so much for the boy and his situation, but because of the discredit he was bringing on others, the children from the workhouses, who, he fervently believed, were of good reputation. "In Canada," he wrote in his report, "no distinction is made between them. They are all 'Miss Macpherson's children' or 'Miss Rye's children'. No one in Belleville knows that the 'arab' boy whom I found, was one of the five inmates of the jail of that town, has not come from an English workhouse..."

As he made his way through the towns and countryside that summer, Doyle came upon farmer after farmer who had applied for a child and received a thief. "The managers of the homes," he reported, "are familiar with numerous cases of complaints of insubordination, falsehoods, petty thefts, and of still graver offences. I confess I was surprised to find how frequently such complaints were repeated by employers during my visits, and how often I heard the determination expressed, 'never to take another.'" His opinion of the harm the children were visiting upon the whole scheme of child immigration—and the reputation of the workhouse children—was clinched one day when, in the course of his investigation, he met with a Belleville politician, A. F. Wood, one of the men who had appealed to Annie Macpherson to set up her home in town. Doyle, who got to know Wood quite well, asked him, now that the home had been in Belleville a few years, for his opinion on the benefits it brought. "That gentleman," Doyle wrote later, "whose sympathies were at first so warmly enlisted in support of a benevolent scheme, and whose opinion is entitled to so much weight, has since repeatedly assured that he felt compelled, though reluctantly, to change his views of it. It would take a long time, he said, to eradicate the evil that had been produced in his own neighbourhood by the class of children who had been imported to it."

Doyle disliked almost as much the ways the children, once they had arrived in Canada, were placed out in private homes. On paper, he said, the policy of both women seemed plausible enough, in that no applicant for a child received one, either for adoption or for indenture, until he satisfied Annie Macpherson or Maria Rye that he was fit, by providing references from trustworthy citizens, including his clergyman. At first glance, Doyle admitted, this seemed reasonable, but then he ripped it apart as flimsy and dangerous. In Britain, he pointed out, no child could be boarded out until a committee of local citizens was convinced that the home was acceptable and guaranteed to take responsibility for the child's welfare once he was there. "As a rule," he then wrote, "the homes in which the children are placed in Canada are not so selected, and it is very certain that great abuses do ensue. Had all the homes been 'selected' by persons who have an intimate knowledge of the locality, children would not have been placed in such homes as those in which I found some of them nor, if strict enquiry had been made both as to the requirements and character of applicants for children, should we hear of such cases as a child being brought back because it was 'too small' then sent to another place 'next day', then brought back 'because the man drank....'"

As for the references that both women said they required, he gave them short shrift. He told the story of meeting a woman who had applied for a child and received one, but who later admitted that, while her minister might be able to describe her family as "respectable", he was not in a position to judge her fitness to raise a child. There was, he said emphatically, no substitute for a committee of responsible local citizens, to decide on suitability and to take responsibility to see that the child was not mistreated. "If Miss Rye and Miss Macpherson," he wrote bluntly, "were less anxious to get the children off their hands immediately upon their arrival, not only would they be able to exercise greater discrimination in selecting places, but they would be able to get them on better terms..."

Still, it was when he came to the supervision of the children, once they were entrusted to the settlers, that Doyle turned up his most shocking evidence and made his most damning condemnation. In the case of Miss Rye, there was actually no system of supervision at all; she simply gave out her children—throughout Nova Scotia, New Brunswick, and Ontario asking a few friends in each area to keep an eye open. She took the view that no news was good news. As a result, large numbers of Miss Rye's girls were never heard from again; what happened to them is left to the imagination of history. Time after time Doyle would go in search of a child and find the home in which she had been placed, only to be told she was no longer there, that she had gone weeks before, drifting, some thought, into the United States, and in some cases into life on the streets.

As for Annie Macpherson's supervision. Doyle reported that, while she had a system, it was quite imperfect. For one thing, she had placed so many children by the time he did his investigation that it was impossible for her visitors, all volunteers, to keep up. (Doyle's observation on Annie Macpherson is also a testimony to her abundant energy: "Miss Macpherson's labours in England are of so engrossing a character that one wonders how she is able to give any time to Canada at all. After three months of the most harassing and anxious work in London, she crosses the Atlantic to pass her winter in Canada, visiting or endeavouring to visit the hundreds whom she has placed out there; then returns to England to organize her summer parties of young emigrants.") Moreover, he argued, there was a crucial difference between the kind of casual visit her workers made and the kind of careful inspection that was required. "The visits," he said, "do not constitute the sort of inspection that is of much use, having a good deal more the character of visits from friends and guests of the employers than of an impartial inquiry into the conditions and treatment of the children." As a result of this superficial gesture, he had encountered numerous cases, not just of missing children, but of abused children, boys and girls who complained of mistreatment that was all too often merely confirmed by their masters. A great many of the men and women who took children also failed completely in living up to their agreement to send them to school, at least for part of the year.

All in all, Doyle felt that the system of supervision was probably the most appalling shortcoming in the entire program of child immigration. Because of Miss Rye's carelessness and Miss Macpherson's limited resources, thousands of British children, already in painful circumstances, were cast adrift to be overworked or mistreated by the settlers of early Canada, who, he had concluded were generally honest, but often hard taskmasters. It could not be continued.

Only one aspect of the work, he found, could be called a clear success: the adoption of children who were very young, under five, who could not be expected to work, and who were therefore adopted with sincerity. (This was not the case with older children, who were adopted, he felt, only as a means of getting them for free labour.) "The mere fact," Doyle said, "that people of good character apply for a very young child to adopt with a view to bringing it up gratuitously as their own is in itself some guarantee that the child will be well done by. And well done by these children certainly are. I visited several, from children adopted into the families of gentlefolks to those, adopted by small, hardworking farmers, and I may say without exception, their condition was in all cases most satisfactory." It was the only pleasant note in his long and grim report.

He told the members of the Local Government Board that, at least in principle, child emigration rightly carried out could work to the benefit of Britain, Canada, and the children themselves. But this could be so only if the work was corrected at every stage, from the initial selection of the children through to their distribution and final emancipation as young adults. Above all, he stressed again and again the need for a system of inspection that was adequate.

One day before he left Canada, Andrew Doyle went to Ottawa and there had a meeting with the prime minister of the day, the solemn, honourable Presbyterian, Alexander Mackenzie. The meeting was attended by Canada's immigration agent in London, a man named Edward Jenkins. Doyle gave them his findings and his judgement. "The result," he wrote later in his report, "will, I believe, be that Mr. Jenkins will be authorized to discuss the subject of the emigration of pauper children with the Local Government Board with a view, if it should be thought desirable to continue it, to place the system upon a more satisfactory footing." But throughout all of that history its footing would be, like its sense of humanity, precarious and uncertain and, in the end, a record of unfulfilled promise.

On March 16, a few weeks after Doyle's report was made public. Maria Rye and Annie Macpherson, their collars drawn high against the punishing Ottawa winds, strode through the snows to Parliament Hill. Both were hurt by the attack made upon them, but beneath that predictable feeling, the deeper response of each woman to all that Andrew Doyle had said was decisively different: Annie Macpherson, moderate and wise, was ready to make change where change was needed, while Maria Rye, angry and proud, was set for a two-year fight with Andrew Doyle, in which she would hurl her disdain and, in turn, draw upon herself a deep discredit.

Once inside the House of Commons on that unhappy day, the women were shown through the corridors and into the committee rooms, where, behind a long table covered with dull green felt, sat the members of the House of Commons Select Committee on Immigration and Colonization. Each member was well aware of the work of both women, and each had read the criticism of Andrew Doyle. They wanted to hear at first hand from Annie Macpherson and Maria Rye, and, in addition, from others—clergy, politicians, ordinary citizens—who would, they supposed, give them a true picture of child immigration and whether it was really as bad as Andrew Doyle had drawn it.

Very early the feelings of the witnesses and the members of the committee began to take a discernible and dramatic form. One of the first to speak was Adam Gordon, MP, a man from Northern Ontario and a member of the Liberal Party of Alexander Mackenzie. The charges, Gordon said, were serious and widely publicized. Therefore, he

insisted that if the committee was to do its job, it must not be content
with staged presentations by the women but must question them closely, scrutinize the record, and let the blame fall where it would. The
committee agreed, and he turned to Annie Macpherson, who was sitting with her friend Ellen Bilbrough of Belleville. She was bit wary, but
calm and assured, as Gordon began his questions

He was particularly concerned with any financial interest he might
have in child immigration. He knew that Andrew Doyle had hinted at
this by reporting that though he asked her for a financial statement,
she did not send one. She told Gordon that the books were open and
independently audited. Then she passed out copies of the most recent
statement, setting out the expenses and the balance at each home, in
Belleville, Galt, and Knowlton. Far from any pecuniary advantage, the
statements showed that after expenses there was virtually nothing left.
(In Belleville, for example, the expenses for 1874 were something over
three thousand dollars and the cash on hand was three dollars.) Several
times in the testimony she disputed Doyle and his findings, but she was
careful, as she did so, not to appear defiant. In fact, she told Gordon
that she had spent that entire winter in Canada with the single purpose
of trying to improve the quality of the program. Nonetheless, she did
feel that Doyle was incorrect in saying that many of her children were
depraved, for she had been assured by those who brought them to her
London homes that none were from the criminal class. For her, that
was assurance enough. She also disputed his claim that she did not see
to the supervision of her children once they were placed, saying that
she had one full-time visitor for her two thousand children and a horse
was kept at Belleville for his use. Moreover, she told the members of
the committee, she had a number of women, friends of hers in Ontario
and Quebec, who dropped in on the children from time to time for
what she called "friendly visits". There is no evidence that Gordon, or
others on the committee, asked her if such visits were independent
enough to be of any value.

When the time came, a few days later, for Maria Rye to testify, the
members of the committee arrived early in the morning with a high
sense of expectancy. They knew that, unlike Annie Macpherson, Maria
Rye was ready to deny everything that Doyle had said and even to
attack him for bad faith and poor manners. They sat quietly as she
strode slowly to her place, a tall woman with an aloof air and a manner
that spoke of class and affluence and friendships in the higher places of
British society. She had, after all, come to this work with the endorse-
ment of eminent people; in Canada, the Anglican Bishop of Toronto

was her generous advocate. As she sat before this collection of motley and obscure back-benchers, who could blame her if she felt, even a little, that her great work was being interfered with and her time wasted, first by Andrew Doyle, who was merely an officious clerk, and now by this bothersome committee of shopkeepers and barristers from the hinterland of the colony.

The report of Andrew Doyle, she told them that day, was ungenerous, unjust, and most inaccurate. She seemed especially incensed—for she came to it so quickly and without any prodding—by his reference to the girl, the one he said was honest, who told him she had been punished by Miss Rye by being placed in a cold, drafty room for eleven days with nothing but bread and water. She said this was not correct. The child had not been there for eleven days, only a few. Besides, she really needed the punishment. After all, she told the committee, the girl had been sent to nine places in four years and had been sent back by every one of them. The members heard this explanation and appeared to receive it with understanding and even sympathy. No man asked, in the light of Miss Rye's admission that she had placed the girl on bread and water, if this might be cruel and harmful. Moreover, no member of the committee seemed inclined to question whether the moving of the girl from home to home nine times in four years might be harmful to her.

Miss Rye then turned to Doyle's claim that she did not keep proper records and as a result had actually lost all knowledge of many of the children she had brought out She admitted that indeed she did not keep a detailed account of the work, for the simple reason that she was too busy. She had hundreds of children coming out every year and had an enormous correspondence. Keeping a register with the names and locations of all the children would be, to her, simply a bit of red tape. As for supervising the children through regular and careful visits, she did not do this because she did not see it as a necessity. After all the children were placed with good people, men and women who would be insulted by the suggestion, implied by inspection, that they could not manage the children.

All through her testimony that day ran a note of confident disdain for everything that Andrew Doyle had said, a feeling not merely that he was wrong, but that he did not understand that he was, in fact, presumptuous to call her work into question. When one of the members— recalling a section of Doyle's report in which he suggested that she was a cruel woman held in fear by her children—asked how the youngsters felt when they were returned to her, her reply was as curt as it was curious: "On the twenty-second of September 1874, when Mr. Doyle was in Canada," she replied, "I invited about 500 persons to meet him and a three week notice was given of the gathering. Had Mr. Doyle been at the home on that day he would have seen some three hundred happy, bright children and been in a better position to have given an opinion on this subject. Children who have been naughty and disobedient and threatened with punishment, finding themselves en route for the home, and Miss Rye who is the very embodiment of punishment, are not likely to have much pleasure in looking forward to a return visit to the home; nor should they."

Into the committee room on those days in the winter of 1875 came others who had requested a chance to appear, to put before the government their view on the work of Annie Macpherson and Maria Rye. A few who could not because of the weather or the distance sent letters through their members of Parliament, and these were read into the record. They were, almost entirely, from men who were politicians or judges or merchants or prelates of the Anglican Church—in short, leading citizens who, to a man, saw in child immigration a source of labour, which was desperately needed and reasonably affordable. There were, it appears, no farmers, none of those who had actually applied for a child and gotten one. Most of the MP's who appeared said with great confidence that, from personal experience in their constituencies, they knew that the children—all but a very few incorrigibles—were treated well and doing well. Taken all in all, said James Young, a Liberal from South Waterloo, Ontario, there was no portion Canada's immigration system that was better for the country than this one, and it was cheap to conduct. Josiah Plumb, Conservative member for Niagara, and Miss Rye's own MP, said that as far as her work was concerned there was really no need for more supervision or inspection, because the evidence did not warrant it. After all, the demand for children was greater than the supply. And the Reverend William McMurray, the Anglican rector of Niagara, sent along a copy of the letter he had mailed to Andrew Doyle's superiors in England. "It is not my intention," he wrote, "to notice at full length the glaring inaccuracies which his report contains, nor is it my object to contradict his statements myself, but to ask you in all fairness to hear the other side before action is finally taken upon it, for a more ill-informed representation of Miss Rye's work here could not, in my humble opinion, have been made by anyone who professed to have examined its merits.'"

The most committed witnesses, however, were two men who were not even friends of Miss Rye—whom they did not even know—but of Annie Macpherson, whose life and work they supported as if it were their own. The first of these was Billa Flint, the senator from Belleville and the man who met Annie Macpherson on her very first visit to his town. He looked upon the committee members that day through large, bright eyes, in which gleamed the faith known only to a true believer. "I've examined Mr. Doyle's report," he said, "I've examined it carefully. I'm astonished that any gentleman could persistently present the dark side of the subject to the people. The system of inspection that Mr. Doyle wants is nothing but a form of red tape. Miss Macpherson and her friends already have an inspection. They don't need another one." And then, in one of those sly sentences betraying the cold rivalry that existed between the two women, he said that really it was too bad that Doyle had mixed up the work of Annie Macpherson with that of Maria Rye, for Miss Macpherson's was quite different.

He told them of that night the previous year when, with the intention of talking about emigration in general, he had invited Andrew Doyle to his home in Belleville. But the evening was a waste of time, he said, for Andrew Doyle couldn't stop talking long enough for him to get a word in. He concluded then and there that Doyle was a man with his mind made up; nothing could be allowed to change it.

Then, toward the end of March, when the hearing was almost over, a man came forward who, more than any other who appeared, would hold the committee in his command and strengthen and confirm all its sympathies toward Annie Macpherson and, indirectly, Maria Rye. He was Christopher Dunkin, a justice of the Quebec Superior Court, the man who had been a minister in the Cabinet of John A. Macdonald.

He was not a large man, but he had fine, strong features and a voice and a style that had set him apart during his years in Parliament as one of the best speakers in the House of Commons. He was a legal scholar and a student of the classics, and had been while a student at Harvard a tutor in Greek. In brief, he was a man of substance. He knew Annie Macpherson well. "I first met her," he said confidently, "in the fall of 1871 and had no hesitation, from what I had then learnt, in at once urging on her the establishment of a second home in my own section of the country, the Eastern Townships. It was thus, in a great part at my instance, that the Knowlton Home was founded. Miss Barber, who took and still has charge of it, is my sister. My wife and our other sisters are, as a matter of course, in instant communication with her, and almost everything of interest as it occurs there is known to me." He knew the work intimately, he said, and he was confident that it was carried out with great care and great charity. As for Andrew Doyle and his report, he dismissed both. He said that of course he had only examined it hastily, but nevertheless he knew it was wrong. "It is full of mis-apprehension and mistake," he said, "to use the mildest terms possible; the work of a reporter prepared to see, hear, argue whatever squared with the prepossessions natural to English poor law officialism, and whose flying stay here and there in Canada has wholly failed to correct these prepossessions."

He knew before he began that he was talking that day to men who felt as he did, that the need for labour was great; that the arrangements were generous, and that the work was done by people of religious motive, and therefore certain to be from the heart. Most of all, there ran beneath all that he said that day a belief, almost a faith, that the men and women into whose homes the children were sent were good people, kind and generous, who lived in communities that were always decent and honest. "Miss Macpherson's workers," Christopher Dunkin told the committee, "do their best to select good homes; and, as a mat-ter of fact, they very generally can and do choose well. If, as must hap-pen, now and then they make mistakes, Canadian social habits are such as to make it morally certain that some neighbor or other, if not the whole neighborhood, will protect any child from wrong."

When its meetings were ended, the members left Ottawa with their faith intact and their indignation stirred by the intrusion of Andrew Doyle. They knew, just as they had always known, that the work of Annie Macpherson and Maria Rye was a credit to them and a boon to Canada. "It results," the secretary of the committee, C. H. Pozer, con-cluded, "with very little exception, in permanent advantage to the chil-dren who are brought out and to the country which receives them."

Yet back in Britain, despite all the words of effusive support—not a single word of criticism had been voiced before the committee—the work of the women had suffered a setback. The workhouses temporar-ily ceased supporting Maria Rye and she would send no children for three years. The influential *Times* of London demanded emigration of children cease until the schemes were reformed. As a result, a supply of help for the farmers, who were the very constituents of the committee's members, was in real danger.

Therefore, while they dismissed Doyle's report as diplomatically as they could by calling it partial, they nevertheless felt that to put it in its place they should call for a Canadian inspection, one conducted by the provinces, which would be much more thorough and thus able to offset what Andrew Doyle had done. So, that same year the first Canadian inspection was undertaken, one that would ultimately claim that child immigration was of shining value to both the country and the children. If anyone at the time wondered what its findings would be, he could have gotten a clue from the appointment, as one of the inspectors, of John A. Donaldson, a federal immigration agent. Weeks earlier, when he heard that the work of the two women was under review in Ottawa, he wrote a letter to Maria Rye, which she placed on record and in which he said: "I have often heard expressed the admiration a those seeking the children, how well they were trained when called on by you to sing their hymns and repeat verses that would compare favourably with any of our Sunday school children…I have no hesitation in saying, with but few exceptions, these children, both boys and girls, are invariably well treated by the parties that get them and that, in the case of the female portion, I have always felt you were filling a gap and supplying a want much felt by the community at large, as they will take the place of domestic servants in a few years."

A couple of weeks after Donaldson's appointment, the St. Catharines *Daily Times,* a newspaper serving the Niagara area of Maria Rye, ran a story dealing with one of her children. "A most horrible and revolting occurrence," the paper said, "has lately disgraced St. Catharines. One of Miss Rye's girls, herself a mere child appearing about 12 or 13—has been delivered of an infant. The poor girl is living in a family which claims to be quite respectable, and therefore no blame can possibly attach to Miss Rye." The article, with its quick and firm defence of Maria Rye, was followed several days later by a letter from one of her ardent supporters, R. N. Ball of Niagara-on-the-Lake, who carried the defence of Maria Rye a step further. He used the incident to take the offensive against Andrew Doyle: "I wish Mr. Doyle could see what a storm of indignation this St. Catharines case has produced; he would be obliged to acknowledge that public opinion is a power in Canada."

Very quickly Doyle became, for the press as for the politicians, the target of the attack. His findings, therefore, could be treated and dismissed as merely passing details along the way to the real business of the day: the discrediting of Andrew Doyle, the officious Englishman who had intruded in the affairs of Canada. The *Ottawa Free Press* was the most vivid and typical example. Toward the end of March, when the parliamentary committee was winding up, it referred to Doyle as an itinerant deadbeat and a professional leech.

"Mr. Doyle," the editor suggested, "seems to belong to a class of persons whom we consider the least desirable to have in Canada—professional leeches who seek to foist themselves into positions in connection with the affairs of this country from which salaries may be derived…He paid a visit to Canada, we have no doubt with the express intention of reaping to himself pecuniary profit out of an agitation which he had initiated in the old country against the benevolent work of Miss Rye and others.... In the meantime, we may state that, before the Parliamentary Committee, every one of the slurs thrown on the work of Misses Rye and Macpherson were proven false, and that the only apparent result was a general impression that the fellow Doyle is simply and only aiming at securing for himself a fat salary and the privilege of inspecting the homes of Canadians, who are generous enough to welcome the waifs and strays of the motherland and who do not wish and who will not permit any taint of the old country poor law to make bitter the sweetness of their generosity."

It was this tone—injured, but righteous and assured—that ran through all of the reporting and comment carried that winter on the work of Andrew Doyle. There was, as well, a view that was as strong as it was unexamined: that the children were a lesser breed who should be grateful for the decencies of Canadians who rescued them from their pitiful circumstances. "Any drearier or more forlorn prospect than what lies before a pauper child or guttersnipe in England is not easily imagined" said the *Globe.* "Almost any change must be for the better, and anyone who knows the character of the great majority of Canadian homes in which these waifs are placed who come to this side of the Atlantic would feel their judgements insulted by any lengthened or grave discussion of the question, whether or not it be for the advantage of such to leave England. Most certainly Canada can much more easily do without them than they can do without Canada."

Then, a couple of weeks later, the *Globe* took deadly, personal aim at Doyle. It chose grounds on which it was sure he was vulnerable to attack, his religious background. He was Roman Catholic. As always, it put its criticism in a shrewd and crafty way, questioning only the principle of it all, but leaving its innuendo unmistakable: "Mr. Doyle who, it appears, is a keen Roman Catholic was sent out to inspect the work or ladies who have not only all along avowed themselves to the Protestant but who, in order to avoid the very appearance of proselytism, have always taken out the children of Protestant only, leaving the emigration of Roman Catholic children exclusively to the benevolently inclined of their own Church. It was, to say the least of it, unfortunate, that the Local Government Board in England should have made such an appointment."

In all that it said that year on the work of Andrew Doyle, the press of Canada revealed a good deal of itself but also a good deal of the Canadian spirit of the time, of which it was merely a reflection. Thus, there was no criticism—not a word from one end of Canada to the other—of the women who conducted the work or of the farmers and townsmen who took the children. There was a comfortable acceptance of the view that all of them were doing a generous work for Canada, for Britain and for the children. Second, it saw the children—the *Globe's* designation of them as guttersnipes was a telling reference—as less than boys and girls with minds and spirits and dreams. They are objects for work, perhaps for pity, but not for understanding, for they required no understanding. Finally, the editorials of that year revealed a society preferring to trust the fates of thousands of children to their masters, with no other check made upon their welfare. To the *Globe*, an inspection system would be a bit of red tape; to the *Montreal Gazette*, it would threaten the authority of the master; to the *Ottawa Free Press* it was merely a ploy by which Andrew Doyle hoped to get himself a job in Canada.

In Britain, the controversies had a moderate and fleeting influence when, following the *Time's* urging, the Local Government Board took Andrew Doyle seriously and said that if Britain was to continue sending children to Canada, the program should "be placed under systematic superintendence and control." Annie Macpherson, much to the regret of Andrew Doyle, withdrew from co-operating with the board and no longer took any children from the workhouses. For her part, Maria Rye, stinging from the harshness of Doyle's attack on her work, sent no children at all for the next three years. In fact, though Doyle probably did not know its dimensions, there was, in the year he came, a small battalion of others—individual and groups—who were sending children to Canada. There was Madame von Koerber, and the Reverend M. Nugent, and Miss Fletcher, and the Reverend Mr. Burgess, and twenty-seven others. All were affected by the criticism of Andrew Doyle. In 1876, the year after his report, the number of children sent from Britain to Canada fell from a high point of 1,124 in 1873 to only 303.

For two full years Maria Rye nursed her grievance with the Doyle report. Aside from her haughty appearance before the parliamentary inquiry in Ottawa, and some sullen conversations with a few friends in Niagara-on-the-Lake—in which she complained at length that Doyle praised her work to her face and reversed himself once he returned to Britain—she remained curiously silent, beyond the reach of any who might have questioned her. Then, in the spring of 1877, the reason for her strange solitude became public. She had spent the months brooding and preparing a rebuttal, one she was sure would put to rest forever the unfairness of the Doyle report. It was, in almost every way, a blunder in both its tactics and its contents, one that left her more vulnerable than ever to Andrew Doyle. He was by then retired, free from the restraining influence of government service and only too ready to reply with a vengeance. Moreover, since he had always regarded her work as far less desirable than Annie Macpherson's, he was privately delighted that now, suddenly, he could point a finger at the real villain, without feeling that his criticism would affect the work of someone else whose efforts, while imperfect, were still deserving.

Her letter, written to the president of the Local Government Board, Andrew Doyle's former employer, was made public in May 1877. It was an emotional piece, at once self-pitying and imperious in its tone, yet overall a revelation of the very fault she sought to deny. Her lack of human compassion, even human understanding, were displayed for all to see. She drew around herself a spirit which she felt to be the shield of religion, but which was merely arrogance and disdain in the of humility. "I need not say anything," she wrote, "about the injustice done to myself, for the great glory of all true work that in the keeping of His commands there is the reward and a thousand Mr. Doyles could not touch me on that point." She was surprised—amazed would not be too strong a word—that the Local Government Board could not seem to grasp the fact that the people in Canada to whom she sent children were of such benevolence that inspecting them and the child, was almost unnecessary. "If you could only understand and realize," she wrote, "the substantial, orderly, comfortable, and a well-established class of people who are the custodians of the children in Canada, you would the better understand the enormous boon you are placing within their reach, and why I think inspection of the children of comparatively so small moment, and the reason I have so largely used correspondence as a means of oversight of the young people when once placed out." Indeed, she said later on, the gravest danger the children faced was in homes where they were treated too gently and too generously.

It was revealing that though she saw the settlers who took children in this benign and kindly light, she did not extend that feeling to the children themselves. Throughout all that she said in that long and often sad letter there ran an attitude, sometimes stark and ominous, that the children were less than appealing and that clearly it was on their shoulders that the blame for failure must come to rest when it occurred. Many of them, she pointed out in strong and heavy terms, had to be moved from home to home before they were found acceptable. "For instance," she said, "a girl may have two, possibly three homes found for her, into neither of which can she be fitted or comfortable, for it must always be remembered that the whole of these children have strongly marked characters and developments; but the majority of these exceptional cases are the cases of girls returned for violent temper, laziness, subordination, and tendencies to immorality. There is also, however, this great fact to be borne in mind on this point, that in Canada we *can* get ten places for such girls."

When Andrew Doyle read the letter of Maria Rye—sent to him as a courtesy by the Local Government Board at the same time that it was made public—he was approaching his seventieth year, living in retirement in Plas Dulas, a bright and comfortable home in a town he had known all his working life, Abergele, a hamlet in the shelter of the Welsh countryside, only forty miles from the British city of Liverpool. He was shocked by her attack on him, for he was certain that it was she who, ever since he had retired the previous year, had helped pass on the rumour that he had been forced out of his job as a result of his report on her work. He knew this to be true, but he also knew that, given the deep and burning resentments of Maria Rye, it was fully understandable. He gave the letter a rapid and preliminary skimming and then moved to his library, where he went slowly over it again, paragraph by paragraph. Then, after going over his own report and gathering notes and figures he had made but had not included in his original judgement, Doyle began to put on paper his reply to Maria Rye and her statements, claims, and opinions that he knew to be either ill-founded or outright misrepresentations. A few days later, on May 14, 1877, it was complete.

Maria Rye's letter, he said, only confirmed his opinion that her work was so inferior, so harmful, that no pauper children should ever be placed in her care for shipment to Canada. He exposed most of her claims to be inaccurate, as, for example, her insistence that only a small number of the girls needed to be moved many times before locating a satisfactory placement. He brought forth his evidence that the actual number was around two hundred and ninety. When he took up her claim that close supervision was unnecessary, he revealed that every country then receiving immigrant children had put in place a form of careful inspection. "In England, Scotland, Ireland, France," he wrote, "the strictest supervision is provided for. All those who take, or have taken, interest in this subject, legislators and administrators, have recognized this as the indispensable condition, Miss Rye appears to be the solitary exception. Regulations that are essential in other countries, and, for other agents, she thinks may be dispensed with in Canada, and on behalf of Miss Rye alone."

Then he made his most injurious thrust at her—one that would appear long afterward as retaliatory and vindictive—by drawing a distinction between her work and that of Annie Macpherson, a distinction not as apparent as he made it seem and one that, in his hands, became the ultimate reproach. "Now, Sir," he wrote, taking note of improvements made by Annie Macpherson in her inspection system, "the wide and varied experience of Miss Macpherson in Canada has led her to the conclusion that no matter what class of children you take out, or in what class of homes you may place them, the strictest personal supervision is absolutely necessary. Even if I could appeal to no other or higher authority than that of Miss Macpherson, hers alone would be sufficient to justify the opinion I have expressed that no children ought to be sent out until a complete and satisfactory system of supervision is established."

Of course, Maria Rye continued to send children, thousands of them. Almost everyone but Andrew Doyle wanted her to continue: the politicians, the press, the people of Canada, and, not least of all, the officials in Britain, those in charge of the poor, who, while worrying over what would happen to them, began once again to deliver into Maria Rye's hands large numbers of workhouse children. Indeed, almost a century after Andrew Doyle's report, a British historian, Kathleen Heasman, would write that contrary to his expectations, the work of Andrew Doyle, by attracting attention to child immigration, actually caused it to grow.

Over a quarter of a century, between 1869 when she began and 1896 when her home in Niagara-on-the-Lake was taken over by the Anglican Church, Maria Rye brought to Canada almost five thousand children. The government of Canada had undertaken its inspection system, but for the most part it was a token, designed primarily to counter Doyle. As for Miss Rye, she steadfastly refused to carry out any such supervision and even criticized those who believed in it. Mostly, she simply stood the children in a line and let the farmers size them up much as they sized up their stock; then they took them away.

Once, in those early years, she brought to Canada a girl named Mary Ford, who, according to someone who knew her in Britain, was a girl of character and promise. Like so many, she was destined to be passed from family to family, rejected by almost everyone; eventually she drifted to Hamilton, Ontario, where she worked as a domestic in a boarding house, then she simply vanished. Maria Rye denounced her as obstinate, impertinent, ill-conditioned, a girl who should never have been brought to Canada. Nothing at all remains of Mary Ford, nothing but a letter written in the summer of 1873 to her brother in London. Maria Rye notwithstanding, the letter casts light upon a gentle spirit and leaves us wondering about a life that might have been:

> Dear Edward:
> I take the greatest pleasure in writing to you these lines, as I suppose you have long been expecting a letter from me, but you must please pardon my neglect; give my best to darling Willie, and tell him that I feel very anxious about him; I hope that both of you may see better days to come; I hope my dear sister Jane has been to see you, and hope, dear, that you are improving in your lessons, as I feel very anxious about you. I have been very sick for a long time as the winter has been very cold, but summer has been very warm, and I hope in time to come that I may be able to take you both out of the poorhouse....
> My pen is bad, my ink is pale,
> My love for you will never fail...
> your affectionate sister
> Mary

Three
Tragedy and Trial

When the coroner, Allan Cameron, arrived at the courthouse in the Ontario town of Owen Sound to give his testimony at the murder trial of Helen Findlay, he barely noticed the size of the crowd—extraordinary for a chill day in the middle of December—so large that it overflowed the aisles and spilled down the steps and out over the cold, frosted courtyard. His mind was occupied. It had been that way for several weeks since the eleventh of November, the day the police came to his office and advised him to go out into the country fourteen miles to Keppel, to the farm of Helen P. Findlay, where a death had occurred in circumstances that warranted a coroner's investigation. He dropped everything and went.

In an upstairs room toward the back of the house, stretched out on two bare boards, he found the body of a child, a fifteen-year-old boy named George Green, an English lad who had been in Canada less than a year. The state of the body and the condition of the room where the boy died were such that they would haunt Cameron's memory the rest of his life. In all is forty years in medicine, including his early days in the slums of Glasgow, he had seen nothing as shocking as his discovery on that grey afternoon in November 1895. Promptly he held an inquest at which neighbours testified that the boy had been severely beaten and systematically starved. Miss Findlay was charged with murder, later changed to manslaughter.

Seated in the prisoner's box, looking out upon the grey and solemn faces, Helen Findlay seemed in appearance much as she was described by her neighbours when the reporters had asked what kind of woman she was. They said she was mannish in her ways—Amazonian was the word that one of them used—the kind of woman no man would want to tangle with. She was forty-one years old, of above average height with a strong chin, weathered skin, and iron-grey hair on which sat a rough cloth cap. She had lived on the farm most of her life, ever since she had arrived in Canada from Scotland with her parents twenty-five earlier when she was fifteen. After her parents died she continued to live on the farm with her brother, and when he was killed in an accident the previous year, she decided to work the farm—about thirty acres of hay, and vegetables, eighteen head of cattle, twelve hogs, eleven sheep, and three horses—on her own. In the spring of that year, to help with the work, she sent to one of the agencies in Toronto that imported boys from England, and that is how, on the seventh of May, young George Green came to live with her.

She made it clear, simply by what she herself told the court, that she did not think too much of the boy, for, as she put it, he was weak on his feet and did not work well in the fields picking stones. She had tried to teach him to mow—he, course, had never seen a farm or its machinery—but he could not even do that. Still, she tolerated him for the few weeks of his trial period, and although she could have sent him back, signed an agreement to keep him for three years, providing him, in return for his work, with food, lodging, and washing, and seventy-five dollars. But he was a sickly person, she said, causing her a lot of extra work, and she admitted that when he was deathly ill that summer, she did say (as one of her neighbours claimed), "I wish the brute would die or get better."

Those who knew George Green said he was an average boy, shy and bashful in his manner and apt to speak only when someone asked him a question. He had been with one other farmer before being sent to Helen Findlay, and they remembered him as a good boy, but one who was not cut out to work on the farm. He was blind in one eye and so, the man said, could not handle a team of horses. After only four weeks he returned him. "I don't wish to keep the boy you sent," he told the home, "on account of defective eyesight."

In the courtroom on that day in December, along with the coroner, the several doctors, and the police constable who had arrested Helen Findlay, were several of her neighbours who had been called to testify as to the treatment she gave George Green and if, as the coroner's inquest had found, it was such as to result in his death. All of them stated that from time to time during the six months the boy lived with Helen Findlay they saw her abusing him—kicking him with her boots, striking him with an axe handle, prodding him with a pitchfork. W. H. Horne, who lived on the next farm, told of seeing the boy, blue and cold in the fall, crying as he was chased by Helen Findlay, a pitchfork high over her head. Mary Brown, a young girl who lived at the same house and worked alongside George Green, said he was a good boy but not quick enough to please Helen Findlay. "In the fields," she said, "he could not work fast enough and she struck him with the prongs of the fork and said if he didn't hurry up she'd run the pitchfork through him. Mr. Horne's wife, Barbara, recalled conversations in which Helen Findlay said she enjoyed beating the boy. "She told me," Mrs. Horne said, "about striking him and he said oh please stop, and she told me that was great fun."

When the time came, on the third day of the trial, for Coroner Allan Cameron—a greying, ruddy-faced man in his sixties—to take the stand, he did so with the confident, assertive style that went with his forty years in medicine and his brusque Scottish temperament. The boy died, he told the court, as the result of neglect, starvation, and violence. Both the defence and the prosecution took him back over the events of November—his discovery of the body on November 11, and his examination of it then and later on November 16 when it was exhumed at the request of Helen Findlay's lawyers for a second autopsy—and his testimony was of a kind to strike horror in the courtroom and, through the press which amplified it, throughout the country.

He was asked, first of all, about the condition of the room in which George Green spent his last days. It smelled more like a privy than anything else, he said. In the corner there was a straw mattress with a large hole in the centre—about ten inches deep, he figured—like a nest into which someone had burrowed in order to keep warm. The hole was caked with excrement. The room was dirty in the extreme, with excrement that had been there for many days creating an atmosphere so foul that he could recall nothing in his career that would even approach it.

As for the body itself, he described it as severely emaciated—"he would have made kid gloves already prepared" was the way Cameron put it—as the result of acute starvation. The skin was covered with welts, scabs, abrasions, and flea bites. According to Cameron and two physicians who had carried out an autopsy that same day, the abrasions were the result of direct violence. One of the physicians, William G. Dow explained to the court that his post-mortem examination, revealed that the boy's internal organs were all normal and it could not be said that his death was the result of any inherent physical defect. It was violence, Dow said, violence and starvation. The excrement that covered the lower part of his body and the bed in which he died was the result of diarrhea, brought on by the pittance of food he was given—a virtual starvation diet, consisting of little else than bran porridge.

When Helen Findlay herself took the stand for questioning by her lawyer, H. G. Tucker, and the crown prosecutor. A. G. MacKay, the courtroom overflowed, not only with spectators, but with reporters from all of the major newspapers, who were there also on behalf of papers in Britain to hear the case that was stirring feelings that were intense and complicated. At the press table, the reporters studying her expression and her style of speaking noticed that though she had what they all chose to call a mannish appearance, she spoke in a quiet manner that was restrained, almost diffident. In their stories there seemed to run a current of sympathy for her as a woman of the land, resourceful and industrious, now faced with a situation that might not be of her own making. "Her features are regular," a reporter from the *Globe* had described her earlier, "the nose clean cut and well shaped, month small, with full red lips, which are firmly set and with the rather sharp chin give indication of strength of character. Her eyes are a light grey, and the brows wide apart over the nose which is not generally a sign of bad temper."

She insisted—just as she always had, both in her personal conversations and at her preliminary hearing—that the boy was useless. And as she described him in court that day, her voice cautious but clear as she listed his many failings, there was in all that she said a view that George Green was to her a kind of primitive and partial being, a boy who had no feelings and knew no dreams and perhaps had no soul. He was, as she put it, defective from head to foot. For one thing, he was cross-eyed. He was also humpbacked. His right hip was drawn in and he sidled along with his right side forward. His mouth was at the side of his head and his lower jaw stuck out an inch beyond the upper, so that his teeth did not meet. Also, she said, he was left-handed.

She denied, of course, the testimony of her neighbours—more than a dozen of them—who said she beat the boy, tortured him, really, and in the end let him die in a bed filled with the discharge of his bowels brought on by the dreadful diet of bran that she fed him. Three physicians testified that the room in which the boy died was indescribable in its filth. But this also she denied. She did admit that of course she shouted at George Green; as she told the court: "This was a different boy. He didn't disobey at all. He only acted in a stupid way."

For the twelve jurors who sat for five days, complaining later of the hardness of the benches they had to sit on, the most crucial evidence came, not from Helen Findlay, but from three physicians who had been called by her lawyer to speak in her defence. Two of them, C. M. Lang and Thomas H. Middlebro, had been authorized to have the body of George Green exhumed and subjected to a second autopsy. They did so on November 16, 1895. The grave and the coffin were filled with water, but both men insisted this would not harm their examination.

Their finding, which they put in highly confident terms, rang in the courtroom with the reassurance of a familiar and popular opinion. They found that George Green had a body so defective it was almost degenerate. "I would say," said physician C. M. Lang, "that he was suffering from struma or scrofulous condition, associated with tuberculosis." He added that struma, in his view, could not be acquired; it was a constitutional defect, a taint of heredity.

In the courtroom that afternoon there were many who had suspected that all along. They were sure, just as their neighbours were, just as the newspapers were, that children like this Green boy, gathered from the gutters of London, were a class so impaired, so defiled, as to be unfit. They did not stir, for they were a silent crowd, but when another physician, J. U. McCullough—who had been asked to see George Green when the boy was unwell but who had said simply there was nothing he could do for him—gave this opinion, they looked each other and nodded in understanding agreement. Dr. McCullough had not examined the victim, but he was reasonably certain he knew the root cause of the disease that led to his death. "I may say," he testified, "that by a great many of the best authorities, struma or scrofulous is considered to be an offshoot of syphilis. I just throw that in by way of explanation."

Shortly before Christmas that year, the *Owen Sound Sun Times* reported the outcome of the trial. The jury was split, divided by the testimony of the physicians, with the result that it could render no verdict.

The case against Helen Findlay simply dissolved, but the case against George Green was to continue in the courtrooms of public opinion for a long time. To the men who wrote the editorials, the politicians who made the speeches, and the unionists who looked for the jobs, it was George Green and those who brought him to Canada who were the dark presence, leading to tragedy among the decent people of Grey County in the autumn of 1895. "The greatest crime is being perpetrated," said the *Owen Sound Sun Times*, in examining the death of the boy, "by the dumping of the diseased off-scouring of the hotbeds of hellish slumdom of England among the rising generation of this country."

When George Green died his lonely death, the newspapers of Canada noted his passing in stories that called him an idiot, a physical imbecile, and a boy who was perfectly useless. The *Toronto Evening Star*, in a story outlining the circumstances in which his body was found, headed the article "A Repulsive Boy." Beneath the caption ran another line: "Disobedient, Dirty, Unable to Work, But a Big Eater". In Hamilton, the *Spectator*, reporting the outcome of the trial, said: "Canada needs immigrants, but we are quite sure that she can spend

money for immigration purposes to better advantage than the importation of gutter angelets."

In their editorials the newspapers reached beyond the tawdry
details of the trial to find in it proof that the bringing of children like
George Green to Canada was a grave and sinister mistake. The *Toronto
Evening Star*, while making passing reference to George Green as nearsighted, lame, knock-kneed, humpbacked, filthy in habit, and deficient
in understanding, denounced the entire scheme and said: "There is a
general belief and strongly defined opinion that Green was not a solitary instance of children with tainted blood being brought into
Canada...and no law too strict can be framed to prevent these waifs,
handicapped by heredity, from mingling with the pure and healthy
children of this country and becoming a burden upon Canada." But the
most important editorial—and to the men and women who brought
children to Canada, the most ominous—came that November in the
Globe. "It is high time," it said cryptically, "the deportation of waifs to
Canada stopped. Until we make a reasonable effort toward solving our
own 'unemployed' problems, we should not be burdened the results of
similar problems in Britain."

The *Globe's* editorial was a sign, not merely of its own changed attitude toward the immigration of children, but, importantly, of the
changed attitude of its constituents—the business and professional
class of Ontario. During the twenty-five years since Maria Rye had
brought out the first children, to be greeted with fulsome praise both
from the press and from politicians, the country, particularly Ontario,
had struggled through two decades in which the economy suffered from
recurring illness. In the late 1870s and the mid-1880s it endured, if not
a full-blown depression, bouts of stress in which, for three and four
years at a time, the economy fell sick, so that men crowded outside
newspaper offices waiting to scan the columns in the hope of finding a
job not already taken. Among the crowds were many immigrants from
Britain, men whose passage to Canada had often been aided by the
government. Their presence among the unemployed provoked bitterness and resentment, not just against themselves but against all immigrants. "That class of people has become a burden upon the people of
Toronto," one labour leader complained. "You will see every morning
large crowds of this class of people around the newspaper office waiting
for the editions of the papers to come out containing advertisements of
situations vacant, showing that the labour market is altogether over-
stocked with that class of people, mainly of no particular avocation,
men who are looking for any kind of odd jobs."

The crisis of the unemployed—always present and always emotional—was not lost on those politicians who looked for a good issue. They could attack immigrants without fear of political retaliation, and of all immigrants, the children were the most vulnerable and the most suspect. With no parents and no education, with no money and no vote, it almost seemed as if they were ready-made to be scapegoats. And by 1880, only a few years after Andrew Doyle had been officially declared a bothersome intruder, that is what they had become, for press, the politicians, the labour leaders, and a wide body of the Canadian people.

The first group to attack them, and in many ways the group that despised them the most, was organized labour. It began in the early years of the 1880s, with occasional criticism of them as unwanted labour. By the end of the decade it was obsessed with them, so that hardly a meeting went by without a speech from D.J. O'Donoghue, the secretary of the Toronto Trades and Labour Council, or A. F. Jury of the same group, denouncing the children as products of a criminal class and condemning anyone connected with their importation. The politicians who permitted it were, according to the labour council, acting like idiots or traitors. In 1884 the policy of labour—one that would prevail until child immigration came to an end in the middle of the 1930s—was firmly expressed in a statement of the legislative committee of the Trades and Labour Council after a Canadian government official had stated in London that the country had a need for juvenile immigrants: "While Mr. Lowe, then secretary of the Federal Department of Agriculture which regulated immigration, may have voiced the policy of the Dominion government on this subject, it is not considered amiss to point out that Mr. Lowe himself, as an authority on immigration matters generally, and particularly as to the asserted needs of Canada in that respect, is most unreliable to say the least of him. Where and why a demand exists for boys and girls justifying this action on the part of the government is not apparent to your committee. They have no hesitation in denying the existence of any such demand except it be for the purpose of placing boys in competition with men where practicable, with the view of still lowering the wages of the latter, if not driving them altogether out of employment...As to girls, it may be said in brief that when those requiring domestics determine on paying reasonable wages, proportionate to duty required, they find no difficulty in securing household servants."

The depth of their hostility to the children and to those who brought them out was never clearer than on one occasion during a visit to Canada by General Booth, the founder and head of the Salvation Army, which by then was bringing children to Canada. The Trades and

Labour Council attacked Booth, calling him autocratic, a man who had appointed himself as grand emigration agent of the poor-law guardians of England —"the parish scavenger as it were". It went on to savage his motives: "No doubt the astute General, in visiting Canada, cast an eye to the fact that, besides the seventy-five dollars per head already paid him by the English Parish Guardians under the existing Dominion immigration system, for every one thousand souls landed by him in this country he could secure a cash bonus of five-thousand dollars out of Canada's public funds."

In the early 1880s the council stepped up the attack by claiming that large numbers of the children were of bad character and ended up in the country's jails, reformatories, and asylums. Britain, one labour delegate told a provincial committee appointed in 1891 to investigate Ontario's prison system, was simply using Canada as a dumping-ground for future criminals. "It may be very well," he said, "for the boys who, coming here, obtain a release from their former associations and have better opportunities of earning a good living they choose to be honest and industrious. But it cannot be good for Canada to absorb such an element in such large quantities. The importation of criminals half reformed or reformed only in appearance, of imbeciles, paupers, and persons of defective physique or tainted with hereditary disease, must necessarily increase the number of criminals and the volume of crime."

Then, the following summer, in June of 1891, labour was given a strong boost in its campaign by a man named J.G. Moylan, a stiff moralist who found his niche in the bureaucracy as inspector of the country's prisons. In the course of his annual report, which included his comments on the vexing question of the use of tobacco by prisoners, he digressed to attack the influx of youngsters from overseas. "Of late years," he said, "our penitentiaries have had a most undesirable— because a most hardened and irreclaimable—class of criminals added to their numbers. This is particularly the case at Kingston and St. Vincent DePaul, where those cockney sneak thieves and pickpockets referred to are numerous. These pests gathered from the slums of St. Giles and East London, after short terms of so-called probation, in a certain notoriously mismanaged refuge, are periodically shipped out to Canada, as immigrants deserving of encouragement and support. With very few exceptions these street Arabs from Whitechapel and Rotherhithe and other like haunts of vice, speedily return to their old habits on arriving in Canada and, as a consequence, become a burden and expense upon the taxpayers of the Dominion in reformatories, jails, and penitentiaries. Steeped as they have been in crime from

infancy, they are found to be the most troublesome and worst conducted convicts that reach our penitentiaries. Their evil influence in
corrupting others is potent and pernicious. The general verdict of the
chaplains and the other prison officers regarding these youthful imita-
tors of Fagin and Bill Sykes is most unfavourable. They consider them
dead to all good influences and that their reformation is hopeless. In
order to protect the community against the depredations of such thoroughly trained malefactors, and our youth, especially against he evil
effects of their example or influence, it was advisable that effectual
means be adapted to prevent mistaken philanthropists abroad and at
home, aiding and encouraging the transplanting of exotics so unsuited
to the moral atmosphere of the country."

Mr. Moylan did not offer evidence to support his claim. He did not
produce a single case or offer a single statistic to show the number of
the children who ended up in the jails and asylums. He did not have
to. For he was playing upon a bias at was broad and deep and permanent. In the towns and villages of the Maritimes and the sweeping
farmland of Ontario and the opening West, the settlers of the 1880s
and 1890s were not given to soft and gentle views of the young, either
their own or those who were born into distant slums and who came to
Canada bearing accents and ways that were different and alien.

Those who knew the children best—the government inspectors who
visited them once a year on behalf of the province or the Dominion, and
the organizers who had brought them to Canada in the first place—
reported regularly that, aside from a tiny fraction, the children were not
in trouble with the law. As early as 1877 John Lowe, secretary of the
Department of Agriculture, said that following the investigation of several inspectors sent out in the wake of Andrew Doyle, it was evident that
the children were an advantage to the country. In 1882, a man named A.
G. Smyth, an immigration agent in London, Ontario, reported that people in his area wanted more of them. "In fact," he said, "double the number could be easily well settled." A few years later, in 1887, Edwin Clay,
the federal government immigration agent in Halifax, said the same
thing, adding: "Good girls and nothing but good girls are what we want,
and there will be no trouble in finding employment for them." Year after
year the government reported in the same vein, less inclined to assure
Canadians that the children were well treated than to assure them that
they were not petty thieves. A report from the Federal Committee on
Agriculture and Colonization, roughly a quarter-century from the time
the first children came to Canada, caught, the spirit of Ottawa's attitude:
"The question of the advantage of these juvenile immigrants has been for

many years past variously discussed before this committee, it having been always maintained by the officers of the Immigration Department that the adverse opinions had invariably rested on the cases a very fractional number of exceptions, while the great bulk of those who had done well and proved of great advantage to the country were not taken into account. It is therefore to be pointed out that a sweeping generalization should not be on the fact of a fractional exception."

Perhaps so. But men and women whose own lives were made hard with toil could not shake deep emotional conviction. And they found their bias reflected and reinforced when they read the opinions of the men who ran the papers in almost every part of the country, especially in Ontario, where most of the children were located. Almost to a man, the editors chose to paint the children as an ominous presence in the life of Canada, one that would poison the clear, pure atmosphere of the new land.

The most virulent of these newspapermen was Edmund Sheppard, a brash, strong editor who owned and operated paper called the *Toronto News*. Founded in 1880, the *News* seemed at times almost anxious to outdo the Trades Labour Council—whose distortions it religiously carried and supported—in its denunciation of immigration in general and child immigration in particular. From his rickety, noisy office at 106 Yonge Street, Sheppard, who later became editor of *Saturday Night*, poured out a stream of venom that ran through two decades and tarred the child-immigration movement as the work of fools or frauds, who were lining their pockets while at the same time dumping among the honest workers of Canada a class of children whom he described over the years as trash, guttersnipes, off-scourings. down-and-outs, and riff-raff.

One evening in May 1884, Sheppard went along to a meeting held in St. Andrew's Hall in Toronto which had been called by the Trades and Labour Council to press its campaign against the government's policy of helping British immigrants—adults as well as children—to settle in Canada. The meeting was packed and noisy. All through the evening the close, fetid air rang with shouts and slanders against the children, the governments both provincial and federal, Sir Charles B. upper (who was that year made Canada's High Commissioner in London and was known as a supporter of child immigration), and in particular those politicians in Ottawa who, inside Parliament and out, were trying to encourage the bringing of waifs and strays to Canada.

The following afternoon, May 6, 1884, Sheppard slipped to his cubby-hole office, shut the door, and, hunching at a cluttered desk, wrote an editorial that was to characterize the spirit of the press toward child immigration for years to come. It was, he wrote, a practice that was wicked and insane. "We have enough orphan and abandoned children in our own streets to look after. The impudence of a large class of pseudophilanthropists who make a trade of shipping outcast children from England to Canada and elsewhere, was well exemplified in the remarks of one engaged in the business, who had the cheek to contend that more immigration was desirable. So long as humbugs of this kind can put money in their pockets by the process they are likely to continue the game which has cost Canada so dearly."

Year after year the readers of the *Toronto News*, those who turned to its lively editorial page, found, among the editorials worrying over the workingman's lot, an angry clamour against the hordes of invading thieves from England. The organizers of the schemes—Annie Macpherson, Maria Rye, and others, who by then had brought to the country more than five thousand children—were, to the *Toronto News*, philanthropic frauds, "a brigade of designing men and women steeped in hypocrisy and cant". To Edmund Sheppard and those who thought like him, their plan was not charity but craft and cunning, a way in which the wealthy class in England, by contributing to the agencies, could rid itself of undesirables: "Upon their return to England their cue has been to appeal to the charitable for funds to aid them in the good of relieving the British taxpayer of the burden of supporting the poor of the land. This appeal is a most cunning one, as under the mask of charity it addresses itself to the selfishness of the wealthy classes, who are always ready to aid in ridding themselves of the worthless and the helpless. They would empty their poorhouses, city slums, and prisons into Canada without a pang, if they could. Thanks to the efforts of Canadian newspapers, some check has been put upon the infamous trade of exporting the lame, the blind, and the vicious to our shores, but those who have been engaged in it still require watching."

Before long, Sheppard's two-fisted opinions were noted by other editors, in Toronto and beyond, where he was recognized even by his opponents as a man to be reckoned with, one whose views—regarded in the atmosphere of the time as radical—were often the forerunners of wide public sentiment. Just a few months after he launched his campaign, a much more moderate voice, the *Toronto World*, began, in the fall of 1884 to raise questions about Britain's practice of sending the children to Canada. "She expends millions annually," the paper said, "for the conversion of Hindoos, Chinese, Hottentots, and even Frenchmen and Spaniards, surely she can do as much for the heathen of her own begetting, who in time might grow up to recruit her army, man her navy, and

push her commercial enterprises to the ends of the earth." Then, less
than a week later, on October 9, 1884, the *Globe* ran an editorial entitled "The Importation of Waifs".

It was in many ways as curious an editorial as it was influential. It
began, carefully it seemed, by making a distinction between itself and
those that expressed more strident opinions. "We have no sympathy,"
it sniffed, "with know-nothingism in any of its phases." On the contrary, it welcomed immigrants, those who were suitable, who brought
credit to themselves and to the land they chose. Nor did it agree with
those who were claiming that Britain was deliberately using Canada as
a dumping-ground for its cast-offs.

But then it made its point: "Canada wants increased population,
but she would not on that account thank any country for landing the
inmates of its prisons and poor houses on her shores." Canada, it went
on, did not want those who could be regarded as "the criminal, the diseased, the pauperized, or the vicious."

For the remainder of that troubled decade, the *Globe's* opinion was
expressed regularly and in ways that were, if anything, more firm, more
dogmatic. The conviction in its editorial rooms had come almost full
circle from those early years in the work of Annie Macpherson and
Maria Rye when it blessed their efforts as a benefit to Canada and a
benevolence to children. "How far," it asked near the close of the 1880s,
"is Canada to be made a dumping-ground for mere helpless paupers and
their unsatisfactory children...Canada has no room for the inmates of
British workhouses whom many philanthropists seem willing to cast
penniless upon the shores of America."

It was the turn in the road, and not just for the *Globe*. Partly because
of its influence among the social elite, the paper was the forerunner of
changing attitudes in the newspapers, professions, and churches all across
Canada. The worry extended even to the academic community, and as
always it was a worry not for the children, but for the country to which
they were coming. The *Queen's College Journal* in June 1888, carried an
article that had within it the seeds of a fear that was by then beginning to
take root in the sentiments of the entire country. "Certainly, adult paupers are not desirable on any grounds," it said. "As regards pauper children, the case is somewhat different. So long as their constitutions are not
hopelessly broken, their moral natures black at the core, and their blood
not poisoned with disease, there is always a possibility of their being converted into good serviceable citizens. But we all know that very many, if
not the majority of these pauper children, carry with them inherited tendencies both physical and moral which no training, however careful, can

eradicate and which may do more harm eventually to the community receiving them than good to the individuals received. Not a few of these imported paupers have turned out to be veritable plague spots in the physical and moral life of the community. We have already so much of the evil element among us that we cannot afford to receive a very much larger influence of bad blood."

Then, within a few years, the mood of the newspapers, particularly in Ontario, began to approach hysteria. In March 1895, the *Windsor Record* singled out both Maria Rye and Annie Macpherson, denouncing both and savaging their parties of children: "It is doubtful if this dumping of the scrapings of waifdom upon us can be allowed to continue at its present rate. Prison statistics indicate that a percentage of this moral refuse, the offspring of rudimentary men and women in many instances finds its level which is in the criminal class and in the ranks of prostitution." In the small town of Milverton, Ontario, the local weekly paper, the *Sun*, ran an editorial applauding a letter in its column that went, "Stunted, starved dwarfed in body and mind and associated with poverty, vice and sin in their most loathsome forms, they are picked out of England's social gutters and engrafted on strong, healthy Canadian pedigree."

The worry that the children were, in their very bones, carriers of some dark defect that was a threat to the country and its people was made stronger because so many physicians gave it sanction. Dr. C. K. Clarke, the superintendent of an asylum and a man whose name was to be given a generous place in Canada's medical history—Toronto's Clarke Institute was named after him—once lectured to a group of students at Queen's College in Kingston and was warmly applauded as soon as he began to attack the inferiority of British waifs in Canada. "A pretty strong proof that the general public has not awakened to its responsibilities in regard to the problems of heredity," the doctor said, "is the fact that in Canada we are deliberately adding to our population hundreds of children bearing all the stigmata of physical and mental degeneracy. And this is being done openly and apparently with the consent of many who are really anxious to prove themselves philanthropists. I refer to the children who are brought to Canada in order to benefit themselves and the country. It is asserted that these children pass a medical examination and are invariably of healthy type. Could anything be more misleading, more untrue?" Dr. Clarke, a man with large, bright eyes and a soft voice, went on to recall that a few months earlier he had been on a train on which some of the children were being taken to the farms. For days afterward, he said, he was depressed, recalling the signs of degeneracy that were so obvious in the entire lot of them. "It is almost criminal neglect on the part of the authorities," he concluded to waves of applause, "to allow this sort immigration to be permitted. And while some may assert that asylum and jail populations have not been materially increased by such importations, they should remember that those who sow the wind shall reap the whirlwind. The next generation must be considered, but the harvest has already commenced—a juvenile criminal here, an insane person there." The next day, the *Mail and Empire* of Toronto declared that his address should be reprinted in every paper in the country.

But if the unionists and the press and a few physicians played up the baser fears of the people, it remained for the politicians—a good number of them—to take this tack to the extreme. One morning during those years, in the old committee room of the House of Commons, during a meeting of the Committee on Agriculture and Colonization, four members of Parliament, all medical doctors with the great influence that their profession afforded them, attacked the children en masse as carriers of syphilis.

Early in the meeting, just after a unionist had labelled the children as delinquents, James Trow, a Member of Parliament from Perth, Ontario, replied that this was not true, that for the most part they were an asset to the country. He was answered by one of the medical men, Dr. John Henry Wilson, who was the member from the Ontario riding of Elgin. "I can understand my friend Mr. Trow," said Wilson, "not being a medical man, not knowing the many ills to which flesh is heir, and being a very careful man himself, unable to understand the condition in which these children are. Any family would be extremely careless and injudicious to allow any of these little waifs to come into the family, because we know that the syphilitic taint, although the child may appear healthy, may be carried to the other children of the family playing with them and they become diseased in the same manner." But Wilson's statement seemed modest beside the remarks of one of his colleagues, Dr. John Ferguson of Welland, who said that if Canada continued to let such children into the country it might as well spread surgeons among the people to inoculate them against syphilis. As Dr. Ferguson chose to put it: "The majority of these children are the offal of the most depraved characters in the cities of the old country."

By then the feeling had become a rage. The papers began to carry notices almost every day of boys who drew knives on their employers or took shots at the neighbours or committed acts of indecency that were left unstated in vague and ominous references. There were stories of girls such as Nellie Wickett of London, Ontario, who was charged with disorderly conduct and given two years in a reformatory. And there was

Selini Hicks, found in bad company near the river—the papers said she was far from good-looking but nevertheless was found in the house of a coloured man—who told the authorities she had been ruined by the hired man. In a great many such cases, perhaps most, the young men and women were not British immigrants at all, but boys and girls who had been born in Canada. Often the stories in the papers would be followed by a letter from some man or woman in the organization named, stating that a check of the records proved that they had not brought the child to Canada. Or else, in a few instances, a humane judge or a fair-minded policeman would, on his own, tell the court that this was not a British waif. But it did no good, for the tide of emotion was too opposite and too strong.

Special to the Mail and Empire.

Ottawa, March 2—In North Gower an alleged case of stabbing, in which a boy from an English home and Mr. George Gibson, a school teacher, figured, occurred yesterday. According to the story, Mr. Gibson was about to inflict corporal punishment on the boy who, having an open knife in his hand, made a lunge at the teacher's throat, inflicting at scratch on the neck. Mr. Gibson caught the lad by the hand. The boy is said to have got the knife in the other hand and stabbed the teacher on the back of the wrist, making a nasty gash.

The boy skipped, and the police are now on his tracks.

Often there were stories of boys who, in the depths of their lonely desperation, took their own lives and in death were used as a further example of why they were unfit to have come to Canada. On a stormy January day in York Mills, a community just north of Toronto, fourteen-year-old Charles Bradbury approached his employer, a farmer named John Blain, claiming that the money he was being paid—it was to be twenty dollars a year, plus his keep—was not enough. The farmer disagreed, saying it had already been agreed upon. A quarrel broke out and the older man threw the boy to the ground and gave him a kicking. Then he left him alone and went to a neighbour's.

About half an hour later, John Blain looked out his neighbour's kitchen window and saw that his cow barn was ablaze. A few hours later when the embers were cool, the neighbours found, in one of the box stalls, the body of Charles Bradbury. The coroner, W. R. Walters, said later that the body—which was afterwards put in a barrel on the doorstep—had the arms and legs burned away, but it was also slashed across the throat. It was evident, he said, that the throat cut had not been fatal. It appeared that the boy had tried to commit suicide, but, having failed, had set fire to the barn, then had died in the flames. An inquest jury agreed, and a caption in one of the Toronto papers caught in simple terms the feeling of the hour: "He Gashed His Own Throat Did the Wilful Boy Bradbury. The farm buildings of the Blains were fired for Revenge by this imported youth, who was of sullen disposition..."

In the leafy districts around the Muskoka Lakes of Ontario where hundreds of children had been placed with farmers near the towns of Gravenhurst, Bracebridge and Huntsville, fear of them reached such a fever that people tried to keep them from attending the schools, even though it was an obligation for the farmers to send them, at least when they were not needed in the fields. Near Bracebridge, not long before the turn of the century, a board of trustees forbade them to set foot in the schools, on the grounds that since they had no parents who paid taxes they had no right to education. On his own, a boy named Frederick Hill, about whom little was ever known, challenged them, and through his sympathetic employer, George Shiers, took the case to court, maintaining that he been guaranteed schooling, and that Shiers was not merely his employer but his legal guardian. The boy lost the case. But the ban on the children did not last long. Even the *Toronto News*, their arch critic, found it a bit unfair: "*The News* has always opposed the importation of this class as being inimical to the general welfare. Having gained an entrance to the Dominion, however, they must be given an elementary education, if on no higher ground than as a measure of protection for Canadians. Ignorance and crime are twins and, while it is not possible to wholly remove the latter, it is possible to render it unnecessary for any child to grow up in ignorance."

Inevitably, as if in the unfolding of a script, there were stories that the children, even those only ten and eleven years of age, were murderers. Once, in the middle of summer Huntsville, a town of few hundred people with more immigrant children than any town of similar size, Robert Webster, eleven years old, was charged with the attempted murder of his employer, Henry Lewis. Lewis, in the habit of refreshing himself with cool tea, took a cupful one day and found it not exactly to his taste. Curious, he took a look inside the pot. The bottom was full of Paris green. Fortunately he managed to throw up. The boy, according to Police Chief McFadden, had it in for

Lewis. As Chief McFadden put it, the boy wanted to "fix" Lewis for not taking him to Huntsville.

The government of Canada and those of the provinces, especially Ontario, feeling the waves of controversy, began quietly and informally to look at ways of containing it, while the same time assuring themselves either that the stories of brutality against the children—charges that occasionally reached them in letters from some distraught or angry citizen were untrue, or, if true, that the brutality had been stopped. There were by then in Ontario alone ten thousand British children, almost all on the farms of the fertile south, reaching from Niagara to the Ottawa Valley and east to the rough grey countryside around the town of Cornwall. Some were children barely out of arms and were therefore adopted, but most—more than nine thousand—were past their fifth birthday and in this hard land were expected to earn their keep, tending barns, milking cows, making hay. Often they would rise before anyone in the house, before the first light of day, and they would work until nightfall.

Each one of them was, in theory at least, to be visited once a year, not just by a man or woman from their organization, but by an inspector of the federal government, a man who would inquire concerning their situation and satisfy himself that they were obedient and that they were being given enough food to eat and an adequate place to sleep. Sometimes, depending on how many calls he had to make, he might take a boy or girl aside and ask if he or she was being beaten or whipped, but most of the time his brief visits took place in the kitchen with the farmer present. There was, of course, no attempt by such men, who were usually immigration agents anyway, to inquire into the child's feelings—the things of the heart—for in the Canada of that time a child was not seen to have hopes and dreams and a personality that could be hurt, sometimes beyond restoring. A child was, after all, an incomplete person, a pilgrim on his way to becoming human; until he reached adult years he did not really have an inner life of the emotions or the mind. The job of adults to whom children were given was to shape their crude material into finished form and to do so through the application of work and discipline. This was not always a pleasant task. As F. Bolton Read, Anglican rector of Grimsby, Ontario, and a friend of Maria Rye, said of her children: "None of them are angels; all of them have human passions to be corrected, and often will give a good deal of trouble to those who undertook the task." Another man said simply that the task of those who received such children was to take them and "drill them into usefulness."

There was, however, a man in Ontario, still in his twenties, who was coming to the conviction that such a view of children was deeply and fatally flawed. He was to bring a new imagination to the attitude of Canada toward children. And he would have an influence upon the lot of immigrant children that, while it had no concrete result, would touch their lives in humane and compassionate ways. His name was John Joseph Kelso.

When he was fourteen years old and growing up in Toronto, John Kelso, whose friends would later call him "J.J.," began dreaming of a career in journalism, even daring to confide to a relative that he would some day occupy the powerful chair of George Brown, the famous editor of the *Globe*. Indeed, by time he was twenty-two, in 1886, he was working on the paper as a reporter, writing stories that exposed conditions in the slums, in particular child prostitution through which small girls sold themselves on Yonge Street and turned their earnings over to parents, often alcoholics. Soon, however, Kelso began to worry that if he were content merely to report on child abuse he would simply be exploiting its news value and not improving the lot of the victims. So, very early in his career as a reporter, and in the face of some cynicism from his colleagues, he organized a movement to prohibit children under eight from working on Toronto streets.

The next year, on February 19, 1887, Kelso was invited, almost as a last-minute joke, to fill in for a speaker who couldn't keep an appointment to address the lofty membership of the Royal Canadian Institute. He spoke on the need to prevent cruelty in Toronto—to animals and to children—and the response was so surprising, even to him, that five days later he called a meeting to organize a group. It was called the Toronto Humane Society. Out of it, in 1891, came the Children's Aid Society with Kelso as founding president. He was still a reporter on the *Globe* when, in 1893; he sat in the gallery of Queen's Park, while the government passed the first bill in Canada to protect children, a bill he had pressed for. A few weeks later, Premier Oliver Mowat asked him to join the public service as Secretary of Neglected and Dependent Children. Kelso gave up his dream of the editorship of the *Globe*; instead, he began a career that would span forty years and would further the welfare of children in Canada in ways unmatched by any man or woman in the country's history.

In the fall of 1894, a year after his appointment, Kelso organized a meeting in Toronto that was to hear the opinions of both the friends and the enemies of child immigration. He hoped to bring the whole movement under the oversight of is office for the good of all concerned, especially of the children themselves. The meeting, which lasted two days, was called "The Conference on Child-Saving Work" and was held not far from his office in a building often used for such gatherings, the Confederation Assembly Hall. It opened on October 8, a morning on which the trees and the streets were soaked and a blanket of fog rested upon the city.

Delegates and observers arrived early, often in twos. Most where from Toronto, but others came from Belleville, Peterborough, Hamilton, Stratford, and Niagara-on-the-Lake, representing various organizations for which they worked as superintendents. Throughout the hall there was an air of expectancy, even tension, since here and there, sitting in tiny clusters of their own, were the avowed opponents of the child immigration movement, unionists mainly, there to denounce the whole scheme and vilify the children. At the front of the hall, talking quietly with the chairman, was John Joseph Kelso, the youngest man in the room, still in his twenties, with bright eyes that peered through steel-rimmed glasses and a head of thick, dark hair. Toward the back, brushing the rain from his felt hat, was D.J. O'Donoghue, the trade unionist from Toronto and the most vociferous of the critics, his ruddy, his eyes cold and wary. Behind him sat Inspector William Stark, chief detective of the city of Toronto. Two other men who were deeply involved in the work with the children entered the room together. One was William Merry, a slender, soft spoken man, the nephew of Annie Macpherson and her superintendent in Canada; the other was the Reverend Robert Wallace, who had married Macpherson's long-time worker in Belleville, Ellen Agnes Bilbrough, and joined her in running the home. As they sat down not far from the front, the chairman, Judge H. S. McDonald of Brockville, tapped the table lightly and announced that the subject for discussion was child immigration.

"This is probably," he said, "one of the most delicate subjects with which we have to deal." He called their attention to page ten of the program, where a number of questions for discussion were listed: Are the children harmful to Ontario? Do most turn out badly? Do they drive out adult labour? Can child immigration be regulated to protect the child and avoid the evils that are complained of?

He took Robert Wallace by surprise, asking him if he would speak first. "Perhaps," he said, "Mr. Wallace will kindly take these questions up and answer them, which will be a practical way of opening discussion on this subject." Wallace came to the front and began by saying he was not prepared to speak but was pleased to do so. He went down the list of questions, taking each in turn and giving a resounding defence of the movement to bring children out from Britain: "Should the importation of English children be entirely stopped? I think not, unless you prohibit immigration as a whole. We must, in fairness, treat all alike, Which is better to bring here, a child who may or may not know something of wickedness, or a man who has grown up and may have been in penitentiary in some of the cities of the old land? Which is the more likely to become a good citizen of this country? Surely, I think, the child who has youth on his side and the possibility of developing good qualities."

It was clear, especially to D. J. O'Donoghue, that Wallace had answered the questions many times before, for his replies had about them the echo of past performances. O'Donoghue, sitting beside his fellow unionist, A.F. Jury, stared wanly at Wallace with the skepticism he reserved for idealistic clergymen as the minister continued.

"Do they drive out adult labour? I think not; any more than the farmers' sons themselves. Why is there such a demand for our children? Simply because in a great many farm homes the boys want to go out into something for themselves, they do not want to stay on the farm, but to become businessmen or professional men, so the home is left without a son and our boys go in and fill the place." He dealt with the remaining questions and then, at the end of his talk, he turned to an idea he knew to be one of the main goals of John Joseph Kelso: that the government of Ontario appoint an inspector to supervise the work of the various child organizations. Wallace was against it. "I think," he said, carefully distancing his work on behalf of Annie Macpherson from that of Maria Rye, "where those interested in the children have at least some fondness for them, that these people would have a greater interest in seeing that they are well cared for than any government inspector would have, who has never seen the boy or girl before."

There was courteous applause and he sat down. The chairman glanced at his watch, then surveyed the crowd as if looking for men whose faces he was not sure of. "I understand," he said, "that Mr. A. F. Jury and Mr. D.J. O'Donoghue are present to represent the labour organizations and would like to be heard on the other side of this question. If these gentlemen will come to the platform we shall be glad to hear from them." O'Donoghue got up. He did not speak for long— about ten minutes in all—and he made three points. First, he said, charity begins at home. Therefore, Ontario should look after its own poor children, of which there were then two thousand, before importing the poor of another country. "We do not hold the children respon-sible for their condition," he said, "but we say that the system which produced them ought to be called upon to care for them and on that broad principle we object to their being brought here." Second, he complained about the expense to the taxpayer. "Year after year," he declared, "in the expenditure of the Dominion of Canada, agents have charged and been paid large sums of money for looking after the con-dition of those children who have been imported." Third, he argued, a good number became criminals: "The expense of those who import them ends practically when they are landed here; after that the admin-istration of justice for Ontario has to foot the bill year after year."

Then, toward the end, after he had attacked the children driving down wages and needled Kelso for showing sympathy toward them, he moved to make a final point, one that was new for labour, and one on which every man in the room, especially John Joseph Kelso, felt vul-nerable. "We have men in the ranks of our labour organization," he said, "who came out under this system but their stories of the treatment they received in the country places before they reached the age of man-hood is of a character to make an ordinary Christian's blood curdle." With that he left.

Kelso knew from his days on the newspapers that most of what O'Donoghue had said was not correct—that the children did not take jobs from adults, that they were not an exorbitant expense to taxpay-ers. Most of all, as a former police reporter, he knew that the accusa-tion that they were mostly a band of thieves had no basis in fact. That was why he was shrewd enough to ask Inspector Stark, the Toronto detective, to attend. Stark spoke near the end of the conference. "During a recent summer in Toronto," he said, "we had an unusual series of crimes. From July until November there were two hundred and thirteen convictions for serious crimes, chiefly burglaries. There was some discussion in a section of the press at the time as to what propor-tion of this crime was attributable to these children who had been brought out from the Old Country and, taking an interest in this mat-ter, I looked it up. Of the two hundred and thirteen convictions, one hundred and ninety-five were boys under twenty. Twenty-seven of these came from the Old Country. Of the twenty-seven born in the Old Country, not a single one had been in any of the homes engaged in the work of bringing out children."

Kelso joined the ripple of applause that followed Stark's statement, but he did so almost diffidently. His mind was occupied with something he felt far more likely and far more worrisome: the claim by O'Donoghue that many of the children were treated cruelly. He had heard enough, especially during his years on the *Globe*, to suspect that this was so. The motives of the people who brought them to Canada—most of them, at least—were decent enough, but too often they simply placed the child with a farmer, visiting him rarely, and even then in a casual way. He hoped that out of this meeting, despite the early objections of the Reverend Robert Wallace, would come a new attitude, one that would support his opinion that he as Ontario's new Superintendent of Neglected Children, would also oversee child immigration, to ensure that the youngsters were carefully placed and visited in some systematic way.

At the conclusion of the presentations Judge McDonald summarized the sense of the meeting. The judge, an old friend of J. J. Kelso's, was obviously aware of his feelings. He said the conference had clearly shown the value of juvenile immigration, but it had also shown the need for careful supervision to protect the children from abuse. Then, as if to answer doubts, McDonald told a story of his own: "A case I am about to tell of was related to me by a clergyman who takes a interest in children. One day, in the village where he lives, he was handed a letter. On opening it he found it was anonymous. The letter said that on the concession in which the writer lived, there was another farmer who had a boy from one of the homes, only eight or ten years of age, who had a fear of swine. This man was in the habit of taking the boy, putting him in the pig pen, standing over him, and whipping him if he attempted to get out, simply to enjoy the boy's agony. Would you believe that in that concession no one had the courage to take the necessary steps and lay any information against him because he was a man of some influence? They did, however, write the anonymous letter to the clergyman who drove out to the farm and told the man that if he did not send the boy back to the home he would prosecute him. The man chose the former alternative and sent the boy back to the home."

Then the meeting ended. Kelso rose quickly. He skirted the crowd and made his way to the back of the room, where he stood nodding and talking with the delegates as they left. A couple of impressions lingered in his mind. For one thing, the meeting revealed that the homes—eight of them were represented—had the support, labour notwithstanding, of the influential men of the courts, the church, and the police. And yet he sensed that these same people shared his worry that the homes were careless of the children, trusting too much in human nature and failing to check on their welfare once placed. It was a spectre that would haunt John Joseph Kelso throughout his entire career.

Four
Enter Dr. Barnardo

On the afternoon when three thousand of his children were to perform at the Royal Albert Hall in London, Thomas John Barnardo arrived very early. His slight, nimble frame, barely five foot three inches, darted across the back of the stage, checking on bakers' ovens, tailors' shops, blacksmiths' anvils, and even, in one corner, waiting its time at centre stage, a miniature hayfield built of straw and wood, ready to show the audience the great things awaiting his children in the golden fields of Ontario.

A few minutes before the program began, at roughly five minutes to three, the huge audience, some of them crowding the aisles of the gallery, stirred softly at the sight of the Prince and Princess of Wales (later King Edward VII and Queen Alexandra) walking slowly through the royal entrance. The audience rose. In the orchestra, beneath a banner that read "Welcome to their Royal Highnesses from the largest family in the world", a choir of 1,600 girls began the National Anthem. The audience joined in as the royal party was escorted to the platform. When they were seated, the choir sang "God Bless the Prince of Wales". There was great cheering and waving of handkerchiefs. The scene was set for the commemoration of the thirtieth anniversary of the work of Thomas John Barnardo, one of the most extraordinary and paradoxical men in the entire history of child care.

When he strode to the front of the platform after a brief introduction by one his supporters, it was clear that despite his diminutive stature Barnardo was a man of presence and style, and above all a showman of supreme skill and confidence. His clothes were of an elegant cut, his silk hat and frock-coat chosen with an eye for the social class he cultivated, and his rather ordinary face was given a strong authority by a waxed military mustache and a pair of penetrating eyes. He explained that on this day—it was the twenty-fourth of June, 1896—he stood before his audience with a record of thirty years' experience in the rescue of destitute children behind him.

Then, like a ringmaster in a circus tent, he began to bring on the acts, beginning with a small army of boys who bounded on stage in the garb of the trade they were learning in Barnardo's homes. Some were dressed in blacksmith's aprons, others in baker's coats, still others as carpenters, shoemakers, tinsmiths, tailors, and cooks. On improvised benches and stools they began tapping anvils, cutting cloth, baking bread, and driving nails, until the air rang with the sounds of no fewer than fourteen trades and the audience erupted in a storm of applause. Then, as quickly as he had brought them on, Barnardo waved them off; he stepped forward, bowed to the waves of approval, and, calling for silence, spoke: "May it please your Royal Highnesses, it will not be our fault if eventually the young tradesmen you have seen are not permanently transferred from the loss to the profit side of the social ledger. But what of their little sisters in orphanhood and destitution? I have close upon five thousand young people under my care tonight and nearly one-half of these are girls."

Then girls, in groups of forty and fifty, came on stage singing ballads, performing drills, ironing and hanging out clothes, sewing dresses, and making pastry. The audience loved them, for they were, as Barnardo described them in his introduction, "neat-handed, white-cuffed, snowy-collared," able to perform for his supporters in the upper class—for whom they might one day work as domestics—all the mysteries of housekeeping. He was, he told them, a firm believer in the virtues of drill, for girls as well as boys. "In dealing with the lawless little people of the streets," he explained, "my first endeavour is to establish the reign of law."

Then swiftly the scenery changed again, this time to a nursery with cribs and cots, rocking horses and playpens; the stage was filled with the babble of infants, some barely a year old, taken for the performance from one of his homes known as the Babies' Castle. But even the pathos of abandoned babies could not really prepare the audience for the heart-rending tableau that was to follow. "It is a pathetic side of our work," Barnardo began in his resonant voice, "that large numbers of my little waifs and strays begin the toilsome journey of their life as cripples, as deaf and dumb, as blind, and as incurably ill. Even the sadness of destitution is mitigated by the possession of health and strength. But, when a waif child is without these, his case is pathetic indeed."

Then the man who would one day be called the father of nobody's children stepped back, the curtains parted, and the audience gazed upon a group of cripples, eight, nine, and ten years old, hobbling about on crutches, trying to play a game of cricket. One boy had no crutches at all; his legs were folded beneath him. He struggled about the floor, crawling on hands and knees. "Once within our doors," Barnardo told the crowd, "it is marvellous how quickly the shadows of their life are chased away and, indeed, there are few jollier fellows than my cripples." The hall burst into wild applause.

Most of the children who performed that day—after weeks of practice in the various homes that Barnardo operated—were retrained in their trades or in the arts of housekeeping, so that day, usually around the time they reached sixteen, they could placed "in service" in England as footmen, retainers, nannies, domestics, pages, or personal maids to the business and professional classes or in the homes of clergymen, usually of the Church of England. For some, however, another kind of future had been chosen, one that was filled with vague but exciting stories of green fields and waving wheat and friendly cowboys. These children, too—whom Barnardo always called "the flower of my flock"—were part of the grand performance before the ladies and gentlemen of London.

It was early evening when their turn came. Through west windows of Albert Hall the sun fell across the crowds so that here and there men raised their programs in the waning light to read the closing number. The heading read simply: "Tested and Trained for Travel: en route to the Far West." Suddenly a bugle pierced the air and Barnardo stepped forward. All over the hall heads lifted. Then, slowly at first but with gathering pace, a line of boys that seemed to have no end began to stream on stage, each one dressed in a common suit of dark, thick wool, each one carrying over his shoulder a small kit bag.

After the boys came the girls, each one in a stark, plain dress and a red hood, with a market bag over her arm. Boys and girls together numbered two hundred and fifty-four.

When the line had ended, Barnardo raised his hand and the crowd fell silent. He spoke briefly, calling upon everyone there to support his work with prayer and donations. Then he turned to the children, some of them not yet in their teens. "May God guide and bless my dear boys and girls," he said, "and bring them all safely to the haven of their dreams." The crowd clapped and a few cheered. Then, when the applause died the band struck up and the children began to march away, bound for the farms of Ontario, where, according to their dreams, they would find happy days and caring friends. The crowd rose as they went; then, toward the very end of the line, a small girl raised a flag with the single word "Goodbye". The men and women watching were swept with a feeling that many could barely contain.

Thomas John Barnardo, who was known everywhere he went as Doctor Barnardo and who was responsible for sending more than thirty thousand children to homes in Canada, was said during his lifetime and for years afterward to be a descendant of wealthy and aristocratic Italians. According to the gossip of the day, his fifteenth-century ancestors owned palaces, one in Genoa and one along the Grand Canal of Venice, where the head of the family, Count John Bernardi, presided over a glittering court of minstrels, servants, gondolas, and fine horses. In time, it was said, the sons of Count John set out on their own as traders, so that by the early 1600s they were independently wealthy and living in Spain. Unfortunately they were also Lutherans, and during the Spanish Inquisition they were driven from the country and lost their fortunes.

For more than a century, so the story goes, the Barnardo descendants wandered through Europe, but in the early 1700s history smiled once more and the men of the family became rich again, this time from the fur trade in Canada and the banking business in Germany. According to one approved biography, by the late 1700s "financiers throughout the world began to talk of the Barnardos in the same hushed tones as they talked of the Rothschilds." The wealth and the power of the family were so extensive that one account states that the Barnardo family was responsible for part of the financing of the Hudson's Bay Company, a firm which Thomas John Barnardo's father is rumoured to have been connected with, indeed, to have represented in Canada. His mother, again according to widely accepted descriptions, was of Quaker stock, a member of a family bearing the name of Drinkwater and having deep roots in the free religious spirit of Irish Protestantism.

Some of this tradition, in particular that which surrounds the misty years of the 1500s, may well be true, but a good deal of the more recent history, setting the family apart as aristocratic, powerful, and wealthy, now appears to be a myth, a legend woven during Barnardo's lifetime and given authenticity by a stream of books purporting to be biography but being in fact hagiography. His family background, while reputable, was also quite ordinary.

Barnardo's father—according to recent evidence offered by the European genealogist Edgar Samuel and the British social historian Gillian Wagner—was not Lutheran in his antecedents, but Jewish, probably German. There is no evidence that he had brothers or sisters;

nor is there any evidence that he worked for the Hudson's Bay Company or that anyone bearing the name was a source of the capital that launched the company. Barnardo's mother was not a Protestant Quaker named Drinkwater but an Irish Catholic named O'Brien. For a variety of reasons, most of them having to do with Barnardo's career and his desire for a reputation of impeccable Protestantism—in which a Lutheran past on his father's side and a Quaker past on his mother's side would be highly advantageous—the true facts of his family background have been passed over or embellished in favour of a more dramatic lineage, one in fashion with his station and in line with his need.

By the time he was born on July 4, 1845, in Dublin, his father, whose name was John Michaelis, a kind and decent man of modest means, was living above his fur store and renting rooms to make ends meet. There were already seven children, lively and intelligent, five of them from a previous marriage that had ended when John Michaelis Barnardo's first wife, Elizabeth, died during childbirth. He waited an appropriate interval, then married the woman who had helped him following his wife's death—her sister, a gracious, religious woman named Abigail.

Barnardo's birth was so difficult that for hours a gloomy silence hung in the halls outside the bedroom and women came and went, nodding quietly on the stairway, their glance at John Michaelis Barnardo filled with pity. In the end, the frail baby survived, but the mother was sent to the country, to the farm of some cousins, where her husband hoped she would draw strength from the clear air. In the meantime the baby was left to be suckled by a wet-nurse until he reached ten months.

From the beginning he was a difficult boy, his appearance—an almost dwarfish body and a face that was very plain—helping to shape a personality that was arrogant and offensive and brought misery to his brothers and sisters, in particular a younger brother whose looks and character were more winsome than his own. One evening, after the boy had been summoned by his parents to sing for some visitors and had been given chocolates in return, he came back to his bedroom, to be beaten by Tom. "You pig," Tom shouted, "you horrid, dirty little pig!"

By the time he was four years old he could be seen, early on Sunday mornings, striding along Dame Street in Dublin with eight brothers and sisters and his parents on his way to Sunday school at St. Werburgh's, an evangelical church not far from their house. Even then there was a certain strut to his walk and swing to his arms that set him apart as a determined, almost combative boy. When he reached his tenth birthday he was sent to a parish school in Dublin, a cold, bleak building presided over by a curate he did not like and where he was remembered by the students, including his own brothers, as an indifferent student and a thoughtless boy who talked incessantly and kept others in turmoil. "He was full of mischief," his brother would tell people years later. "He gave no end of trouble to his teachers." Then, when he reached his teens, he was sent to St. Patrick's Cathedral Grammar School, the oldest school in Ireland and one that prepared boys for university and business. He not only hated St. Patrick's but developed a lifelong contempt for its master, a chilly disciplinarian named the Reverend William Dundas whom Barnardo, when he became a man, would remember as "the most cruel man as well as the most mendacious that I have ever in all my life met. He seemed to take a savage delight in beating his boys."

When he left St. Patrick's in the afternoons, he would come home, often alone and almost always filled with anger at the routine of the school but in particular at the cruelty of Dundas. It was to remain engraved on his mind forever and tempered his own personality and his treatment of children.

In his private moments on the third floor of the house over the fur store, he began to read not religion, but philosophy, especially the works of the secular thinkers Voltaire and Rousseau. He found them more exciting and more acceptable than anything he had ever heard from the church or from the parish school. As a result, he surprised his father one day when he was seventeen years old by telling him that he no longer believed in God. He was, he declared, an agnostic.

By then he was out of school, a carefree and conceited boy—"just as cheeky as a young fellow can be", he was to recall many years later— and already expressing his fondness for fashionable clothes, gleaming white shirts, fine silk scarves, and, no matter where he went, a top hat to lend height to his short stature. Employed by a wine merchant, he cut a memorable figure, strutting to work every morning, a seventeen year-old youth whose stylish, measured step was made almost theatrical by a walking stick.

In the evenings, when he was not reading Voltaire or arguing with his brother George, a brilliant boy who went to Trinity College, or with Fred, who attended the School of Medicine, Barnardo would sit diffidently with his father, listening to that kind and gentle man as he spoke of the things of his faith. He spoke particularly of the religious revival that was then sweeping Dublin and drawing thousands of people to meetings at the Metropolitan Hall on Abbey Street, an echoing hippodrome of a building in which hundreds of men and women every evening were pledging themselves to new lives. "I wish," his mother would say softly, "that you might come with us, Tom. Just come." For several nights he did. But as he sat on his seat and looked down on the distant stage, the pleadings of the evangelists seemed too heated, too fevered. He would glance at his father and mother and feel a mingling of sympathy and sorrow for the simplicity of their lives.

One night, following a service on a spring evening in 1862, a Dublin lawyer named William Fry invited him to his home for coffee and conversation. Fry, a zealous supporter and organizer of the revival meetings, was even more zealous in his commitment to the tenets of the Plymouth Brethren, a strict Calvinist sect that had no clergy and stressed Christ's imminent return to earth and the terrible urgency of salvation and obedience. Fry talked with Barnardo, not aggressively, but kindly, as if he could sense that only a gentle and subtle style could breach the wall of arrogance that the young man had built around himself. The two talked well into the night, and when Barnardo finally got up to leave he was, though not persuaded, led to reconsider the confidence of his agnosticism.

Three weeks later, on the twenty-sixth of May, Barnardo walked with his brothers George and Fred to the Metropolitan Hall, where, along with thousands of Irish Protestants, he heard an actor, a man named John Hambleton, recount his life story, including the story of his conversion or, as Hambleton chose to put it, his return from the gates of Hell.

When Hambleton, his face flushed and sweating, finished his dramatic sermon, he began pleading for souls, beseeching men and women to come forward, to declare their sins, to be washed in the blood, to begin life anew. Barnardo did not stir, but he watched, his eyes moving from the stage to the seats; as the actor's voice rose and fell through the shadows of the hall. "Is there not one more, now," he pleaded, "one more for Jesus? Is there not one here who is wondering, one who is at the threshold, one almost ready to share His burden and take His cross? My friend, come. Come now." Barnardo did not move.

It was very late when he left the hall that night, silently strolling among the crowds with his two brothers, each of whom, being converts to the Plymouth Brethren, had prayed aloud in the meeting that Tom, too, would come to the Lord. He said nothing all the way home. But, after they had reached the house and each had gone quietly to his own room, so that they would not wake their parents, Fred decided to try once more. He went to his brother's room and there at his bedside he began to entreat him to accept the Lord, reminding him that Jesus loved him, had died for him, and held out the promise of eternal life if he would but follow Him. Soon George too was kneeling in the room, pleading, beseeching, and begging Thomas to accept his "free and full salvation".

It was a scene that secular men and women would never understand and, a century later, would view with the deepest skepticism and disdain. But on that spring evening in 1862, in a room over a fur store in Dublin, two teenagers so deeply influenced their younger brother that he would, as part of his new life, change the destiny of hundreds of thousands of British children and, in doing so, have a deep and complex influence on the life of Canada for a full century. That night, Thomas Barnardo became a religious zealot.

Within a few months, Barnardo, driven by his conversion to a new sense of mission, felt called by God to an immediate and special kind of ministry. Though only seventeen years old, he sat at his table one night and wrote a letter to a man named George Muller, a member of the Plymouth Brethren who was revered for his work with children in Bristol, England. To him Barnardo poured out his overwhelming desire to do something at once for God and for man. His letter revealed not only his own state of mind but a mind that was typical of converts to the Plymouth Brethren, one that believed that men and women must be saved before it was too late.

"Living in the heart of the City of Dublin," he wrote, "I see daily around me numbers in a dying state, dying because the have not life eternal, and I am anxious, with God's help, to do something to arrest them on the brink of ruin, but I am so very young, being a lad of only seventeen years; but I have been thinking lately that if I, in connection with young Christian friends, were to have a room for one night in the week and there with some friends hold a Revival prayer meeting, the Lord would bless us."

For weeks Barnardo would come home from the shop where he worked with his father, a job he now found unrewarding, to hunt for Muller's reply. When it finally came, it was a crushing disappointment. Muller in effect dismissed him. He told Barnardo to wait until he grew up, and in the meantime to keep a tighter rein on his feelings.

Naturally Barnardo could not. He rented two rooms in downtown Dublin and announced that three nights a week he would be preaching. In fact, he did little preaching, relying instead on older friends among the Brethren who had the confidence—in fact, the courage—to face the nightly congregations of hooting, jeering crowds, some of them so drunk they took to throwing bottles at the preacher. For three years, from the summer of 1863 to the winter of 1866, he kept up a strange and punishing schedule, working for his father by day, and at night handing out pamphlets or climbing on platforms, a short, plain youth exhorting men to salvation while there was still time.

Then, one snowy evening in February 1866, he met a man who was to touch his life, first with excitement, then with disappointment. The man was Hudson Taylor, a noted missionary whose famous words "a million a month dying in China without knowing Christ" was to become part of the very language of the missionary movement. They also filled Thomas Barnardo with a flaming desire to go to China to save souls. He announced to his father that he was leaving the business and leaving Dublin. He would go to London, he said, and there hope to be accepted as a candidate for the China Inland Mission.

The men in London who were in charge of recruiting missionaries for China were baffled by the young man who presented himself that April in 1866, urging that he be sent immediately to the fields of the heathen. He seemed, for all his slight stature, to have energies that were almost beyond his control and equaled only by his almost overbearing sense of self-confidence. He expected to go to China immediately and was surprised and somewhat hurt to learn that, for him at least, a period of training was deemed necessary. Already, people around Barnardo were sensing in him a headstrong personality, and one man was so struck by his almost defiant independence that he doubted that the youth would ever be satisfactory as a missionary in China, where he would be part of a team and not a one-man band. "His bearing," another man remembered, "was that of a thoughtful, resolute, obstinately persevering man."

Still, Barnardo knew that if he were ever to be accepted for China, he had no choice but to train, and so, his ambition still strong, he began to ponder the sort of skills he should acquire to make certain that the China Inland Mission would take him. He would, he decided, study medicine as a means to that end. He presented himself as a student at the London Hospital.

Early each morning, six days a week, he would leave his cluttered room, strewn with tracts, and make his way past dingy offices to the hospital, a sooty, deteriorating building in which the operating room was so primitive that a piece of wood was shoved under a leg of the table to keep it steady. A washtub filled with wood chips sat beneath the table to catch the blood that splashed while the surgeons worked. The floor was bloodstained and uneven; the students drank. Barnardo was appalled, but he was also disinterested. His mind was elsewhere, in China, where a million a month were dying without salvation.

He was determined that within three years, by 1870, he would be qualified as a physician and therefore acceptable for China, probably as the administrator of a medical mission. And so, three days a week, he made rounds at the hospital prescribing medicines and supervising dressings. The patients saw a solemn young man, one who, while only barely into his twenties, rarely smiled and moved about as if he had the cares of the world pressing upon his lonely shoulders. His fellow students were not taken with him, not merely because he was so aloof, but because he was so religious. "He is something of an enigma," one of them told some friends. "He is the most hardworking among the students. He appears to have abounding energy for his work. At the same time, it is obvious that his heart is not in his work, that his mind is on other things." Then one night, in the midst of a cholera outbreak only a few months after he began work at the hospital, some of the students came upon him one evening standing atop a wooden crate on a street corner, exhorting men and women to come forward. "Won't you now take that great step forward," he was saying, his voice rich and strong, "that first step toward your free and full salvation?" The students stared, some jeered. Then they walked on, certain that Barnardo was nothing but a crank who would bring disrepute upon their hospital and their profession. They decided there and then to ostracize him.

Despite his eagerness, it soon became clear to the men in charge of assigning missionaries to China that Barnardo was not suited, mainly because of his personal style and his religious dogma. His personality was too self-centred and authoritarian, and his religious attitude, so deeply and finally influenced by Brethrenism, made him unwilling to submit to any form of church government. He was even critical of the way the men to whom he was applying ran the China Mission. But with his overflowing sense of confidence he had no idea that in the offices of the missionary organization he was viewed with growing skepticism. "As far as I am concerned," he wrote them one day, pleading to go to China as soon as possible, "I look forward, God willing, to leave about October or November next....I am now in my second winter session and with God's help I have worked hard, having been up to this date (January third, 1868) been enabled to dissect two complete subjects and think I am well up as and man of my year....Beloved brother, pray for me."

Shortly afterward, a man named W. T. Berger, who was in charge of the mission's office in London, put on paper his deepening doubts about Tom Barnardo and, in doing so, touched upon traits of behaviour and character that were to mark Barnardo's work all of his life. "While he is a very talented fellow," Berger wrote to Hudson Taylor, "he is so overbearing that it tries some of us a little. He is doing great work in the East End of London and gaining valuable experience, especially in the wise use of money, for he is naturally fast and spends his money far too freely and unthinkingly. He has been in great difficulties at times as to means for carrying on his work and gets behind in his payments, so he will not be so forward to judge others who may do likewise."

Then, a few months later, as gently and as diplomatically as he could, Berger told Barnardo the disappointing news: he would no longer be considered a candidate for missionary work in China. "Thomas J. Barnardo and I spent some four or five hours together last week," Berger reported to Hudson Taylor. "He is carrying on a great work in the East of London and neither he nor I see how he can leave it....So we agreed to consider him as no longer a candidate; he will go on for MRCS and MD so I trust he will have a means of support whether he should go as a missionary or not."

For several weeks he was crushed with disappointment, laid low by a kind of depression that would remain with him forever, hovering like a cloud at the edge of his life, coming and going but never far away. He spent his mornings aimlessly, wandering the streets near his room and then drifting toward the mission he had founded a few months earlier as part of his training for China, calling it simply the East End Juvenile Mission, where in the afternoons he held classes for children and in the evenings climbed on a makeshift platform to preach to the boisterous crowds.

He gave up all his plans to become a physician, though his vanity and his need for prestige would not permit him to forsake the title he had used in his student days: "Doctor". At the time, he was a full year away from qualifying as a physician, and his practice of referring to himself as Doctor Barnardo (or signing his articles and letters as Thomas Barnardo MD) was to be, within a few years, the source of an ugly and painful controversy, one that would diminish all who took part in it. It was, his friends worried, merely a manifestation of some deeper need to be seen as an authority, a man before whom ordinary people stood in respect. Even his mother, his most generous advocate, worried over her son, so convinced of his religious faith but so overbearing in his personal ambition and conceit. "Are you seeking the praise of men?" she asked in a telling letter during those months. "Do you love to be approved by them? Do you indulge the flesh as to food, dress, frivolity, excitement?"

It was as if his restless, driving energies, now thwarted in one direction, moved immediately and entirely in another. His spare time religious work became his complete commitment and within a few weeks he was expanding it, taking children off the streets and vowing to make his life work among them though in these early years his concern was primarily with their souls rather than with their need for food, shelter, and decent care. He was an evangelist to children. Then one day he met Annie Macpherson, already at work in the child field, and his imagination was fired with what needed to be done and what could be done. It became an obsession, driving him with such force that along with his children's mission he founded a congregation. At the same time he began his lifelong career as a writer, pouring forth a Niagara of articles and stories, of children and adults, telling of his work, all for the purpose of securing financial support and a modest income for himself.

Most of his writing dealt with reports of his street work or took the form of direct appeals for financial aid. But one piece published in *The Christian* in the summer of 1872 just as his work in child rescue was becoming widely known, was called "How It All Began" and purported to be an account of his first meeting with a destitute boy, a child named Jim Jarvis. The story caused a sensation when it appeared and began the romantic legend that would some day entwine his name.

According to the story, Barnardo rented an old donkey stable in a depressing area of the East End called Stepney, put a floor in it, whitewashed the walls, and, two nights a week and all afternoon and evening on Sundays, opened it to children who came in droves for lessons and scriptures and, more probably, the warmth and force of Barnardo's personality. One night, just as he was closing up the building, he noticed one boy remaining behind, as if he did not want to leave. He asked the boy if he shouldn't be on his way since his mother would be waiting for him. The boy—his name was Jim Jarvis—replied that he had no mother. Barnardo asked him where he lived. He replied that he lived nowhere. "Now, my lad," Barnardo replied, "it is no good trying to deceive me. Where do you come from? Where did you sleep last night?" The boy said that the previous night he had found a deserted cart and the straw that had been left inside it made him a more comfortable bed than usual. Barnardo looked at him closely, a thin wisp of a boy, with eyes that were wise to the streets. Barnardo went on to ask if there were others like himself, without parents and without homes. "Oh yes, sir," Jim answered, "'caps of em! More'n I could count."

Barnardo took the boy to his own plain room, gave him food, and drew out the rest of his story. He had been on his own, he said, for several years, ever since his mother died when he was five. He had scavenged a farthing here and there, trying at the same time to avoid the police, who, when they found him sleeping outside, would take him before a magistrate who would have him locked up, usually in the workhouse. Barnardo, always the zealous evangelical, then asked the boy if he had ever heard of Jesus. The reply, given Barnardo's deep reservations about the Roman Catholic Church, not only stunned him but probably caused him to redouble his efforts. For the boy replied: "He's the Pope of Rome."

It was then past midnight. Barnardo, still wondering if the boy's story of children sleeping in the outdoors was true decided to set off with him in search of the hideaways where they spent their nights. The account of that late night wandering as Barnardo rendered it is still vivid: the young student in his black cloak, a silk hat on his head and a lantern in his hand, heading off with the boy, barefoot and in rags, on a mission that would make history. They made their way through alleyways filled with trash, beneath windows through which drifted the moans of the drunk and the dying, until at last they were standing beside a shed off Petticoat Lane. Suddenly the boy shinnied up the wall of the shed, stood on the roof, and reaching back with a long stick, helped Barnardo to the top of the building. There, under the cold light of the moon, he discovered a pathetic scene.

"The roof was dome-shaped, and adjoining and communicating with it was a large hayloft, used by dealers in china for packing their wares. This loft was closed, but a good deal of straw had dropped from it into the gutter, and was put to use by the lads, whom we saw lying there asleep. With their heads upon the higher part of the roof and their feet somewhat in the gutter, but in a great variety of postures, lay eleven boys huddled together for warmth—no roof or covering of any kind was over them and the clothes they had were rags which seemed worse than Jim's."

Barnardo said nothing. The boy spoke up cheerfully saying there were lots more in other places; he offered to take Barnardo to them. But the man in the top hat did not answer. He was, he told friends later, too shocked to speak. His imagination, for so long taken up with thoughts of China, began slowly to sketch a new vision of his future. "That awful night of discovery," he was to write later, "was not forgotten, for again and again the faces of those boys, their destitution and their mute appeal for help entered into our soul until, leaving ourselves and our future career in the hands of Him who ruleth all men's hearts, we were enabled to renounce a life of usefulness in another and a distant land." His China dream was at an end.

That night, according to the popular legend, Thomas Barnardo took the first child, Jim Jarvis, into his care. Within a few weeks, by December

1870, he had opened a refuge—three small houses near his East End mission—where thirty-three boys from the streets, mostly thirteen and fourteen years of age, came to live. He put them to work chopping wood, so that quickly they began to realize a small income to help pay the cost of the rent and the food, most of which was borne, as would be the case throughout his life, by donations. Then, one day in the spring of the following year, he chose about a dozen of them—those, he said, least likely to find a decent life in London—and delivered them into the hands of Annie Macpherson, a fellow evangelical who was taking children to the farms of Canada. Thus, Jim Jarvis, Barnardo's first boy, so the story goes, embarked in May 1871 for life on an Ontario farm.

There is unfortunately no way of tracing the life of Jim Jarvis to authenticate the details of his meeting with Thomas Barnardo or his subsequent life in Canada. But now, a century later, with no evidence but Barnardo's own renderings of the story, it is fair to ask if it is more a parable than an actual event, a myth woven in the colourful imagination of Thomas Barnardo to symbolize and dramatize his work before the public whose support he coveted. There is, for example, aside from the lack of independent and confirming evidence, some reason for wonder at Barnardo's surprise and shock at the discovery of children such as Jim Jarvis living in the streets. After all, Barnardo's own rendering of the incident—published in *The Christian* in 1872—makes it clear that it took place some time in the winter of 1869, after he had been in London for more than three years studying at the hospital and doing street evangelism. The latter brought him into regular contact not only with the poverty and distress of East End London, but with some of the people, among them Annie Macpherson, whom he was helping (at her Home of Industry) as early as 1867. Given his association with Annie Macpherson, who began rescuing children as early as 1866, it is hard to understand Barnardo's sudden discovery of homeless waifs three years later. It seems likely that the validity of the famous story of Jim Jarvis is more in its symbolism than in its historicity.

Moreover, in much of his written work—and indeed in some of the treatments given to his work by others—it is strongly suggested that Barnardo was instrumental in bringing the existence of waifs and strays to the attention of Lord Shaftesbury, the nineteenth-century earl who was one of the most influential figures in the history of social reform in Britain. Shaftesbury, so the hagiography maintains, hearing of a talk Barnardo gave on destitute children, invited him to dinner for the purpose of having a dozen other people—including a couple of Annie Macpherson's workers—hear at first hand of the terrible conditions that Barnardo was reported to have discovered among destitute children. "Barnardo had no suitable clothes," wrote one of his biographers, relying, of course, on Barnardo's own account of the evening, "nor even, the price of his fare at that moment. Until he received his next allowance from his father, he was down to his last shilling, a predicament to which he was well accustomed. Since the invitation promised much, he borrowed a dress suit from the house surgeon and walked the greater part of the way to Lord Shaftesbury's Mayfair home."

After dinner, so the widely accepted version has it, the gathering adjourned to the drawing room. Then Shaftesbury, signalling for silence, turned to Barnardo in what must have been a memorable tableau: the famous earl, then in his sixties, his fame vast, his influence without equal, seeking the advice of a young man still in his early twenties and barely known. He asked Thomas Barnardo, a bit skeptically, if the statements he was reported to have made—about a boy named Jim Jarvis taking him to a nest of urchins sleeping on a rooftop—were in fact accurate.

Barnardo, of course, said it was true, every word of it. The rest of the group Barnardo recalled later, quickly gathered round. Shaftesbury still doubted. "I suppose," Barnardo recalled him saying, "that you would have no difficulty in finding a group of such boys as you speak of tonight." Barnardo said he would not. And so the great man, still finding it hard to believe, went with him that very night, said Barnardo, and of course was appalled when shown that children were living in crates and barrels and on the roofs of warehouses; Barnardo remembered it well and told of it afterward. "All London must know of this," Shaftesbury told him. And then: "God bless you and lead you, young man. Continue with your good work."

It does not diminish the life and work of Thomas Barnardo, his compassion, his vision, or his energy, to suggest that this meeting, with all its drama and prestige, was probably a creation of his theatrical imagination, embellished by devoted followers. Shaftesbury, after all, had been crusading for social reform for many years. He entered Parliament in 1826. Then, in 1841, three full years before the birth of Thomas Barnardo, a friend took him to see at first-hand the horrors of life in the East End of London. That visit marked him for life, arousing in him a deep concern for the men, women, and children of the East End who were broken by the influences of industrialization and urbanization. As his biographer, Edwin Hodder, has shown, he knew the East End intimately, and was in daily contact with others who knew it intimately. It is highly unlikely, therefore, that in his late sixties he would need anyone to show him that children were living in the gutters.

On a damp, grey day in June 1870, Thomas Barnardo, then twenty-five years old and a mature young man with a commanding, serious style, strolled into Stepney, a corner of East End London that he knew as well as he knew his old neighbourhood in Dublin. It was a place of rotting tenements and sour-smelling rooms in which thousands of men and women looked to a future of despair and death. Their children, many of them, were delivered to the streets and, as the work of Dickens would later make vivid, became scavengers of food and servants of thieves.

Barnardo himself was at a crucial passage of his life, one in which he had been driven deep within himself and left with vague notions that his destiny was being altered in ways that were indefinable but certain. The door to China seemed permanently closed. And his work with destitute children—teaching, preaching, and sheltering a handful in his mission—seemed somehow incomplete and unfulfilled. "The future," he scribbled in a brief note a few days later, "even to our most hopeful lads, is dark and unpromising." What they needed, he came to feel, was not merely a refuge, but a home, a place that would look after their needs, not just for shelter, but for moral upbringing, so that their steps could be set upon the paths of righteousness forever. He resolved to provide one.

He chose a huge, vacant house in Stepney, one that had been empty for several months and for which the rent was less than sixty pounds a year. He had only a few pounds of his own, which was soon used up in paying the carpenters to rip out the walls and turn the many small rooms into large dormitories, five in all. But within a few weeks, through his articles in the religious papers and his budding friendships with wealthy evangelical laymen, he was able to have the building renovated to include not just the dormitories, but a sunny, spacious kitchen, a large communal washroom, and an apartment that would serve as living quarters for the two adults who would supervise the home. There was room for seventy boys.

Some time in the early weeks of September 1870 he began to search for the children who would become the first residents of his new home. For two nights he strutted up and down the streets that spread like a cobweb from his Stepney home, peering into stalls and carts in the silent dark, Almost always, he said, he found a boy, usually ten or eleven, with no parents and no shelter, and after a brief conversation he took him to the home, where his supervisors cleaned up the child, replaced his rags with a suit of clean, plain clothing, and assigned him a bed in the dormitory. On the seventeenth day of September 1870, twenty-five boys, scrubbed and barbered and acting like members of a cadet corp, filed into a room in the dormitory and sat in a circle around Thomas Barnardo. He led them in a simple service that was the official opening of Dr. Barnardo's Home.

There is every reason to believe—given the record of his life—that in those early days he drove himself recklessly, with a moral passion that was sincere and deep and an abandon that constantly threatened his health. In the beginning, his literalist interpretation of the scriptures—in particular an injunction to owe no man anything—forced him to keep the number of children in his care low, no more than he could pay for out of the money he had on hand. Thus, one night, after he had filled five vacancies—made available by an increase in his funding—he met a boy named John Somers, eleven years old, abandoned by his father and used as a scavenger by his mother, who took whatever pennies he brought home and spent them in a gin shop. The boy begged Barnardo to make room for him, but, adhering to his iron principle, Barnardo told the boy he would have to wait his turn. A few days later, the boy's body was found in a barrel near London Bridge, his death the result, the coroner said, of exhaustion, exposure, and lack of food. For days Barnardo sat in his room at the Stepney home, staring gloomily into space, depressed by the loss of the boy and driven to question his conviction that he should always remain out of debt. In the end, he emerged from his room and had the carpenters erect a sign outside the home that would become the famous slogan of Barnardo's to this day: "No destitute child ever refused admission."

For the next two years Barnardo drove himself relentlessly, raising funds, enlarging his work, and in the nights, often from midnight until five in the morning, scouring the streets for the children for whom his religious and moral fervour grew deeper with every search. Often he took with him one of the children already in his care, a boy who, he reasoned, would be able to assure others of his age and kind that Dr. Barnardo's Home was not a jail or a court but a safe, sure refuge. Once, in the first weeks of winter in 1871, with a slight dust of snow on the buildings of East London, he and one of his boys stopped at the doorway of a rickety tenement only a short distance from the Thames. Afterward, Barnardo recalled the incident as merely typical of his nocturnal excursions, and if it is tinged with moral assumption, it must also be seen, in its time and place, as an act of lonely courage. "Into one house my little conductor entered stealthily, returning shortly and requesting me to follow him. I entered a long passage. I advanced quietly turning on the full blaze of the lantern, but could at first discern nothing except what looked like a dark bundle of old rags in the far-thest corner under the stairs. The odour of the passage was uninviting and one might have imagined that what I saw was really what it seemed—a pile of cast-off rags, unworthy even of a beggar's notice; but well I knew that this was not the case and, reaching forward, I felt beneath the rags, and soon grasped the thin, spare arm of the boy. [Then] my guide whispered. 'Look behind, sir, quick.' I observed that hidden in the corner there was still another little bundle of rags under the stairs, and the sad little bundle proved under examination to be another boy some two and a half or three years younger. A very few words of explanation and encouragement to the older boy was all that was required. Away we went, reaching, about four o'clock in the morn-ing, that dear old refuge in Stepney Causeway, into which many storm-tossed little barques had now hidden in safety. The two boys crept, just as they were, into some old hammocks in the receiving room, and slept undisturbed till about twelve the next day. Then, after the necessary cleansing and rehabilitation in clean, wholesome garments, they were formally received among the other inmates of the Home."

The boys, whose numbers were now overflowing his accommoda-tions—there were by this time over one hundred and thirty of them, some as young as six, others as old as seventeen—spent their days in an atmosphere that was humane but Spartan and strict. From rising at six o'clock until bedtime at nine, their lives were governed by a spirit that was militaristic in its adherence to rules, schedules, duties, and penal-ties. In the morning, after washing and making their beds so that a penny could bounce from the covers, they sat at long wooden tables, had daily devotions, and ate a breakfast that was almost always meagre and tasteless—bread, porridge, and tea. Then they began their routine, which was divided into two basic activities: work and study. Their work, designed personally by Barnardo, was planned as both a moral benefit to the boy and a financial benefit to the home. And so, along with all the household duties—baking, cleaning, and scrubbing—they spent their afternoons in a trade school where the fruits of their labour (shoe-repairing, tailoring, bread-making, and so on) could be sold and the money used to enlarge Barnardo's work. In the mornings they went to a school on the premises where they were taught only the most ele-mentary, reading, writing and scripture. It was clear from Barnardo's attitude that he did not believe deeply in education and at times open-ly wondered if it might be a disadvantage for his boys. In time, he hoped, they would be suited for a trade somewhere in industrial England. He also set them to work as messengers among the offices and factories, billing them in circulars as the City Messenger Brigade. All through the 1870s, small boys, wearing the vivid Barnardo uniform (a tunic, a pair of red-striped trousers, and a hat like that of a Salvation Army officer), could be seen darting up and down the stairways of London, bearing papers and parcels.

Overnight, Thomas John Barnardo was a name to conjure with in the circles of religion and philanthropy in England. He had arrived. By now he was widely recognized, known not only as a man of deep religious zeal and moral commitment but as a daring fundraiser and a brilliant, if sometimes arrogant, administrator. Early on he had rejected the notion that he should rely on prayer alone for his financial support, and in spite of many raised eyebrows he began to campaign for contributions in the pulpit and in the press. Thus, in the space of a single year he more than doubled his receipts, from about seven thousand pounds in 1872 to over fifteen thousand pounds 1873.

The money did not go to improve the quality of care for the children he already had, but to extend his work. Soon, within three years of the official opening of the home at Stepney—which was quickly swallowing up nearby buildings so that one day it would occupy half the street—Barnardo was operating, along with the home, free schools, Sunday schools preaching missions, and, most daring of all, his own church. Known as Edinburgh Castle, the church had been a huge rambling gin palace which he bought amid much publicity. During the week he served coffee and cocoa to working men and on Sundays he preached in a great hail to thousands of evangelicals who rejoiced that Barnardo had brought about "the fall of the Citadel of Satan". By the end of 1873 his church had two thousand members and was serving both as a revival centre and, in its coffee house, as a social club for the working class: stevedores, factory workers, and men employed at the nearby slaughter-houses.

That summer, when he was twenty-eight, he also married a bright, serious woman of twenty-six, Syrie Elmslie, a teacher. Her parents were upset at her decision, worrying that Thomas Barnardo, who called himself Doctor but wasn't qualified, was in fact an adventurous romantic whose schemes, while gathering great publicity, might also be reckless, expensive ventures that would drive him into disgraceful debt. Nevertheless, on a sunny day in June, with a soft breeze wafting through the windows of the crowded six thousand seat Metropolitan Tabernacle— then the citadel of history's greatest evangelical preacher, Charles Spurgeon, Barnardo married Syrie Louise Elmslie. Naturally he saw to it that the event was accompanied by wide publicity, which in turn worked to his advantage. A man named John Sands, a wealthy lawyer who shared Barnardo's Plymouth Brethren beliefs, sent word that he was providing the couple with a private home in Barkingside, a pleasant village a few miles from the boys' home at Stepney.

A few days after they had moved in, Barnardo was seen by some neighbours standing by a coach-house in the back garden, his hands behind his back, studying the size and structure of the building. Now that he had a wife, he was ready to undertake a part of child care that until now, as a single man, he'd been reluctant to embark upon: the rescue of homeless girls. The following morning, carpenters began ripping walls, building staircases, and widening windows. That October he placed an announcement in *The Christian:* "Through the great goodness of God, a Home has been placed at our disposal in which it is our united desire to rescue little female waifs and train them as domestic servants for establishments of the better class."

Before long he took what was, for his time and society, a wise and enlightened step. He concluded that the placing of girls in a single large institution was not in their best interests, that they would benefit more in smaller groups and smaller homes, each home presided over by a house mother who would treat the children in her care as her family. Thus, in the leafy village of Ilford, only a short walk from his new home, and with some help from his father-in-law and a few wealthy benefactors, he set to work building fourteen cottages, each with four bedrooms, a playroom, a kitchen, and a small apartment for the woman he placed in charge. Today, more than a hundred years later, these houses still stand amid wide and quiet lawns, their halls still alive with the voices of children. They are part of the memory of thousands of Canadian women who recall, often with deep emotion, their early childhood at the Girls' Village Home of Thomas John Barnardo.

By the time he marked his thirtieth birthday at home with Syrie and their first son, Barnardo had, outwardly at least, all the hallmarks of great achievement. When he sat at his table on that evening in July 1875, he was a genuine celebrity, a famous figure in the field of evangelical religion, which, unlike our own time, carried with it an aura of glamour and prestige. His juvenile mission in the East End, providing meals and scripture lessons to working boys, was one of the fastest growing in all of London; his schools were crowded and busy places where hundreds of children every day learned to write and were given a bowl of soup; his Stepney Boys' Home boasted six hundred inmates and even its own infirmary; his Girls' Village Home had just opened; his articles appeared regularly in *The Times*, the *Manchester Guardian*, and papers overseas; and, most telling of all, he stood almost every Sunday in the pulpit of Edinburgh Castle, the former gin palace, preaching to the working men and women of London who crammed every corner of its three thousand seat hall. In a word, he was a hero.

Yet with his prickly personality (he was so impatient with one of his female volunteers that he said, in front of her and others, that women were by nature stupid) and his success so vast and so rapid, it was inevitable that Barnardo would inspire jealousy. What shocked his friends—and came perilously close to destroying Barnardo both personally and professionally—was the extent to which his enemies were driven by their hatred. They sought to destroy him through character assassination.

They began, naturally enough, with the charge to which Barnardo was most vulnerable—that he was not entitled to call himself, as he always did, "Doctor" Barnardo. But that was a detail. In the end, Thomas Barnardo had to face a public scandal that accused him of dishonesty in his handling of money, cruelty in his treatment of children, deception in his appeals for funds, and, finally, of having lived, before his marriage, with a woman who earned her living as a prostitute.

Five
The Scandal of the Pious

E ven his friends of those years began to sense in Thomas Barnardo an ambition that had about it an air of vanity and excess, as if in some part of himself he was seeking, not so much the welfare of the homeless, as the power of achievement and fame. His great benefactor John Sands, a man of means who had given him much, began in private to shake his head, not merely at Barnardo's vain style, but at his overbearing ambition and his near obsession with beginning new ventures: an evening club for factory women, an infirmary for his children, a hostel for cabmen, even a reading-room near his headquarters where the people of London could read dramatic accounts of his rescue work on the streets of their city.

It was, however, his decision to open a second coffee house—he was already operating one at Edinburgh Castle, where, in the early hours of the evening, he could be often found strolling between the tables, handing out pamphlets and advice to the dock workers—that struck John Sands as unwarranted and indeed unfair, since he chose to open it in an area of London where other evangelicals were already at work in the same kind of programs.

One of them was Frederick Charrington, twenty-three years old, a tall, light-haired man with a broad, strong face, who was, in many of his ways, akin to Thomas Barnardo—opinionated, ambitious, and above all, emotional. He was five years younger than Barnardo and had been born to wealth, being the son of a famous brewer. When only twenty, Charrington had been converted to evangelical faith and the cause of the temperance movement, a cause that, in one of the many ironies of his life, he did not hesitate to promote with some of the money that came to him from his family's brewing wealth. He knew Barnardo, and while there was a measure of rivalry between them as men who were emerging as leaders of the evangelical movement of the day, their dealings were generally cordial. Often, particularly when Barnardo had the famous preaching team of Dwight Moody and Ira Sankey speaking to his congregation at Edinburgh Castle, Charrington would be there, a rather curious presence, his aristocratic bearing standing out among the rough-clothed dockers and factory hands who came in great numbers to hear the two preachers remind them of the wrath that was to come.

One day in the spring of 1875, Charrington opened his paper to read that Barnardo, already so well situated in other parts of London, was planning to open a coffee house on Mile End Road, a part of the city that Charrington, because his family's brewery had been there for years, regarded as his own. He had established his work there: a school, a mission, and, like Barnardo, a home for destitute boys.

His face darkened as he read of the boastful ambition of Barnardo, who seemed bent simply on widening his horizons no matter at whose expense. In his imagination he began to visualize local funds—all of which he badly needed to support his school, his mission, and his home—being drawn away by the flamboyant appeal of Thomas Barnardo. For the rest of the day, Charrington could be seen moving along Mile End Road, stopping in shops and offices, his proud figure barely containing his frustration, a man forced to couch his anger in pleas for sympathy, complaining that he, Charrington, was almost ready to open a mission hall on Mile End Road. In fact, he said, he had already bought the land on the very day that Barnardo was so selfish and thoughtless as to plan one less than five minutes away. "It is," he would say, "ungracious and uncharitable and harmful to all of us who have worked here so hard to build our own mission."

Then, within a day or two, he went to see Barnardo in person. He sat in Barnardo's office a long time, pleading, reasoning, and demanding. Barnardo listened, and years later when he recalled the meeting he claimed to have been sympathetic and ready to compromise. But Charrington did not remember it that way. He said that Barnardo was as arrogant as people thought he was, refusing to listen and going ahead with his plan to build a coffee house—thus establishing himself as a temperance worker and preacher—right in the neighbourhood of other evangelicals.

Charrington was not alone in his resentments. Along Mile End Road, in a tiny church that had only thirty members and was known as the Cave of Adullam, a slight man with large, suspicious eyes, George Reynolds, a former railwayman turned preacher, looked on Barnardo with the same helpless fears and the same rising jealousies. With his little band of followers and their pittance of financial support, Reynolds saw all too clearly that if Barnardo were to establish a mission and con-

gregation near him, his church would not only be dwarfed but probably destroyed as its members were inexorably drawn toward the mag-
netic personality and growing fame of this young man. On some days
Reynolds would meet Charrington outside his curious church building
and together they would nurse their shared grievance. In time they
were driven toward a course of common action that, no matter how it
was viewed, brought disgrace on them and indirectly on the character
of evangelical work at the time. One day, during one of his sullen and
gloomy visits to Barnardo, Charrington held out an ominous hint of
the depths to which they would soon sink: "There is something behind
which you do not know of, Barnardo, and which you will be very sorry
for." Barnardo heard him out, but as usual he was so preoccupied with
his own plans, so insulated by his own self-confidence, that he paid little heed and therefore had no idea of what was to come.

At the same time, in another part of London, people with other
plans looked upon Thomas Barnardo and did not like what they saw,
either of him or of his work. These were the members of the Charity
Organization Society, a group of men and women, mostly from business
and the established church, founded only a few years earlier and claiming for themselves the job of overseeing all work among the poor and,
in particular, defining the roles for local government and for private
agencies such as Thomas Barnardo's. For the most part they were well-
positioned men and women and their views were conservative—
Frederick Charrington was one of their members in the East End. They
took a predictably critical view of Barnardo's free-wheeling approach,
convinced that he was so ready to aid any and all destitute children
that he was actually helping to create a class of people who were taking advantage of charity and, in the process, having their own wills
destroyed and replaced with lazy dependency. It was, of course, an
opinion that would always divide those who worked in the field of
social welfare—whether to make their programs open to all or only to
those judged to be in dire need. Very early in his career it was clear that
Barnardo, whatever his faults of personal style, was among the progres-
sives who were unwilling to apply a means test to those who came to
his door. Moreover, Barnardo's growing popularity—the result of his
great gift as a preacher, writer, and publicist—was seen as a direct
threat to the Charity Organization Society, whose efforts to find public acceptance were, by comparison, pedestrian and plodding.
Nevertheless, no matter how deep their frustrations or how reasonable
their views—they did have a case obviously in feeling that the work of
social welfare should not be left to some of the will-o'-the-wisp entre-

preneurs who came and went at the time—their willingness to be used by Frederick Charrington and George Reynolds in their campaign against Barnardo was breathtaking in its lack of judgement.

It began in the springtime of 1874 with a campaign of whispers that spread the rumour that, when he was a student at London Hospital, Barnardo had lodged in the home of a prostitute, a mysterious "wicked woman" known only as Mrs. Johnson. According to the gossip, he had formed an intimate relationship with her, and had even suggested that some of those helping in his work come to live there as well. The father of the rumour was the Reverend George Reynolds, who knew Mrs. Johnson slightly (she was then living in his neighbourhood), drew her into conversation one day, and manoeuvred her into implying that when he boarded at her house Barnardo had been involved with her sexually. Barnardo, always too wrapped up in his work to have time for common talk, had no idea that the story was circulating until one day, when he was away preaching, a letter written by a friend of both Reynolds and Charrington arrived at his home, charging him with the scandal. Since he was travelling, his wife opened his mail, and, after reading its surprising news, she sent word to Barnardo of this great Christian charity from his brethren. Naturally Barnardo denied the allegations, but Charrington and Reynolds simply ignored him and stepped up their activity, and within weeks people all over the East End of London, were reading anonymous letters, handbills, and tracts, all carrying, not just the story of "Barnardo and the Wicked Woman", but new charges that depicted his home for children as a chamber of horrors.

He was, for the first time but certainly not the last, a man under siege. He began to show it. His brisk stride seemed less confident and his colourful presence less evident as he spent hours and sometimes entire days trying to reason with Charrington and Reynolds. Or else he was listening to the advice of friends who were worried, not just for Barnardo and his health, but for the future of evangelical work, which was slowly becoming soiled by the venom of the controversy. There were some who argued that he should sue for libel, and, in fact, on two occasions he would take the first step and have a writ drawn up, but always he would fail to press it, believing, as a member of the Plymouth Brethren, that Christians were enjoined to stay out of the courts of law. "It is," he would say sternly, "an action that is forbidden by the very Word of God Himself in Holy Scripture."

So, for more than three years, beginning in 1874, while the number of children in his homes grew to almost a thousand and the money he handled went into five figures, Thomas Barnardo weathered an attack on his character and work that at times drove him into the dark corners of depression. In letters to the editors of small local papers in the East End, Reynolds, who, having no reputation to lose, became the ruthless aggressor for both himself and Charrington, began to suggest that Barnardo was not a philanthropist so much as a profiteer, lining his pockets from the misery of children and the generosity of supporters. Reynolds savaged him for living in a comfortable home: "Let the truth be known," he wrote, "Dr. Barnardo, instead of sacrificing all for the Lord's sake, has raised himself on a pedestal of his work." Then, in what turned out to be a shrewd ploy, Reynolds drew the Charity Organization Society into the fray: "It is hoped that the Charity Organization Society may go thoroughly into these matters and the law of the land may soon be altered, so as to enable them to grapple effectually with many of these societies."

When he read the letter in his newspaper, sitting in his office at Stepney Causeway, Barnardo got up and walked slowly to the window and looked out over the empty playground of his home. He stood there for almost an hour, hurt by the bitterness engulfing him and yet not able to grasp its full depth—unable, for example, even to suspect that at that very moment the Charity Organization Society had in its possession material it would use in an attempt to discredit him. He would scarcely be able to believe it when, within months, the society would announce a list of men contributing to a fund backing Reynolds in his campaign, a list headed—to Barnardo's lifetime regret—by no less a man than the great Lord Shaftesbury.

He was unable to see that his self-centred way, his domineering style, his one-man rule; all were leading to the abyss. Despite the growth of his work, there was no board of trustees, no audit that was independent, no statement that was issued yearly, only a report on the state of finances made by Barnardo himself when he finally got around to it. His sense of pride and his passion for independence were carrying him into dangers that he would forever regret.

It was as if his enemies knew every part of his life and work that was open to criticism. Reynolds, for instance, knew only too well that Barnardo, for all his bravado, was highly vulnerable on his use of the title "Doctor", a designation he not only assumed for himself but also requested that others use when addressing or introducing him. In truth, Barnardo was not then a physician—not in those early years of the 1870s—having abandoned his studies to further his evangelical work before he took his final exams. In time, after several years of hectoring by Reynolds, Charrington, and the Charity Organization Society, he did complete his academic work and received his diploma in medicine from Edinburgh University in 1876. But the harm was done and the suspicion lingered that, for a period in his life, Thomas Barnardo was willing to engage in a degree of deception to enhance his authority.

Often on Sunday afternoons, following his services at Edinburgh Castle, in which he would be buoyed by the satisfaction that comes from speaking to a congregation of thousands, Barnardo would emerge from the building to find George Reynolds circulating among his parishioners, handing out leaflets that contained the most slanderous accusations. Sometimes Reynolds, who by now was driven by a bitterness that was as reckless as it was burning, would actually try selling the leaflets, and once, in a gesture that proved his nerve, he thrust some of them into Barnardo's own hands.

He was questioning, of course, not merely Barnardo's use of money and title, but his treatment of children. According to Reynolds, Barnardo was systematically taking children from their parents, refusing to return them, and in fact subjecting them to abject cruelty. Moreover, said Reynolds, the methods Barnardo used to gain support for his homes—photographs of each child taken before and after admission to show their impoverished state and their subsequent improvement—were outright fakes. Barnardo, Reynolds charged in his leaflets, smeared the children with soot, mussed up their hair, and tore their clothing, all in a calculated effort at making them appear more ravaged than they actually were.

For months Barnardo could scarcely leave his office or open his mail without facing some new, frightening charge against his work or against his character. He withstood it for a year, but then the whole episode took a turn that was to make the controversy not only sadder, but more notorious, to raise it beyond a mere local squabble to a national incident.

It began on September 11, 1876, when a small local paper, the *East London Observer,* carried a letter to the editor, signed with a pseudonym (Clerical Junius) and purporting to be written by an Anglican minister who was coming to the defence of Thomas Barnardo against his critics. "If Dr. Barnardo determines to be silent," he wrote, "nor again to reply to antagonists who under the cover of an assumed name attack him and his work, all must feel that his dignified self-respect has guided him aright, but his friends, at least, need not be bound by similar considerations." The letter then went on to praise Barnardo at great length and in extravagant terms, outlining his membership in a distinguished family, his ambition to become a missionary, his decision to set his dream aside in favour of his country's own needs, and his rapid and inspiring success. Then, a couple of weeks later, on September 25, another East End paper, the *Tower Hamlets Independent*, carried a second letter, longer still, written by the same correspondent, this time containing, along with all the fulsome praise of Barnardo, an attack on Reynolds and Charrington, which, although veiled in allegory (Reynolds was called Rev. Swino Reynard and Charrington was depicted as Mr. Brewgoose, "who had not quite the brainpower to succeed"), was extreme in its use of sarcasm to impugn the motives and abilities of both men. It was, as a method of rebuttal on behalf of Barnardo, a monumental mistake. It not only inflamed the controversy—which was precisely what aided a crank such as Reynolds—but also gave Reynolds a further opportunity to cast even more serious aspersions on Barnardo. Within a week Reynolds retreated to his church building and began to write a sixty-two-page booklet containing all the stories and all the slander that he could compile against Thomas Barnardo. He would call the booklet *Dr. Barnardo's Homes; Startling Revelations*, and he would peddle it all over London at a shilling apiece. Its accusations and its influence would be such that Barnardo and his friends would be beside themselves with despair.

One damp morning in November of that year, one of Barnardo's friends knocked on his door early and handed him a copy of the booklet. He leafed through its first pages, reading, as in past handbills, Reynolds' plea that the homes be placed in the hands of a board of trustees, with a treasurer and an auditor, and what he called a kinder régime. But it was not until he reached page twenty-eight that Barnardo's face turned white. He sat down slowly, almost disbelieving. There, in the form of an affidavit, was a statement from one of his former employees, a man named Edward Fitzgerald, claiming that the author of two controversial letters signed with the pseudonym Clerical Junius, praising Barnardo and damning his critics, was in actual fact Thomas Barnardo himself. "On or about the eighteenth day of September, in the said year and following nights," Fitzgerald's declaration said, "I was in the back parlour of the said Thomas John Barnardo, at his said house, and on those evenings, I heard the said Thomas John Barnardo dictate to Frederick Fielder, who was then in his employ as clerk, a letter which afterwards appeared, to wit, on the twenty-fifth day of September, in the *Tower Hamlets Independent*, signed Clerical Junius. The extract from the *Tower Hamlets Independent* now produced and marked with the letter A, contains the substance of what I heard the said Thomas John Barnardo dictate to the said Frederick Fielder; and in many places I recognize the exact expressions used by the said

Thomas John Barnardo. I was in the house when the said Frederick Fielder left it, professedly, to take the said letter to the offices of the said *Tower Hamlets Independent;* and I saw him leave the said house dressed in such a manner as to represent the appearance of a clergyman. And I further say that this was done with the knowledge and sanction of the said Thomas John Barnardo."

Other than Barnardo, the man most distressed by the ominous turn of events was John Sands, the wealthy and generous evangelical, who sensed that Barnardo's style and manner would sooner or later bring him into trouble. Along with that, Sands worried, was the possibility that the entire evangelical cause—then in a serious, if diplomatic, struggled with the Charity Organization Society over the control of social work in London—was being dragged deeper and deeper into the mire of a disgraceful dispute. Sands decided it was time to act.

He had believed, even before the Reynolds booklet, that Dr. Barnardo's homes were of such a scale of operation and finance that they could no longer be run as one man's concern. And so, being Barnardo's major supporter, with an influence that was thereby larger than any other, Sands went to him and put before him the case for a board of trustees to which Barnardo would be responsible. For a few minutes Sands was almost certain that he was to fail in his argument, that Barnardo was so fiercely wedded to his independence that he could not countenance supervision by a board. But slowly, as Sands argued well into the night, he came round, if not to approve the idea, at least to accept it. But he did not like it.

Within days the board met at the Stepney Home, most of them able, vigorous men who were first of all willing to face the mounting sea of controversy. Barnardo, more subdued than any of them had ever seen him, entered the room and quietly took a seat at the end of the table, facing the chairman, Lord Aberdeen. The chairman looked at him, as did a few of the others that evening, with a strange mixture of frustration and wariness, as if they were ready to exert their authority but unsure of how to do it. After all, they had before them a man who had built such a reputation that he carried a large portion of public opinion with him; and yet, in the minds of thousands of Londoners, he was a man under a cloud, an evangelist alleged to have consorted with a prostitute, lied about his credentials, and profited from the miseries of society. Aberdeen called the meeting to order. Quickly it became apparent that the men in the room were ready to support Barnardo, but only on two conditions: first, that he assure them that he had an answer for every charge that had been laid against him; second, that he assure them, in so far as it was possible to predict, that there were no further allegations to come. Barnardo did not hesitate. He told the nine men that he could answer every charge, and while he could not be certain that other slander would not come from the warped mind of Reynolds, he felt, as much as it was possible, that Reynolds had exhausted himself.

For the first hour the talk was brisk and candid as they admitted to each other that they were facing a deep crisis, not just over the work and character of their friend Barnardo, but over the definition of charitable work among the poor. One man, Harry Nesbit, an aloof, almost grim lawyer who was made secretary of the trustees, told the others that the appearance of Reynolds' pamphlet was a special blessing to the Charity Organization Society in its campaign against Barnardo. "They are now saying," he told the others, "that they are receiving inquiries from all over London, from people who contribute to you, Barnardo, who wonder if they should continue their support. And the society is saying they don't recommend it. They are saying that you are on their 'cautionary list'. They are blacklisting you."

Barnardo, his voice for the first time rising with tension, stood up and looked at them one by one as he spoke. "I know that. But let me tell you something about it. We are dealing with a society that is, to a very large extent, influenced by two men who, for their own reasons, spend a large part of their time seeking to destroy my work. I mean Charrington and Reynolds. Both are members of the society from this very district. We should be clear about what we are facing. The charges about an immoral relationship between Mrs. Johnson and myself are baseless. So is their claim that I do not have my medical qualification. Their claim that the homes are profitable to me in a personal way is baseless."

He was, when speaking of the alleged affair between himself and Mrs. Johnson, speaking to a group of men who already believed him. For, even before their first meeting, some of them had visited her, questioned her, and come away convinced that she was a hysterical and unstable woman. As for his medical background, he had, it was true, just a few months earlier secured his diploma. As to his alleged profiteering, a team of auditors was called in—Turquand, Young and Company—and, to its astonishment, found in his books meticulous records of no fewer than sixteen thousand separate donations, ranging from those of a few pennies to a couple that were over two thousand pounds. The auditor's report was unqualified: "Examined the books and found correct."

Still, for all this anxious inquiry, the trustees knew that something further was needed, some public action that was official and definitive, if they were to lay to rest, once and for all, the suspicions that Thomas

Barnardo was a fake and a tyrant who ran homes that were little more than jails. They faced, however, one strong and emotional obstacle: Barnardo's resistance, on religious grounds, to a full-fledged libel action. Finally, late one night, after he had sat through a tense session with John Sands and Arthur Kinnaird (an able member of Parliament who was to be a crucial influence in the trying months ahead), Barnardo agreed to a plan by the trustees, one that was bold and risky, but that in its final outcome would prove to have been brilliant in both conception and execution. They would go to Reynolds and, first, invite him to make his charges formally, not in a court of law but before a committee of independent arbitrators, Christian leaders, approved by each side; and, second, advise Reynolds, who was as poor as a pauper, that all costs would be borne by Barnardo, all except the fee for Reynolds' own lawyer and witnesses, a cost which, as it turned out, Charrington and the Charity Organization Society covertly paid. Thus, John Sands and the other men who believed in Thomas Barnardo were able to bring matters to a formal hearing, while at the same time avoiding the kind of civil prosecution that Barnardo could not accept and that would have brought even greater publicity to one of the most embarrassing episodes in the history of the evangelical movement in Britain.

Some time around mid-morning on the eleventh of June, 1877, a clear, cool day with a trace of the rain that was to pour that afternoon, the hearing opened in a large, rather forbidding building, the Institution of Surveyors, set among the offices that lined Great George Street in the heart of London, just of Parliament Square. At the front of the room—a big, sombre chamber with high ceilings—sat three men who would hear the evidence, pursue it further by visiting all of Barnardo's homes, and then render a verdict on the character of Barnardo and the integrity of his work. Seated there, amid the austerity of the surveyors' institute, they seemed misplaced and uncertain, as if the job before them was one they would never have chosen. In the middle of the three, flanked by his two lay arbitrators, sat the lawyer who would preside over the hearing, John Maule, a bright-eyed, gifted man who came from Leeds, and who would prove to be an incisive and vigorous adjudicator. On his left, leaning forward slightly, was a large, ruddy-faced priest of the Anglican Church, Canon John Miller, who came from outside London, a man who, aside from his gifts as a preacher among working-class people, was known to have a shrewd sense of business practice. To the right of Maule sat a slight, serious man, William Graham, a Presbyterian, a former member of Parliament, a man of the arts, and yet a man of serious commitment to evangelical causes. These were the three who, during the sweltering heat of that summer, sat through the melancholy parade of accusation and counter-accusation, and sifted the claims and counter-claims that flew between Barnardo and Reynolds, Charrington, and the Charity Organization Society. Around the room, seated on hard-backed chairs that lined the walls, were the interested spectators, a group that grew in number as the hearing neared its close and that included, not merely friends, but, almost every day, leaders of the Charity Organization Society, especially a man named C. J. Ribton-Turner, who, it would turn out, had been collecting evidence against Barnardo with the zeal of a detective.

From the middle of June until the middle of September the three arbitrators sat, almost always uncomfortable, not merely from the suffocating heat, but from the melodrama played out before them. George Reynolds' case, put before rite arbitrators by little-known lawyer, St. John Wonter, took twenty-seven days, and drew upon forty-seven witnesses, most of them former boys who had been expelled from the homes, former employees who had been fired, or parents who claimed, sometimes with deep passion, that Barnardo refused to return their children or even to permit them visits. The case on behalf of Barnardo was taken by Alfred Thesiger, a slender man with a boyish face, who, though still in his thirties, a reputation as a brilliant counsel and was sought all over London in civil litigation. He was a busy man, and his willingness to take on Barnardo's case was a sign of the influence of the powerful men who had gathered together as trustees to protect Thomas Barnardo. From the very beginning, Thesiger, who brought sixty-five witnesses to the stand, was in command, a man whose style was quiet and modest, but whose grasp of the case neared perfection and whose plea was couched in the most lucid and concise language.

The case for George Reynolds did not go well. Several of the witnesses, among them a man named John Hancorne who had circulated with Reynolds the story of a boy who was said to have been beaten, dragged downstairs, and flung onto the streets by a Barnardo supervisor, were shown to be disreputable. Hancorne himself had been fired for immoral conduct. When Edward Fitzgerald—Barnardo's former assistant, who claimed that Barnardo had had an affair with Mrs. Johnson and that Barnardo himself had written the Clerical Junius letters—took the stand, Thesiger began to expose the flimsy nature of Reynolds' campaign and the secretive backing of the Charity Organization Society. Fitzgerald, a large man with an impressive bearing, was, in fact, a drunk who had been let go by Barnardo, but who was, as Thesiger revealed through his questioning, in the pay of Barnardo's enemies even before he left him. He not only supplied them with material but also tried to foment trouble. Once on the stand, Fitzgerald fell apart, told conflicting versions of his story, and, in the end, in Thesiger's hands, turned out to be an ace card for Barnardo. Even Reynolds was forced to admit, under questioning, that Fitzgerald was a drunk. Thesiger next compelled Charrington to admit that he had employed him, as had the Charity Organization Society. Then, quietly and deliberately, Thesiger began to lay out the position that would bring permanent discredit upon the actions of all three: Reynolds, Charrington, and the Charity Organization Society. "This man," said Thesiger, referring to Fitzgerald, "foul as he was, had been taken into the confidence of Mr. Charrington and Mr. Reynolds and, I am sorry to say, by several prominent members of the Charity Organization Society." The air in the room seemed charged with tension as he turned to the three men at the arbitrators' table and said pointedly that he regretted that on that particular day the leaders of the Charity Organization Society were not present. "I cannot help thinking," he said, "their eyes would have been opened and they would have been ashamed of joining these persons who have been guilty of such deceitful conduct as those two gentlemen have been guilty of all along."

Reynolds, he said, was a reckless man, from whom nothing but malignancy could be anticipated, but Charrington was even worse, for from him more could have been expected. "One heard of a young man with an opportunity, if he thought proper, of pursuing a lucrative business, turning from that business and giving himself up to operations of a kindred character to those that were carried on by Dr. Barnardo. One only started with a feeling of respect for Mr. Charrington, and I must say it is only his own fault if that respect has been removed from the minds of those who have heard this case....Malignant as Mr. Reynolds has shown himself, he has come forward boldly and openly....Mr. Charrington has pursued a course which, as regards the prosecution, I shall show you is identical with that pursued by Mr. Reynolds, but he has not pursued it openly...." Charrington, to his great embarrassment, was shown not just to have employed Fitzgerald in his effort to undermine Barnardo, but to have helped Reynolds publish his notorious pamphlet *Dr. Barnardo's Homes: Startling Revelations*.

It was August, late in the month, in the middle of the hearing's most sweltering days, when Thomas Barnardo entered the witness box. Since the beginning in mid-June, he had come by carriage from Stepney Causeway to the Institute of Surveyors. He would sit and listen, sometimes getting up and striding from the room, his frustrations running over at the tirades of Reynolds and the slanders of men whom he had fired for the most scandalous reasons. By now his moods swung like a pendulum between white anger and dark depression. His eyes, usually bright and curious, had about them a weary glaze, and people noticed that his usual natty appearance seemed frayed and his shoulders slumped as he sat.

St. John Wonter, Reynolds' lawyer, realizing that his crucial witnesses had failed him, now saw in Barnardo his final, uncertain hope. On the morning when Barnardo was due to testify he reviewed in his mind the direction his questioning would take. He knew that his plan to discredit Barnardo on the basis of his medical qualifications had been diminished since Barnardo had, albeit only a few months ago, received his diploma in medicine from Edinburgh University. Therefore, decided Wonter, the more crucial issues, the ones on which Barnardo's integrity was most shaky, were his use of deceptive photographs to publicize his work and, above all, his role in the writing of the two letters signed Clerical Junius, on which, if he could be held responsible, his moral stature could be virtually destroyed. Wonter knew, however, that on the matter of the photographs, just as on the matter of his medical degree, Barnardo and his trustees had already outflanked him, at least to a degree, by circulating a description of the purposes of the photographs which explained that some of them were posed in order to achieve "an exact likeness" of the child at the time of discovery. Moreover, Thesiger, representing Barnardo, had almost put the issue of the photographs to rest by calling as a witness a poor woman whose three children had been used by Barnardo in his photographs and who approved of it. Her story, drawn out with great drama, was so pathetic that John Maule, the head arbitrator, could be seen wiping his eyes. Thesiger had to control his own feelings and, incredible to everyone, Wonter, the prosecutor, was seen offering her a few shillings to tide her over!

And so, Wonter was left with one issue, an issue that could, he thought, destroy Barnardo's credibility—the authorship of the infamous Clerical Junius letters. After Barnardo took his place in the witness box, Wonter rose and approached the slight, weary man seated before him, convinced in his own mind, as were many others, that Barnardo was, in fact, the author of the scurrilous epistles which praised himself, damned his critics, and yet left him protected in the cloak of anonymity. Slowly, carefully, Wonter raised the crucial issue. First, he outlined what was already known, what, in fact, Barnardo had already admitted or what had been revealed by earlier witnesses: that Barnardo had supplied the writer with certain documents, facts, and details; that he had done so in the full knowledge that a letter defending his person and his work was being prepared for the local newspapers; and that, as one witness, a lady named Mrs. Guinness, had said, he had read both letters before they were submitted to the papers and in fact had actually delivered one by hand to his close friend, the editor of the *Tower Hamlet Independent*. All this Wonter reviewed, calmly reminding the arbitrators that Barnardo either had admitted what he was now telling them or had not denied it when others said it.

Then he levelled his gaze at Barnardo and asked him simply who wrote the letters, who the true author was. There was a pause, brief but charged. Barnardo shifted slightly and then, in a calm, confident voice, he replied tersely: "I have already declined to tell." Wonter asked again, who, tell the truth now, who is the author? Barnardo, this time quickly, shot back: "I refuse to tell." Wonter, looking for a trace of insecurity, closed in once more and asked his question. But Barnardo was adamant. "I refuse to say," he told Wonter, "though I distinctly and fully accept the entire responsibility for the authorship of the letter, but I decline to inflict an injury upon the real author by giving his name."

By now the three men on the committee of arbitration had been sitting for almost three months. They had come to their work, not out of interest, but out of duty. Their strength of will, their patience with all the pettiness, were never strong, and now with this abrupt turn of the hearing they were bewildered. John Miller, in particular, the Anglican clergyman who had to come many miles every day to the hearing, could be seen mopping his brow and slumping over the desk, clearly a man who was weary of it all. He looked at Barnardo, rigid in his refusal to give the name, and he came as close as an Anglican cleric could come to losing his temper in public. "This is a very mournful thing," he told them all, "and sad, for a head of a great Christian work like this to appear in the witness box and refuse to obey the law of the land." He said he was certain that Barnardo was duty bound to answer that the question of who the letters was the most crucial the arbitrators had to face. "I must say frankly." Canon told Barnardo, "that I regard it as the most important because it reflects confidence in you and, as we all know, if the result of any trial or arbitration is to destroy that confidence, it would destroy the institutions as they presently exist."

Thesiger, too, was baffled. He was, after all, Barnardo's counsel, but he was also a leading jurist committed to the processes of the law, and he found himself agreeing with the prosecutor and the arbitrators that his client should, in the interests of all concerned, reveal the name. He suggested that to Barnardo, but got nowhere. Barnardo, looking straight at him, replied that he refused to do so, since it would bring ruin upon a man he had promised to protect. Then, Wonter announced that since Barnardo had refused to give information the arbitrators required, he, St. John Wonter, could see no sense continuing and he therefore would ask no further questions. Thesiger, his mind grasping the possibility that the entire proceeding would fall apart, moved immediately for an adjournment saying there were "persons to be consulted", meaning quite obviously the influential trustees who were handling Barnardo's public problems. The hearing adjourned.

The next morning it was no better. The air in the room was filled, not merely with stale air, but with the frustrations of stubborn men. Barnardo was utterly intractable. Wonter refused to go on. Moreover, Canon Miller was ready to up his hands and return to his parish and his summer holidays. At that point, William Graham, the quietest of the arbitrators, cleared his throat and began to offer what was to be the most crucial opinion of the entire three months of hearing. It was obvious that he had met during the adjournment with the Barnardo trustees and he now argued that, first, Barnardo should give the name, but in the event of his refusal, the three arbitrators should still agree to listen to the summation of his counsel, Alfred Thesiger, and only then decide if they could reach an opinion on the life and work of Thomas Barnardo. In short, said Graham, Reynolds and Wonter should continue; the arbitrators should hear the case to its conclusion. Then they should render a decision. Graham's plea saved the hearing from foundering; Wonter and Reynolds left the room, but Miller stayed and the hearing continued.

Thus, early in September, Alfred Thesiger, the brilliant defence lawyer, found himself in the strange and delicate position of summing up and making a plea without his adversary counsel, St. John Wonter, even a participant in the proceedings, a fact that Thesiger set forth cleverly, saying that it made his work, not easier, but more difficult. He spoke for two days during that first week of September, wisely presenting the arguments of both sides, but nonetheless leading to ruin the conclusion that "on the whole these institutions have been carried on with the utmost propriety by Dr. Barnardo, that they are institutions which have not been carried on for his own ends, but have been carried on through his own unselfish desire to benefit the class of children he has taken into the homes." The hearing then came to an end.

For the rest of that month, and on into October, Thomas Barnardo endured not only the anxiety of the long wait for the decision of his judges but, to his amazement, another attack by his enemies in the Charity Organization Society, who began to peddle a new circular claiming that the arbitration hearing had broken down and that Barnardo, by his refusal to answer the critical question, had in effect revealed his guilt. Barnardo, his nerves frayed beyond endurance, could scarcely believe it when someone showed up at his door carrying the new attack. He wrote an angry rebuttal and then, his spirit almost broken, he retreated to his office and was hardly seen for weeks. He was waiting.

The decision came on October 15. It was delivered by hand to his office. He was sitting at his desk, his eyes red from lack of sleep and his hands listlessly riffling some papers. He did not open the award but instead passed it wordlessly to Lord Aberdeen, the chairman of the trustees, who had come to him. Aberdeen tore open the envelope and, stepping into the light that fell through the window, read silently for what seemed a very long time. Then, slowly, he turned and handed the award to Barnardo, pointing to a sentence that became the most famous ruling of the tribunal: "We are opinion that these Homes for Destitute Boys and Girls, the Barnardo Institutions, are a real and valuable charity worthy of public confidence and support." Thesiger triumphed.

For almost all of that day Barnardo sat at his desk reading over and over again the twenty-five foolscap pages of the award, as if, in its judgements, he found not just relief, but an almost physical strength. It was signed, he noticed first by all three men, including Canon John Miller, who had been so hesitant and difficult over his refusal to name the man who had written the Clerical Junius letters. It said that because of Barnardo's attitude, the arbitrators' opinion on the matter of the two letters was not as soundly based as they would have preferred. But, given what they had to go on, they concluded that Barnardo was "as he has acknowledged" morally responsible. It was, he knew, as much as he dare expect. Moreover, when he leafed through the pages looking for their opinion on his practice of photographing the children before and after admittance, he nodded to himself, for, while they condemned it ("this use of artistic fiction to represent facts is, their opinion not only morally wrong but might in the absence of very strict control, grow into a system of deception"), he had, on his own, already abandoned it.

For the rest, their opinions on all the major issues favoured him. They dismissed the claims that he abused children or profited from their misery. They took a soft attitude to his use of the title "Doctor", noting that then, just as now, it was the custom to refer to medical students as doctor. They disbelieved the rumours about him, particularly about his supposed liaison with Mrs. Johnson, saying that the allegations were ill-founded in the first place and unsupported during the hearing. And they clearly put the blame for the creation of the controversy at the doorstep of the furtive man in the background who manipulated George Reynolds, Frederick Charrington: "There existed on the part of Mr. Charrington and so many of his fellow workers an unbecoming jealousy of the existing and extending work of Dr. Barnardo." Had it not been for their envy, said the arbitrators, the whole quarrel and might have been solved through compromise rather than confrontation. Then, going on from the specific issues, they made two major recommendations: one, that from now on the homes should have a management committee rather than the one-man rule of Thomas Barnardo, but even more important, that the ugly and defamatory tactics used in the conflicts should be seen for what they were and relegated to history. "We have now only to commend to the earnest consideration of the parties affected by it," they concluded, "our remonstrance against the spirit and temper which has pervaded this scandal controversy. To the extent of our power we decide and award that the circulation of defamatory charges by either side shall henceforth be entirely discontinued, and we venture to add the expression of our earnest hope that all the persons implicated in this quarrel may henceforth be induced to conform more nearly in the prosecution of the work in which they are engaged to the standards of conduct recognized among gentlemen and to the dictates of Christian charity...."

It was almost midnight when he finally set the manuscript aside, rose from his chair, and went out onto the street, walking as usual through the old streets of the Stepney neighbourhood that he regarded almost as his own. He paused briefly beside a tenement, smelly and decaying, where only a few weeks before, in the midst of the controversy, he had gone with one of his workers to remove a small girl whose mother, a prostitute, had decided to give her up. He glanced toward the windows, open to the warm night air, and heard again the sounds he knew so well, of men and women and clinking glass, human beings in the rapture of false escape. He walked on, wrapped in his thoughts, a man trying to find again confidence that he once possessed and now desperately needed.

He had at that moment more than a thousand children in his care. Even in the midst of his trials he had, like a man driven by a neurotic compulsion, enlarged his work still further to include a monthly magazine, *Night and Day,* and to the astonishment and concern of his friends he was even trying to raise money to buy a ship on which he planned to train for a future life as seamen.

He was certain that—as the great newspaper *The Times* would say a few days later—he had been given a judgement by the arbitrators that was "the kind of judgement the people wanted". Still, his exhilaration at the decision was tempered by a worry that would never leave him: that he was now in debt so deeply that he might never recover. The bill for the arbitration—which he and the trustees had largely assumed—

ran to more than two thousand pounds, a figure that he would never be able to raise and that tormented him almost as much as the agony of the battle. When he finally reached home that night, he settled in a chair in the living room and sat there until the first glimmer of the sun fell through the window, a man whose spirits moved between despair at his situation and excitement for his future. His dreams were at war with his debts.

A few days later, on October, *The Times* ran the decision, and then the next day an editorial supporting him, and for weeks afterward he was like a man struggling within himself to forget his worry and acknowledge his fame and triumph. "In the end, as our readers saw yesterday," ran the long editorial, "they have fully acquitted Dr. Barnardo of the gravest of the original charges made against him. They can find no proof of dishonest management or of intentional concealment of the real state of the homes. They are satisfied with the moral and religious instruction given in them; and their conclusion, based upon the evidence taken in court and upon personal inspection of their own, is that the homes are doing a work of real philanthropy and that they can show, accordingly, a good title to public support."

All over London that day, the men and women of the evangelical movement read the *Times* editorial, just as they had read the decision the day before, with a feeling that they too, like Barnardo, had been vindicated. For the award of the arbitrators and, almost as important, the endorsation of *The Times* meant that religious charities such as their own could now be viewed in secular society as valid and worthy organizations. Here and there among the supporters of Reynolds (who simply vanished from public life) there were those who, like Shaftesbury, were left with nagging uncertainties over the character and work of Barnardo. But most, like Annie Macpherson, the woman who was in some ways his mentor, read the editorial as a vindication of work by evangelicals among the outcasts of the city.

Annie Macpherson was, at the time of the award, a figure of authority and respect among all the workers of the East End. Unlike her contemporary and rival Maria Rye, Annie Macpherson found in Thomas Barnardo a friend and a kindred spirit. Often, when she returned from one of her many trips to Canada with children, she would go to Edinburgh Castle, sit in the crowded hall, and listen to Barnardo's appeals, and then, in a room beyond the hall, she would visit with him, telling him of the demands for children in Canada and most of all of the opportunities, especially in Ontario. Among the numerous papers and pamphlets filed neatly in his bookcases was a copy of the circular she had written eight years earlier in 1869, the one she called *Emigration, the only remedy for chronic pauperism in the East of London*. He had read it when she first sent him a copy, and one sentence above all the others remained in his memory. Now, as he looked to his future, it surfaced again in his mind: "We who labour here are tired of relieving misery from hand to mouth and also heartsick of seeing hundreds of their families pining away for want of work when from the shores of Ontario the cry is heard, 'Come over and we will help you.'" For the past few years he had been sending small groups of boys—including, he would always say, his very first child in care, Jim Jarvis—across the Atlantic in Annie Macpherson's keeping. "What such children need," he said to her when he sent his first group in 1872, "is a new heaven and a new earth—the fresh conditions of colonial life."

But now, with the arbitration decision behind him and his stature regained, he began to take so many children in his care that both he and Annie Macpherson felt it was time to begin an emigration program of his own. He had, after all, followed her work closely as if it were his own, and he knew, detail by detail, her methods, her problems, and, in particular, her differences with Andrew Doyle. He was certain, therefore, that on his own he could carry out an even larger work and avoid the pitfalls into which his friend, through inexperience, had fallen.

He told his trustees of the scheme and, his old confidence beginning to return, gave them a lecture on why he believed they should support him in his plan to send children, hundreds of them, perhaps thousands, to Canada. They were, for the most part, wary at first, feeling as they always would that he was taking on too much, too much for his resources and too much for his health. But they could not help being impressed as they looked at him, still young but aged by the strain of the past year, yet putting before them a proposal that, though no one in the room could have known it then, would turn out to be the most famous child emigration scheme in history. As they heard him out, even the most hesitant men in the room could not resist being swayed by Barnardo's presentation, not merely because it was delivered in his vigorous and persuasive style, but because he had thought it through so carefully, so minutely.

"A rescue home," he told them, his short arms rising and falling with each phrase, "must be continuously gathering in fresh inmates, else in a single generation it would be compelled to close its doors and write in the face of new applicants, 'No admission.' But to secure the open door in front, it must maintain its exit door in the rear. "The exit door was the door that opened toward Canada. "We in England," he said, "with our four hundred and seventy inhabitants to the square mile are choking, elbowing, starving each other in the struggle for existence. Yet the British Colonies over the seas are crying out for men to till their acres, to feed their national life, to add to their human resources. Canada alone, with an acreage nearly equal to the whole of Europe, possesses only the population of London. Here is a boundless field for settlers, and for just such settlers as can be selected from my family—boys and girls of good physique, of tested moral character, of upright habits, able to make trained use of their hands with few ties to bind them to the mother country, and at an age when they are easily adaptable to almost any climatic extremes." Furthermore, he pointed out, the cost of settling a boy on a farm in Canada was not high, given the help provided by the government there. "For the sum of nine pounds, he told them, "I can now fully equip, outfit, and pay all expenses connected with the emigration of a boy or girl to any part of Ontario."

Some time in the early weeks of summer, in the year 1882, with the full approval of his board, he called the superintendent of his boys' home into his office and told him to choose a group of youngsters—"the flower of the flock" was the way he described them—and accompany them to Canada, to a children's home loaned to him temporarily in Hamilton, Ontario, from where they could then be placed out on the farms of the province. The superintendent picked fifty-nine boys, ranging in age from fourteen to seventeen. On the evening of August 8, in a YMCA building at Aldersgate, he led them in a brief service of worship, gave each one a Bible containing a photograph of himself and a personal message, and reminded them of their responsibility to uphold the good name of Dr. Barnardo's Home. Then, the next day, he went with them to the port of Liverpool and boarded a tender that took them all out into the harbour to the steamship *Parisian*, ready for sailing to Quebec City. He helped them all on board, shook hands with each one, wished them God's blessing, and then stepped back on the tender. The boys gathered at the rail, the first party of Barnardo children bound for Canada, pioneers of an organization that, before it ceased emigration in the 1930s, would send over thirty thousand children to this country. They waved to him as he stood on the tender, and then, in a scene he would always remember, they began singing the words of a hymn he loved:

> Jesus, Saviour, pilot me
> Over life's tempestuous sea…

Six
Thomas Barnardo in Canada

July day in 1884, when the sun was high and hot and fell upon the streets of Toronto with the heat of a furnace, a tall, sturdy man with the bearing of a police inspector stood on the railway platform in Toronto awaiting a train from Montreal. He was Alfred de Brissac Owen, in his early thirties, a clergyman's son from England who, just a year earlier, had been appointed to his position as superintendent of the Canadian work of Dr. Barnardo's Homes. Now, on this scorching summer afternoon, he was standing alone, tense with expectation, for the train that was due any minute was carrying among its passengers from the liner *Parisian*, which had just landed in Quebec City, none other than the man himself. Thomas Barnardo. It was Barnardo's first visit to Canada to see the country, to survey his work, and, most important of all, to plan for its expansion.

He was, Owen thought as he watched him step onto the platform, a most fastidious dresser, a colourful figure with his expensive grey suit, his starched collar, and his gleaming cuffs. The two men shook hands. Then they set out for the home of the Honourable Samuel Hume Blake, Q.C., a former judge and leading member of the evangelical wing of the Anglican Church (he helped found Wycliffe College in Toronto), who had offered to head a group of advisers of Barnardo in Canada, and act as host during his visit.

That evening, over dinner in the quiet elegance of Blake's home in a comfortable neighbourhood of Toronto, surrounded by men and women who shared his vision and coveted his presence, Barnardo was like a man who had found a well of inspiration. He held forth, regaling the dinner guests with dramatic accounts of his adventures, his clashes with the Charity Organization Society, and even the details of his eight-day journey across the Atlantic. He told them that he had met on board a gentleman named J. W. C. Fegan, who, like himself, was engaged in the work of rescuing children and placing them in Canada.

"He had a party of fifty very nice lads along with him," Barnardo said, "whom he was taking to place in situations over here." Most mornings and evenings on board he attended services, usually conducted by Fegan, who he felt to be a very godly man. As always when he spoke of those who, because they worked in the same field, could be seen to be his rivals, Barnardo was unfailingly generous, even to the point of referring to Maria Rye's work as "well-managed", a description he knew to be at least questionable.

For most of the evening the conversation ran to talk about the controversy always stirring in the newspapers over the influence of child immigration on the character of the country. The issue was excited anew by stories of one organizer in Britain who, just weeks earlier, had shipped to Canada a load of men and women one guest described as loafers, drunks, and women of doubtful virtue. Barnardo listened thoughtfully, and then he began to speak. "These poor creatures," he said, "were of course deceived by promises of easy work and high pay. I believe that most of them paid for their passage out by begging or borrowing to get the money. The evil that results is obvious. In the first place, the people themselves were deluded. But in the second place, the widespread opinion is created all over the Dominion that all emigration societies are engaged in collecting the vicious, the immoral, the drunken, in fact, the useless debris of large cities in England and dumping them in Canada." Around the table the men and women sighed and some nodded. But one man, tall and greying, with the look of a banker, shifted slightly and spoke what was obviously on the minds of everyone else. "We know that is the impression, Dr. Barnardo," he said. "We face it wherever we meet people who know we support you. But what can be done about it? What can we do to offset it?"

Barnardo surprised them with the tone of his response, which was brief, brusque, and almost disdainful. "Our own work, of course," he replied crisply, like a man anxious to get on to other things, "is of a vastly different kind to that. All of our children have been carefully trained in our homes, many of them for years. They are sent out to Canada under watchful oversight, on arrival they are placed in homes that are chosen with the greatest care and, even after that, they are visited by qualified persons and looked after for years after they have left our homes." There was a respectful silence, as if they were not sure of his willingness to discuss it further, but then the man who had asked the question cleared his throat and spoke again, suggesting that everyone knew the children were decent and the care was wholesome, but still, what was necessary to convince the critics? "I intend to travel the length of this country," Barnardo answered tersely, "to speak to the people through meetings and through the press. I'll fight this prejudice that has been brought about by the errors of others for which I am in no respect responsible." It was clear to everyone that it was a subject that touched his sensitive and autocratic personality in ways he did not like.

The next morning he rose very early, slipped out of the hotel, and, before the heat of the day, began to explore Toronto on foot, the city about which he had heard so much from Alfred Owen and especially from Annie Macpherson, who told him often about its crowded churches and its streets where, on the Sabbath, nothing moved. "The tramcars" she had reported approvingly, "do not run on Sundays." He walked along Yonge Street, pausing to stare at the store of the great Methodist merchant Timothy Eaton, and then at the next corner, Farley Avenue (later Richmond Street), he turned to look for number 214, a red-brick building that Owen had said a group of Toronto churchmen was prepared to make available to him at a nominal price for his Toronto headquarters. He spotted the number, crossed the street, and there, in the damp quiet of dawn, stood all alone, studying the building that shortly became Barnardo's Canadian Office and Distributing Home for Boys, a dwelling that thousands upon thousands of small boys from Britain would remember as the place in which they stayed on their way to the fields and farms of Canada. It was, Barnardo could see, a large, deep building, running well back from the street; in his mind he could imagine that once some of its interior walls were removed its upper floor could be used as a dormitory to accommodate the large groups of children as they arrived and stayed a few days before being sent by train to their employers.

Later that day he had lunch with Samuel Blake and Alfred Owen, and after some preliminary talk about the city (he said that Toronto reminded him most of all of a flourishing English city of the second class), he began to outline for both of them his ambitions for his Canadian visit, which would last three months, and his plans for a tour that would take him all the way to British Columbia and then Chicago, New York, and Boston. He wanted above all else, he said, to get a sense of Canadian life—the attitudes toward children, religion, education—so that he could be confident of the atmosphere into which he was putting his children. "I want to be sure," he had, told Owen even before he left England, "that if I'm removing them from one set of influences I am replacing it with a set of influences more beneficial."

He was fortunate in that the railway companies, in particular the Canadian Pacific and the Grand Trunk, had told him that wherever he travelled on their lines, in Canada or in the United States, he could do so free of charge, a policy he felt to be inspired not just by charity, but by the railways' interest in fostering immigration programs like his own. He told Blake and Owen that he would probably spend a couple of weeks in Toronto, where, with their help in opening doors, he wanted to speak at public meetings and visit schools, hospitals, churches, prisons, and the homes of both the poor and the rich, all with the intention of learning Canadian attitudes and of countering the prejudice against his children that he was convinced was as unjustified as it was unwarranted. Then, that evening along with Owen, he met with a group of reporters, so that the next day the word of his arrival and the outline of his plans could be made available to the public. "I want to point out," he told the men who sat with him that night, "the great difference between the children we sent out—carefully trained, carefully selected, carefully placed, and carefully supervised—and the shiploads of helpless, enfeebled men and women who have been shunted into the country in defiance of humanitarian considerations and social-economic law." Someone asked him, just as he had been asked at the dinner at Blake's, what he intended to do to prevent his work being tarred with the bad brush of other schemes, and his reply was calm and diplomatic: "I believe that by temperate and wise letters to the press, replying to such criticisms, by public meetings in some of the large cities, and by correspondence with leading men, I'll remove these false impressions. The character of the children I've sent out is excellent. All you need do is look at the record."

He liked Toronto. Each morning until the end of July he was up early, as if he felt he must use every moment of the day, and he made his own way all across the city, even to the reformatories and jails, where he talked to prisoners and guards and watched the inmates making brushes in one of the workshops. He regarded the workshop as one of the most hopeful signs of penal reform he had ever witnessed. "The prisoners are treated as men and women," he wrote in a note that evening in his hotel room. "They are not treated as automata-guilty men and women, to be sure, deserving punishment, but having human sympathies, hopes, and fears, through which they may be reached and benefited." The churches, where he attended and sometimes spoke, were usually full. But what impressed him most was that the members—so many of who took him to their homes for meals—were invariably strict abstainers. One evening after he returned from the home of one of them, Barnardo, his attitude toward liquor shaped by the alcoholism he knew so well in Britain, put on paper his appreciation of the temperate life he found among the people he met in Toronto: "I have been a guest in many families, but I have never once been offered beer or wine, and I never once saw it on the table in any private house where I called. In the hotels, too, this is very remarkable. At the luncheon, dinner, and supper hours, one almost invariably observes the greater part of those present drinking water or, perhaps, milk with a lump of ice in it. Very occasionally, indeed, will some gentleman be seen taking wine or beer, and I have generally found that these, for the most part, are English or American visitors."

It was early in August when, along with Owen, he boarded a coach of the Ontario-Quebec Railway and set out for Peterborough, the small town in southern Ontario that was to become so much a part of his work in Canada. He was anxious to see the town, which had then a population of seven thousand, but in particular a large home on its outskirts which, in November of the previous year, George A. Cox, a railway executive, and later a Liberal senator, had donated to him rent free for his work. As soon as he had received it, even before he made his first trip to Canada, Barnardo had designated the building—a large, impressive dwelling known as Hazelbrae, overlooking a green ravine on what was to be known one day as Barnardo Avenue—as his distributing home for girls, and had already sent out almost a hundred of them who stayed a few days at Hazelbrae before being placed in homes throughout southern Ontario as servants, companions, or, in some cases, ordinary farm labourers.

As the train pulled out of Toronto station, Barnardo talked seriously to Owen about the need to overcome the prejudice in Canada that portrayed his children as tainted waifs who contaminated the families and communities that took them in. It was obviously a deep worry to him, one that, he told Owen, he had gone over time after time with his trustees, some of whom knew Canada and had even raised the matter with Sir Charles Tupper, Canada's High Commissioner in London and a supporter of the work. As he talked, Barnardo got up, took down a briefcase, removed a sheaf of papers, and handed one to Owen. "Here," he said. "Here are the principles on which we will base our Canadian work. I believe they are principles that will reassure those who condemn the children." Owen took the paper—it was called the Charter—done in Barnardo's ornate hand and obviously written since he had come to Canada. It was the guarantee he offered both to children and to Canadians, and it guided his work in this country as long as it lasted; whatever the flaws that were inherent and inevitable in the practice of sending small children to Canada, Barnardo's charter was an indication of how seriously he approached his work. Owen settled back, reading silently and nodding over each of the six clauses:

First: That no child shall be sent out manifesting criminal or vicious taint.

Second: That no child is to be sent out who is not at the time in excellent health, and without tendency to disease.

Third: That all such children (excepting, of course, the very young ones who go out for "adoption") must have been passed through a period of the most careful training, not only in industrial pursuits, but also of a moral and religious character.

Fourth: That as regards all children who come up to the standard of the three previous conditions, only the flower of our flock are to be sent to Canada.

Fifth: That upon reaching Canada all children are to come under the care of properly qualified persons connected with our institutions on the Canadian side, by whom they are to be distributed carefully into well-selected homes; and that even then our work is not to be considered complete, but that regular communication shall be maintained with these children for years by personal visitation of experienced assistants, and by a system of written reports from the child and its employer. That careful statistics shall be kept showing frequent reports of their whereabouts, progress, and general welfare, until they have reached an age when they no longer require our supervising care.

Sixth: That if, in spite of all these tests, precautions and safeguards, it is found by experience that some particular child, after having been placed out in Canada, becomes definitely immoral or criminal, then every legitimate means is to be adopted to recover possession of that child, and to return him or her at the earliest opportunity to the old country.

Owen read the paper once more, told Barnardo that it was much to the point, and then reached into his coat pocket and took out a clipping, one he had saved, not because it was unusual, but because it was so typical of the atmosphere in which they were trying to do their work. He showed it to Barnardo, a column from the *Toronto Evening News* of a couple of months earlier, reporting on a large meeting called by the Trades and Labour Council. Barnardo read it, his head shaking slowly as he came upon its most venomous and insulting reference, one calling people like Barnardo humbugs and pseudo-philanthropists.

Thomas John Barnardo, the energetic founder of Barnardo's Homes, whose organization placed 30,000 children in Canada.

(Barnardo Film Library)

The indomitable Maria Rye brought the first group of British children to Canada in 1869 and housed them in a refurbished jail on the out-skirts of Niagara-on-the-Lake.

William Quarrier, founder of the Orphan Homes of Scotland. Over 7,000 Scottish children were sent to Canada from this children's village just outside of Glasgow from 1871 to 1938.

James W. C. Fegan, founder of Mr. Fegan's Homes for Boys in North Buckinghamshire, England.

Nobody's Children.

A BRIEF ACCOUNT OF

WHAT IS BEING DONE TO SAVE THE ARAB CHILDREN OF OUR GREAT CITY,

TO WHICH IS ADDED A CHAPTER ON

THE WAIFS AND STRAYS OF LONDON STREETS.

By T. J. BARNARDO.

With Two excellent Photographs

TAKEN FROM LIFE,

LONDON: MORGAN AND SCOTT,
(OFFICE OF " The Christian,")
12, PATERNOSTER BUILDINGS. E.C.
And may be ordered of any Bookseller.

Price 6d., or two copies free by post 1s.

Nobody's Children, one of the many pamphlets published by Barnardo and sold to the public to raise funds.

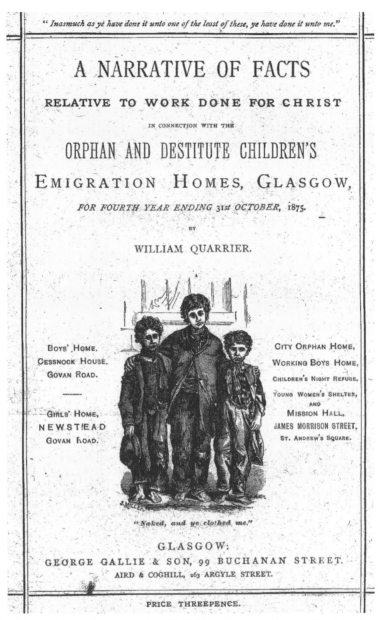

" Inasmuch as ye have done it unto one of the least of these, ye have done it unto me."

A NARRATIVE OF FACTS

RELATIVE TO WORK DONE FOR CHRIST

IN CONNECTION WITH THE

ORPHAN AND DESTITUTE CHILDREN'S

EMIGRATION HOMES, GLASGOW,

FOR FOURTH YEAR ENDING 31st OCTOBER, 1875.

BY

WILLIAM QUARRIER.

BOYS' HOME,
CESSNOCK HOUSE,
GOVAN ROAD.

GIRLS' HOME,
NEWSTEAD
GOVAN ROAD.

CITY ORPHAN HOME,
WORKING BOYS HOME,
CHILDREN'S NIGHT REFUGE,
YOUNG WOMEN'S SHELTER,
AND
MISSION HALL,
JAMES MORRISON STREET,
ST. ANDREW'S SQUARE.

" Naked, and ye clothed me."

GLASGOW:
GEORGE GALLIE & SON, 99 BUCHANAN STREET.
AIRD & COGHILL, 263 ARGYLE STREET.

PRICE THREEPENCE.

The Narrative of Facts outlined William Quarrier's work with the destitute children of Scotland and the emigration scheme to give them a new opportunity in life.

Left: The back streets and alleys of Glasgow were similar to many other large cities and were filled with homeless and destitute children.

Above: Barnardo stirred controversy with the use of photography to dramatize the plight of children.

Left: The first Fegan boy admitted to Mr. Fegan's Home for Boys in Deptford, England, the day of its opening in 1872.

Mr. Fegan's Homes for Boys at Stony Stratford, originally built as a college in 1899 but unable for financial reasons to open. Mr. Fegan bought it for £4,000 in 1901.

The Fegan receiving home at 295 George St. in Toronto. Over 3,200 Fegan boys passed through this non-denominational sponsoring agency from 1884-1939.

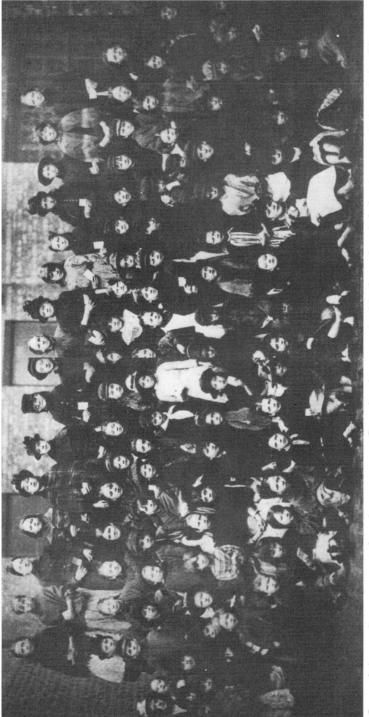

One of the earliest groups of orphans sent to Canada, photographed before they left for Liverpool aboard the SS *Hibernia*, August 1873. (Gwen Davies, Liverpool)

A party of boys from the Orphan Homes of Scotland leaving their homeland for a new life in Canada.

Girls in the forefront, boys at the rear, a party of immigrant children disembarks at the landing stage, Saint John, New Brunswick.
(Public Archives Canada 41785)

In the early days very young children were sent to Canada and adopted into families. An early party of boys and girls arrive at Quarrier's Fairknowe Home in Brockville, Ontario.

All the parties from Quarrier's posed in front of Fairknowe Home for a group photo. In later years the boys and girls would often return to Fairknowe to meet with their friends from Quarrier's village in Scotland.

An arriving party of boys from Mr. Fegan's Homes waits patiently for the Toronto train, circa 1912-13.

The headquarters of Barnardo's Homes in Canada on
Jarvis Street in Toronto.
(The James Collection, City of Toronto Archives)

Hazelbrae, Dr. Barnardo's receiving home for girl's in
Peterborough, Ontario.
(Ivy Sucee)

Fairknowe Home, Brockville, Ontario, the receiving home for children who came from William Quarrier's The Orphan Homes of Scotland.

Farm life in Canada was vastly different than life in the industrialised cities of Great Britain.

Home boys at work on a farm at New Brunswick, 1910.
(Wilson Studio, Saint John, New Brunswick)

Loneliness and hard work were part of the day to day experience in Canada for many of the Home Children.
(Barnardo's Archives and Home Children Canada)

Young boys were an important part of the economic success of many Canadian farmers. The Home Children were a cheap and accessible unpaid labour force to help build Canada.

Some of the home children today:
John Seely, Toronto (top left), Lillian
Bradley of Brantford (top right),
Charles Goddard, Toronto (bottom
left), Margaret Crooks of Ancaster,
Ontario (top centre).

Maria Rye escorts a group of girls to Sunday school at
Niagara-on-the-Lake.

Barnardo said nothing; Owen, in the manner of a man who knew he must learn to live with a prejudice he could not change, said simply, "It's nonsense, that's all it is, nonsense." Then they fell into silence and watched the green carpet of fields passing beyond their windows.

It was past noon when the train lurched into a station bearing a sign that caught Barnardo's eye and provoked his curiosity. It read simply: Pontypool. He got up and strode with Owen to the front of the car and asked how long the stop would be. When he was told, he nodded to Owen and the two stepped down onto the platform, where Barnardo strode up and down, watching the handlers unload the baggage and stuff a stagecoach with sacks of mail. He asked Owen about Pontypool, and his interest peaked when he was told that it was a place where large numbers of his boys, including some of his very first shipment two years earlier, had been placed. They went inside the station and there, on a map on the wall, Owen pointed out the towns along the line, Claremont, Burkdale, Bethany, saying that in every one of them, and in the countryside surrounding them, there were scores of children who had been sent out from his home. He studied the map carefully, noting not only the towns and villages but the great open countryside, where there was room for so many more people and a need for so many more of his children. "And they are far enough from the city," he said in a reference that was a deep conviction. "Cities are no place for our children."

During the rest of the journey, which was slow and tiresome, Owen told him of the kind of men and women who lived on such farms and who took the children. They were first of all, Owen said, hard workers, believing that work was necessary not only to make a living but even more to build character. It was good for their own children (though most in that period had small families), and in particular for the children who came to them from Dr. Barnardo's Homes. Most of the boys, Owen said, certainly those who were past their eighth birthday, were up before dawn and worked until dark, lighting fires, carrying water, feeding animals, milking cows, picking potatoes, stacking hay, and cleaning stables. This, both men knew, was the way to encourage strong character, this and regular attendance at church and Sunday school. A stranger, had he been seated near them and able to overhear their conversation that day, would have been struck by their confidence—a confidence that was part of the faith of all Canadians of their time—that for such children, most of them abandoned and many of them heartbroken, work and church were the most essential elements to their lives.

When they finally arrived in Peterborough early that night, with the scent of wood smoke softening the summer air, Barnardo and Owen were met by one of the workers from Hazelbrae and taken by carriage to the sprawling timber mansion on the edge of town, where Barnardo made his lodging for the next two weeks. They had dinner, and then, with the crackle of a distant bonfire the only sound in the descending darkness, the four of them—Barnardo, Owen, and Mr. and Mrs. Annersley, the superintendents—sat out on the veranda where Barnardo held forth once more, stressing his plans, explaining his policies, and, most of all, asking, with an urgency that gave his voice a peculiar tension, about the girls he sent to Hazelbrae—how they were placed, how they were visited, and especially how they were supervised. Some time shortly before midnight he suddenly got up, said he would have to rise early next morning to begin the most important part of his visit to Canada, and excused himself.

The next day, a Friday, he spent the morning studying maps and writing directions to Lindsay, to Bowmanville, to Orono, to Cobourg, and to a dozen places that were mere crossroads in the country but places where, in the preceding ten months, almost two hundred girls had been placed. He drew up a list with the names and addresses of those who had been in Canada the longest, and that afternoon he set out alone on the train, like an old-time peddler heading out to his territory, ready to go door to door in village after village to visit as many of the children as he could manage in a couple of weeks. Sometimes he would have trouble finding them, and once or twice farmers met him at the door and dismissed him as a bother and a meddler. But more often he could be seen standing in front yards and back gardens, smiling and nodding, as farmers and their wives came out to greet him as a man whose fame had gone before him. He would introduce himself, sit first of all with the husband, asking how the child, Jane or Emily or Ethel, was working out—was she a good girl, a good worker? And then, as he would insist of all his workers, he would meet privately with the child, at least for a few minutes, asking for her opinions of her situation in the family. His visits, because he tried to make so many, were brief and hurried, sometimes less than half an hour, so that an observer might have wondered—in view of that and in view of the awe in which the children and their employers almost always greeted him—how worthwhile they were as checks on the welfare of the girls. But this was a question no one asked, for it was enough to be told by the farmer that the girl was behaving and to be told by the girl that she was fed, clothed, and not physically abused.

Late one Saturday night he arrived in a small, obscure town a few hours by train from Peterborough, and after taking a room in the local hotel he got out his list and went down the names, making plans to visit the next day after church two girls whose names he noted only as Jane K. and Frances B. "I walked down a long and beautifully shaded street," he noted after his visit, "and knocked at a detached, old-fashioned house, standing apart from the others and back from the road. The door was opened by an elderly lady, one of those sweet, genial women of advanced years whom it is at all times a delight to meet. Such peaceful quietness seemed to dwell in her face and peeped out of every fold of the neat cap and apron!" He introduced himself, was profusely welcomed, and, seated in the quiet front room, began to ask her about the girls, their manners, their obedience, their willingness to work. There was, in all he asked her that day, no feeling that perhaps an elderly woman living alone, one who had never had a child, might find it hard to provide mothering care for two small girls, each one under twelve, each one in need of affection and security. "They are comforts to me," she told him that day. "I hope you have not come to remove them or unsettle them." As he knew before he went to see her that day, she had provided Alfred Owen with the usual letter of reference from her minister and had agreed, like all the others who took his children, to pay an amount of money each year to the Barnardo Home in trust, which would be given to the girls when they reached the age of eighteen years. He assured her he was not about to remove the girls, and then, sensing that time was slipping by, he asked her if she would mind calling the girls so that he might meet with each one alone.

It was, for the children, a touching and affecting moment. He knew, because he made it his business to know, more of their early lives than they would ever know, how Jane had been left on the street by her mother, a pathetic alcoholic, and how Frances, when he took her into his care, had been so sickly that he was certain she was about to die. He stood up, removed his glasses, and smiled as each girl, silent with the shyness of the meeting, was brought into the presence of the great man. He spoke gently, kindly, to each of them, asking if they were going to church and reading the Bible—the one he had given them, the one with his likeness and signature on the frontispiece—and finally, in a request that was sincere though brief, he asked them to do their best to live the Christian life. Then he shook hands all round, and with the girls standing silent and holding back tears he bowed, kissed the top of their heads, and left. "They were no longer little," he told someone later, "but they had grown so tall and well, and looked, oh, so nice!" He was sure, he said, that with the attitude of their mistress their futures were full of promise, so much so that "it seemed to me as if they could not be my little Jane and Frances of long ago."

One Thursday evening in Peterborough, near the middle of August, after he had visited scores of his children—and told people that in the main the farmers expressed "great pleasure, great satisfaction, and thankfulness in having a little maid from our home"—he spoke to a crowded and curious audience in the town's opera house. He was introduced and gave a brief sketch of his life and some of his more exciting exploits in London, but then, to everyone's surprise, he began talking of what he called "the great North West" and how, if the government gave him the land, he was going to open a farm there, one to which he would send boys suited to the life of the frontier. It was the first time he had spoken of it publicly and to the men and women who crowded the opera hall that night it added new colour to his reputation as a bold entrepreneur among evangelicals. He told them he had discussed the idea before he left England with Sir Charles Tupper, a former Cabinet minister and a close friend of Prime Minister John A. Macdonald, who assured him that he would do all he could to help in the necessary arrangements to acquire the land. Barnardo did not mention it that evening, of course, but his approach to Tupper—a Baptist, a minister's son, and, in his public persona at least, a proper evangelical—was not to the man's Christian generosities so much as to his interests in a good deal. Back at the hotel, among Barnardo's papers was a crinkled copy of the letter he had written to Tupper just a few weeks before he left for Canada, a shrewd appeal, ending with a tough alternative. First of all, the letter set forth the advantages to Canada in granting land for such a farm in an area of the West then in need of men to clear the territory and build its future. It then appealed for help, not just in the form of land, but in the form of assistance in transporting the boys from Quebec to Ontario and on to the West.

"I need hardly point out," his letter to Tupper had begun, "the great advantage of a society like ours undertaking such work. First, our lads would not be deserted and allowed to fight each one the battle for himself. In a new country like Manitoba, where the winter is so severe and where even a small amount of capital seems absolutely necessary in order to a colonist becoming independent, it must be of the greatest possible advantage to immigrants of the class I refer to, that they should have a powerful institution as their friend who would be disposed under certain conditions, afterwards to be developed, to advance them a small capital as a loan so as to enable those who are able, to avail themselves of any allotment of land that would come to them as emigrants, to attempt work in the future on their own behalf." He went on to assure Tupper that the boys—who would be in their mid-teens or older—would be of sound mind and character, thus providing Manitoba and the West with new citizens of high quality. But in return he made it clear he wanted a grant of land, and not just any land: it must be desirable, fertile, and sizable, so that in time it would be productive and profitable. "My committee," he had told Tupper bluntly, "some of whom have considerable Canadian experience, would not be prepared to accept any land which might be allotted to them by Government. They would ask, if their proposal was favourably entertained, that they might have the option of choice as it is notorious that much of the land would be unfit for the purpose, whereas other portions of it in special localities would be exceedingly admirable. As my committee is advised, we consider that from three thousand to five thousand acres would probably be needed for the purpose of an institution in which from forty to fifty lads or young men would be constantly kept while others were being passed through the home..." He ended by saying that if Canada did not come through with a satisfactory offer, "I am instructed to make my way to the United States...."

He left Peterborough in the latter part of August, took the train back to Toronto, and there met for an evening with Samuel Blake and a few others, giving final approval to the purchase of the house on Farley Avenue, the one that he had inspected and that would serve for more than thirty years as the headquarters of his work in Canada. Then, a day later, his pass on the Grand Trunk Railway in his coat pocket and his vision of the West strong in his imagination, he boarded a train in Toronto that would take him across the border at Sarnia, into the United States, and on to Chicago. There he would change trains for St. Paul, Minnesota, and then head north to his first destination, the city of Winnipeg. He was alone for the journey west, a dapper man in a frock coat, a bit aloof from the roughly dressed men and women crowding on the trains to Manitoba, then the promised land of Canadian immigration. Sometimes he would get up and stroll down the aisle of the ornate coach car, with its brass fittings and plush upholstery and on into the spare wooden cars that carried the colonists westward. His eyes, alive with curiosity, would move from family to family, and sometimes he would stop briefly at the seat of someone who recognized his familiar face. But mostly during the four days it took to get to Winnipeg, he sat alone staring out of the windows, a man whose eyes had known only cities and crowds, now intent on gathering in memory the magnificent distance and the great endless sky of the West. His journey to Winnipeg was a journey into new excitement as he sketched in his imagination the vastness and opportunity that awaited his work in the expanding country. His farm—which would be known all of its life as Dr. Barnardo's Industrial Farm—would, he was certain, absorb thousands of his boys and thus fulfil one of the basic tenets of his philosophy of child immigration: "An ever open entrance to the Homes demands an ever open exit." The trip west, however, was also a time for sober and serious examination of where he stood. In the nights, as the train lurched through the never-ending darkness of America's small towns, he sat up late beneath the glow of the oil lamp by his chair, his seat strewn with papers, letters, and financial statements, some of them the cause of worry that he tried to set aside so that he might savour the optimism of his westward trek. But his worries would not leave him; he knew that back home in London contributions to his work had fallen drastically, so severely that the accountants were puzzled as to where the next month's funding would come from. Yet everywhere he turned, the pressure was on him to expand, to enlarge, and to increase. It came from the children in London whose numbers and desperations were growing daily around him; but it also came from the Canadian farmers who were writing in such volume, asking for a boy or a girl, that he could not come close to meeting the demand. (Before the decade was over, his Toronto records would show that in a single year, 1889, he had almost a thousand applications and could supply only two hundred and fifty-eight children.) He reached toward the seat facing him, rummaging among the mass of papers spilled over the rich velvet, searching for a document Owen had given him, a note he knew to contain good news, a message that, even on a second reading, would distract him from the pain of his obsessive fretting over money. He found it. It was a brief notation, made by Owen, on the corner of a sheet of correspondence dealing with the policy governing the placing of every child brought to Canada under Dr. Barnardo's Homes. The notation read simply: "more and more people in government believe this policy should govern all child emigration to Canada." Barnardo, his small hands holding the paper in the glow of the oil lamp, read again the policy he had drafted in London several months before. "The form of agreement in use," it said, "is drawn in simple language.... The employer undertakes to receive the child for a period beginning and ending on specified dates: to provide it during that period with sufficient and proper board, lodging, clothing, and necessaries, and to pay a stated sum of money at the expiration of the period to the representative of the homes, to be held in trust for the child and for its sole use and benefit." It went on to say that for younger children (by which it meant, those between seven and thirteen) the payment would be an annual one; in the case of those over thirteen, some of the salary would be dispensed on a monthly basis, providing enough for the child to buy clothes, the remainder coming at the end of the year. The agreement made no mention of the amount of money to be paid, saying only that "the arranging of the terms gives rise to a good deal of bargaining and correspondence," since Canadian farmers were notorious as hard bargainers, out to serve their own interests. The spirit of the agreement—which was in reality a letter of indenture binding the child for a period chosen by the farmer—was summed up best by one sentence that spoke not of the needs of the child, but of the necessities of life: "The general effect aimed at is to ensure by a written covenant that the child is supplied with the necessaries of life; that the authority and responsibility of the homes as its guardian is duly recognized, and that the child shall be fairly and justly paid for such services as it is able and expected to render."

Barnardo folded the memorandum and slipped it into the inside pocket of his frock-coat, keeping it handy for the meeting he was to have within a few days with some of the Winnipeg officials, who would, he was certain, help him acquire the land he needed for his farm. He could show them a letter from Tupper, one of the most influential Canadians of the day, who had put in writing his faith in Barnardo, his belief in his work, and an introduction to the Minister of Agriculture in Ottawa, a shrewd, tough politician named John Henry Pope. (Pope was soon to become even more of a mover in the corridors of John A. Macdonald's government as minister of railways.) He felt, as he reviewed such facts, that the old worries were only nuisances at the edge of his life, and that, at its heart, his principles were sure and his future was clear. He was certain—now that he had his home in Peterborough and one about to be purchased in Toronto—that he would soon be sending several hundred children a year across the so-called "Golden Bridge, that marvellous structure which spans the ocean with its Highway of Hope, one pier of which rests amid the gloom of Darkest England and the other set among the glorious plains and limitless possibilities of our great Colonial Empire." In time, Owen told him, he should be sending out a thousand a year; the demand for them was, to use Owen's own word, insatiable. Thus, he reasoned to himself, with almost a dozen applications for every available child, the opposition to his children from labour and parts of the press could be seen for what it was, the hostility of a clamorous minority. Above all, he insisted, virtually all the children did well, Before they left the homes in England to board the ships, he would always remind them in his farewell talk that once in Canada, in return for what he called "the necessaries of life", they must render good service to their farm employers. He took out a piece of paper and there, in the quiet of his coach hurtling on through the night, he made a brief note, one he would later put in his magazine *Night and Day:* "As may be imagined, all employers are not equally pleased with the children, nor are all our children equally satisfactory in their demeanor and conduct. Sometimes, a change of situation is absolutely necessary; but not infrequently, a girl, placed out at first in a situation where nothing has seemed to go well for her, has given the greatest satisfaction when removed and sent elsewhere."

There was, of course, no way in which Thomas Barnardo could have known Margaret Crooks, the child who came into the care of Dr. Barnardo's Homes when she was a mere infant in England, and then, when she was twelve years old, and a girl full of life and promise, was sent on her way across the Golden Bridge to Canada, arriving one autumn evening along with thirty other girls at the lovely house in Peterborough known as Hazelbrae. She had never been anxious to come to Canada, for, after entering Dr. Barnardo's Homes as a very small child, she had been placed by the staff in a foster home, with a man and woman who owned a small fruit farm in the countryside of Britain. They loved her and regarded her as their own. She did remain with them from the time she was five until she reached the age of twelve, coming to love them and to call them, as she would all of her life, "dear Ma and Dad". She was never sure why, when she reached twelve, she was taken back Dr. Barnardo's Homes and sent to Canada, but she was told it was because, as Dr. Barnardo himself always said, an open door at the front of the home demanded an open door at the back. Margaret's place in the foster family could be taken by some other child, just as soon as she was on her way to Canada.

In Peterborough she stayed at Hazelbrae only a few days. Then she was put on the train with her small trunk and told that the conductor would put her off at her destination, a place called Tillsonburg. There she was to be met by a farmer with whose family she would stay a few years, doing light housework, and receiving, in return, her food and shelter, her schooling, and a salary of twelve dollars a month. But she did not do housework, and she did not go to school. She was needed on the farm, since the farmer was not well, his boy was not strong, and there wasn't a hired man to be had in the whole district. So, in her first winter in Canada, Margaret tended the barns, drove the cattle, milked the cows, and, in the depth of the January cold, spent much of her day pumping water in the barnyard and carrying it to the animals. One afternoon in March, when the yard was a sea of mud and the wind was cold, the lady visitor from Dr. Barnardo's Home arrived and found her there—her hands so numb they were stiffened in the shape of the pump handle—and said that pumping water in the winter was no fit work for a little girl. Margaret, she told the family, must be returned to the home. A week later, buying her own ticket from the pittance of allowance she was given, Margaret Crooks, still only twelve and not yet a year it Canada, began a long and burdened journey from farm to farm in Ontario. She went from Tillsonburg to Long Branch and then to Pickering and then to Beeton and then to South Monaghan (she was still only thirteen) and then to Mohawk and Brampton and Perth. In most places she did not stay very long; sometimes it was less than three months when the visitor from the home would come and decide that in her own interests she must be moved on.

In some places conditions had been so bad that she would go to her room in tears and write a note to the Barnardo Home—she had learned to write in England before she came to Canada—telling them that she could stand it no longer. Once or twice a neighbour—often the station-master, who seemed to take an interest in children such as Margaret—could see that she was being worked too hard or abused too often, and would tell her that it was time to go back to the home. Once, in a place that is almost driven from her memory, she was doing housework for a man and woman who were often away, so that, at fourteen, she was left alone with an elderly man who lived with them. His intentions toward Margaret were not good. One day, his eyes flaming with anger at her resistance to his advances, he pursued her through the house, until she raced up the stairs, ran into her room, and locked the door. Quickly she packed her trunk and lowered it out the window with a rope she had hidden under the bed. Then she tied the rope near the windowsill and lowered herself, first to the roof below, and finally to the ground. Then, driven by her fear, she ran wildly across the snow-dusted fields to the station. The station-master, a gentle, protective man, took her in, calmed her trembling, and sent someone for her trunk. That night he put Margaret on the train and sent her back to the home.

A few days later she was sent to another farm, and not long afterward to still another. Eventually she was sent to one in Perth, near Smiths Falls, Ontario, and there at last she found a family who treated her fairly and almost as one of their own. But for the rest of her life she would look back, not on one childhood but on two, one with her foster parents in Britain, the other a bewildering, lonely adolescence in which she was passed from farm to farm, twenty-one times, all over southern Ontario.

In those same years, Katherine Major, barely a teenager, was also being shunted from one farm to another in Ontario as a child of Dr. Barnardo's Homes. She found, in places such as Uxbridge, Bradford, and Port Hope, that she was treated not as a child but as a servant—kept for a few months, sometimes a year, and then, when no longer wanted, sent back to the home in Peterborough until someone else wrote in for a girl. Thus it happened that one year, early in the winter, Katherine, who was then fifteen, was sent to a farm near Brampton, to a life that would be so revolting she would never find words to describe it.

Often, when she did not do the chores well, because she was too small or because she was unwell, she was not scolded but beaten. Once, in the middle of that first winter, when the farmer could not get the outdoor pump to work, he called to her to come from the kitchen to hold the handle while he primed the pump. She began to look for her gloves, but he yelled at her to forget the gloves, to come right away. When she did, and placed her bare hands on the frozen pump, they froze fast to it. Whereupon the farmer doused them with hot water. Katherine, the flesh now peeling from her hands, ran screaming to the kitchen and fainted.

One day, during a difficult period in her puberty, she was told to go to the far pasture for the cows. She said she was not feeling well, where-upon she was punched, pushed to the ground, and kicked. She ran away, was found by the police, was sent back, and was beaten again. When the inspector from Dr. Barnardo's Home made her twice-yearly visit, Katherine told her what was happening but nothing was done. The farmer declared that Katherine was lying.

In the end it was not the beatings that made her childhood so ter-rifying. Instead, it was what happened to her on those days, usually Saturdays, when the farmer and his wife went to town and left her alone in the house with the drifting hired men who would come to work on the farm. Many times she was forced to fend them off. Once, on a Saturday evening when she was in the front parlour, one of them began to molest her and a second man—a quiet, passive person she would always remember—grabbed him and they began a fight that left the room almost in shambles. Late that night, when the farmer and his wife returned, Katherine met them with the only request she ever made: a hook to put on her bedroom door.

Like Margaret Crooks and Katherine Major, Winnifred Morrison also spent the best years of her childhood in the pleasant cottages of Dr. Barnardo's Girls' Village Home in Barkingside, near London, where she was taken at the age of five by her mother for reasons she was never told. She would always remember the cottages fondly, as she would the women who were the cottage mothers, but she would try to forget the later years after she came to Canada and began, when she was only ten, life on a long series of farms, where she rose before everyone else and worked in the house, the barn, and the fields.

She was just twelve years old and on her second farm—a very lonely girl who kept to herself and wept a lot in her room—when she faced the ordeal that was to mark her personality forever. Several times, despite her youth, the farmer had made advances toward her which, because of her bewilderment and her small stature, she had great difficulty handling. Then, one day when she was doing the dishes at the sink, she looked up to find him staring down at her, demanding that she accompany him to the barn. She refused. From behind his back he brought out a whip and raised it. Winnifred flung the scalding water at him and ran. That afternoon in her room, overwhelmed by all that was happening to her, Winnifred swallowed a dose of strychnine. She threw up before it killed her and in a week she was removed from her wretched situation, but she took with her a memory that would haunt her always.

It was not yet dawn when the train carrying Thomas Barnardo westward made its way north from the Minnesota border into the town of Emerson and the grey Manitoba morning. From his window he watched the sky, flecked with rain, begin to clear, so that the slow currents of the Red River seemed to shine in the prairie sun. Soon, some time before the middle of the morning, he caught sight of the outer buildings of the sprawling, bursting centre of Winnipeg. It was by then a city of ten thousand people, the ambition of merchants and the dream of immigrants, the great gateway to the west and the north, with its granary, its railway, and on its edge a clamorous shantytown into which flowed a river of newcomers from Hungary, Germany, and the Ukraine.

Barnardo stayed in Winnipeg only a few days, putting up in one of the several new hotels. In the company of some of the aggressive and confident men from the Manitoba Club, he saw all of the city, from its wide, raw Main Street, where the carts stuck in the mud, to the warehouses spilling over with grain. He sensed in the city an attitude that left him ambivalent, appreciating its energy, but doubting its moral stability because of its newness, boldness, and transient peoples. It was not, he reasoned, the place for his children, at least not then. The more distant, the better. During dinner in the quiet and comfortable rooms of the Manitoba Club, he received the advice of men who knew where he should look for the land he might acquire, one way or the other, to build the farm for his boys. They suggested he follow the flow of settlers toward the West, along the old North Trail, until he reached the lush and open land of the Assesippi country, where, beside the banks of the Shell River, a new town called Russell had been established the previous year. A couple of days later he climbed aboard the CPU coach and left for Portage la Prairie. There he caught a train that took him through the rolling flatlands to Minnedosa. It was late when he arrived in Minnedosa and, on his own, he found a place for the night. It had been less than a day's journey to this serene and peaceful village, a world away from the clamour of Winnipeg; still, the hardest leg of his journey lay before him, the eighty-five miles to the new town of Russell. There was no train, nothing but a road that was a river of mud, and no conveyance but a cart and a team of horses. Next morning at first light he was up and about and within an hour had hired a driver and a team. They made a strange and memorable spectacle when they left town, the small, dignified man in his starched collar perched beside the driver as the horses heaved through the thick gumbo. It took them three days to reach Russell.

He found his land a few miles from the raw town, mile after mile of fresh prairie, green and rich and rolling even farther than his eyes could see, much of it along the Assiniboine River. It was dappled with the autumn foliage of larch, birch, and, here and there, young oak. The greater portion of it was owned by the railway (the Manitoba and Northwest) and the government of the province, both of which would grant it to him in return for some public work by the boys he planned to send. He spent several days in Russell, staying at the small, plain hotel, but he was rarely seen there, for usually he was out on the prairie, sometimes slogging across fields in the cart, but often standing alone and silent on the banks of the river, sketching in his mind the huge home, the barns, the fields, the pastures on which his boys would raise tons of grain and graze huge herds of cattle. He knew there were adjoining lands he could acquire by purchase from the railway, the government, the school, and a few squatters. He would do so. And when he did, Dr. Barnardo's Industrial Farm would cover fourteen square miles.

He would send to the farm, not his younger children, but older boys, those who had passed their seventeenth birthdays and had come to live in what he called his "labour house", a residence for youths who were growing up on their own on the streets and were apt to be, as he himself put it, rougher than the others. He thought it best to place them outside of Ontario lest they drift back to Toronto and the tempting and destructive influence of the city. The farm near Russell was ideal for them, rigorous enough to stimulate their physical growth and isolated enough to protect their characters. Once they had been trained in farming, he reasoned, they would be hired throughout the West or, even better, they would be given land by the government and become prosperous farmers on their own. But beyond all of this, he and his trustees had agreed, the farm would not just pay for itself, but with its sales of grain and livestock would turn a profit that could help the work back home. The number of children in care and the slender support from government and the public meant that the London office was fighting a constant battle to survive.

It would take him a couple of years to acquire the land, build a dormitory, and place a man in charge who would be there to oversee the first shipment of youths and direct them in the initial work of clearing and cultivation, as well as the erection of barns and fences. Nevertheless, the feat was accomplished. In the summer of 1887, about forty boys with husky frames, some with furtive and uncertain faces, were met at the train, which then reached into Russell, by Edmund A. Struthers, a CPR land inspector whom Barnardo appointed manager of his work in Manitoba. They were taken in large wagons the three miles to the farm gate, where just inside stood an immense wood building two storeys high, with a large attic and many narrow windows. When they filed silently through the large door at the front, they found themselves in a wide hallway, off which ran several rooms, the largest of them a mess-hall—a plain room with a high ceiling, white walls, and a raised platform at one end—that would also serve as a place for meetings and a church for worship. It could accommodate two hundred boys. On the same floor was an office for Struthers, a staff dining room, a spacious kitchen, a bakery, and at the very back a space for storing the wood. From the hallway an ornate stairway made of oak led to the second floor, where, to the right, there was a huge dormitory with double bunks from one end to the other and rows of lockers along the sides. On the opposite side of the hall were several small rooms, including, every boy noticed, one with bars that would be used, fairly often it turned out, as a jail. Finally, a tiny, cramped stairway led to the attic, an open space for storage from which two gabled windows looked down on the front lawn and the laneway. It was by any standard a plain building, serviceable but rather severe. A reporter who would one day visit it and be given a tour of all its rooms would make a reference that was telling, both of the home's régime and of the attitude of his generation: "Then, as the pièce de résistance, the *Colonist's* representative was led to the dungeons. Into one of these the *Colonist* man allowed himself to be closed for the space of just about a minute, and the narrowness of the confinement and the darkness made that minute quite enough for him. And yet the house master informed him that he had known boys to endure that dark, narrow confinement for two and three days at a stretch before they would yield to some trifling point of discipline. Such dogged obstinacy, where applied against legitimate authority, of course, has a very bad look, but it must not be forgotten that strength of will of that kind may turn out to be an invaluable characteristic in the man who had his own way to make in the world."

The boys who came that first autumn were put to work after only one day in the residence, building the first fences and clearing the land close to the property for a vegetable garden that would in time cover more than twenty acres. They also began to put up one of the first buildings, a creamery in which they would turn out butter that would quickly achieve a reputation all across the West and then, shortly before the turn of the century, win a gold medal at a world's fair of the time. For every boy there it was a hard and punishing winter, with snow that came early, settling on the land and becoming so hard that it seemed no longer snow but ice. From the north the wind swept the fields, shivering windows and frosting timbers so that even the fire seemed to have no warmth. The boys, who did not know the world could be so cold, were numb and some wept with pain when, in the darkness before dawn, they took an axe to smash the ice around the pump to get water for the animals. The months passed slowly, their days spent only in hard and monotonous work, relieved sometimes in the evenings when they would rearrange the dining room benches and sit, silent and stoic, while a minister from Russell gave a sermon or a travelling official gave a talk on the great future of the Canadian northwest.

Then, after a hymn and a prayer, they would file out quietly and go upstairs, leaving it all behind in the blessed oblivion of sleep. In time, when the weather broke and spring came, Struthers would say simply that they had survived, that all of them had "proved their pluck and suitability in a most encouraging degree." Almost regularly, every summer and fall, the new boys came and the old boys left, hired by farmers in the West and becoming, most of them, nameless and forgotten men who helped to clear the land that other men might prosper. The farm grew, two hundred and fifty acres opened each year, so that in time boys would rise before dawn and spend the entire day miles from the home, yet still on the farm. In the nearby town, men and women grew accustomed to seeing them, boys with something curious and awkward about them, riding homeward in the wagons at twilight, their smiles hesitant, their voices muted to the level of whispers. Over the years, on the property surrounding the home itself they would build two huge barns, one for hay and one for animals; the creamery; a home for Edmund Struthers; and several other buildings, some to store vegetables and others to house tools and equipment. Often, on fine summer evenings, men and women from Russell would ride out to the farm simply to stroll through its grounds, as green and sparkling as any in the north-west, and to visit the great cattle barn, its ceiling as high as a cathedral, where boys, so quiet, so shy, would be combing the horses in their stalls. Some of them would notice that between the boys and the animals there was a bond that seemed at first surprising, but then quite natural. Barnardo himself noticed it one day when he visited the farm, and later he told his trustees that nothing he saw on his visit to Canada was as memorable as the kindness of his boys to the livestock at Russell. "Many of these lads," he wrote, "have, in their early lives, lacked love and kindly care; but now, with human hearts that yearn for something to love, they have lavished their sympathy upon the first loving crea-ture that was able to appreciate and return kindly care." Yet they were, like his children in Ontario and other such children elsewhere in Canada, surrounded by vague controversies and sullen persecutions, so that no matter how honest their character or exemplary their work once they were hired, they were rumoured all over the West to be vil-lainous and criminal.

Once, a youth in Brandon, not a great distance from Russell, was arrested and charged with the murder of his employer, a district farmer. He was a local boy, born and raised in Manitoba, but immediately upon his arrest the claim was made in the newspapers and by certain politi-cians that he was from Dr. Barnardo's Farm. All through the trial, and indeed after the conviction, the opinion persisted that the murderer was one of the orphan boys from England. The belief became a nation-al conviction as newspapers in Ontario, reflecting the opinion in the West, reported the story and ran editorials denouncing all child immi-gration. Finally, the *Manitoba Free Press*, responding to the hysteria, spoke up shortly before Christmas in 1893: "It was not just to say that the lad now under sentence of death at Brandon for the murder of his employer and benefactor is a Barnardo boy as was said at the time of his arrest and has ever since been widely believed. He is not a Barnardo boy, but a Canadian boy, born and bred; a product of our own soil. Similarly, many other youthful criminals who have figured in our courts have been no more Barnardo boys than this one, although in the great majority of cases they have been so adjudged in the public mind." But it was a sentence earlier in the editorial that caught clearly and concisely the prejudice that had settled and hardened in the minds of Canadians everywhere, and that confronted Barnardo with a problem that vexed him all his life: "A good many of our people have the impression that every Barnardo boy is a bad boy and even worse than this, that every bad boy is necessarily a Barnardo boy."

The opinion of the *Free Press*, as lonely as it was courageous, was correct. Its truth was borne out, not in debates or testimonials, but in the less dramatic and therefore dry evidence that comes from statistics. In the spring of 1896, after years of attack on his children and their characters, Thomas Barnardo wrote a long and candid letter to officials in Ottawa, in which he included a set of statistics that proved that the children from his home were less likely to be law breakers than citizens born and raised in Canada. First, he reported the number of children he had sent to Canada during the previous ten years, 6,128. Then he reported the number who had been convicted of an offence, 52 or 0.136 convictions per thousand. Then he compared this rate with the rate of convictions provided by the Canadian government. It was 0.775 per thousand. He used Canada's own statistics to demonstrate once and for all that the children he sent to this country, though perhaps broken in spirit, were not broken in character. As the *Colonist* wrote shortly after his letter came out: "A striking piece of statistical evidence has been advanced in favour of the boys, showing that, in an equal time, a larger number of past and present members of the Dominion House of Commons had been convicted in a court of law than boys who had been through Doctor Barnardo's Home."

But the prejudice was hard and set forever. For years afterward the papers would carry articles and letters that portrayed immigrant children in dark, villainous ways. Occasionally one of the boys, grown to young manhood, would have the courage to write a letter, as Henry Gammon of the town of Binscarth did to the *Free Press*, saying that the boys were not tainted but were more often than not abused and even cheated out of their pittance of a wage. "It seems, to me," Gammon wrote on the day after Christmas in 1894, "that there is a set of people in Manitoba given to everlasting grumbling. Not only have they the Barnardo boy as advantage to themselves as regards to cheapness, but oftentimes treat him with as little indifference as their canine friends....If the lads were treated with due consideration, such as human beings ought to receive, rest assured, the lads would turn out a credit to themselves, to God, and to man."

Barnardo left Canada after that first visit—it was by then the late fall of 1884—his worries over money having receded to some corner of his mind, pushed there by his growing enthusiasm for the state of his work in Ontario and the promise he sensed in Manitoba. He went home through the United States (after a side-trip by steamer from Tacoma in Washington to the new town of Port Moody in British Columbia), where his energy and his boundless curiosity took him to Chicago, New York, and Boston; in these cities, usually in the company of a detective, he would visit the seamy and sordid neighbourhoods, comparing what he saw there with what he faced in London and concluding that, at least in Chicago and New York, things were worse than at home.

Just past the middle of November he arrived in Liverpool, met at the ship by a few friends, who the next day escorted him to his great hall in London, Edinburgh Castle. There, before an audience of four thousand who turned out to welcome him home, Thomas Barnardo preached for two full hours and told them all of the weary prospects that awaited his children in Canada.

He would visit Canada again in 1887, in 1890, and in 1900. Often, when he came to this country, to Toronto, to Peterborough, and then across the great distance of the West, he was met by men and women in their twenties who were once the children he sent across the Golden Bridge. Sometimes he was moved when they would come up to him in the halls where he was speaking, bringing wives or husbands, showing him children, and asking if he remembered them, which of course he always did. Once, in Peterborough, while he was staying a few days at Hazelbrae and visiting in the towns nearby, the superintendent sent out word that Dr. Barnardo was there and, on a forthcoming Sunday afternoon, would be pleased to meet all who could come to a tea. A great many did come, and the lawns around Hazelbrae were filled with buggies and with shy men and women carrying children in their arms. The short, ebullient Barnardo moved among them, speaking to each of his old girls, as he called them, meeting their husbands, admiring their children, and most of all enjoying the goodwill that flowed around him as the women recalled, not so much the farms of Canada, as the kind, warm days in London, at the Girls' Village Home.

In the winter of 1896 he enlarged his work, opening a home much like the one in Toronto on Pacific Avenue in Winnipeg, a large square building with long, narrow windows. To this home he and his staff would send hundreds of boys ten to thirteen years of age, younger than those sent to the farm near Russell. His superintendent in Manitoba, Edmund Struthers, explained candidly in a letter to one of Barnardo's benefactors, W. Sifton (father of A. L. Sifton, who became the premier of Alberta in 1910), the reason for the new home: "Doctor Barnardo has recognized for some time past, that a great demand exists among the farmers of the North West for boys of this age...."

Barnardo was not well when, in the summer of 1900, he came to see his Canadian work for the last time. He arrived in Toronto during Exhibition week, and Owen, who met him as usual, could see that, as Barnardo himself would admit, he was not the same man he had been when he came to the country sixteen years earlier. He was a bit over-weight, his immaculate clothes were a bit tight, and though still a rel-atively young man—he passed his fifty-first birthday while in Canada—he was by then having trouble hearing. He carried an ear trumpet, and often, in the middle of meetings, he appeared slightly eccentric, his head turned to the side, his trumpet cocked in one ear.

Owen took him on that last visit to see J. J. Kelso, then well estab-lished as Ontario's superintendent of neglected children, in which role he inspected agencies such as Barnardo's. The three men sat in Kelso's cluttered office, the sun streaming through its bare windows, and for the most part they were of one mind on the benefit of Barnardo's work to children and to Canada, though Kelso had some minor doubts because the emigration scheme was becoming so large, so wholesale, having sent by then over ten thousand children to Ontario alone. It was not their first meeting. Barnardo, with his interest in publicity and his exceptional memory, easily remembered Kelso, who stood out in his mind as the young reporter from the *Globe* who had shown such inter-est in his work when he had come on earlier visits to Canada.

As they talked, Kelso said that simply from his own observation he felt more of Barnardo's children were failures than either Owen or Barnardo would admit. "Your figures, Dr. Barnardo," he said, his face smiling and sympathetic, "are after all just that, your figures. We have had so far no independent statistics, so there's no way of computing the degree of success. For example, girls who fail are lost sight of, they don't show up in your statistics, because they may not end up in court. But often, they are failures. The same with boys who run away. And some do. I recognize the value of the work, but there are, you'll have to admit, a few more bad cases than you and Alfred are ready to recognize because naturally, you don't want to harm your work." Yet, as he talked, it was also clear that Kelso, for all his progressive idealism and humane instincts, was accommodating toward the practice of placing children hither and yon, without the most careful scrutiny of those who accepted them. For example, he told the other two men of an acquaintance of his, the Reverend C. W. Watch of Brighton, a small Ontario village, who was a founder of a local Children's Aid Society. "He has had," Kelso told them, "considerable experience in child-saving work. And he's found that a number of persons anxious to adopt children are not willing to risk close supervision, so he decided to engage in home-finding on his own. He simply announced in the press that he'd receive applications for children, and in response he received over one hundred applications. And on the other side, he's received from parents and relatives the legal transfer of a number of children and has placed them and undertaken himself to maintain a record of their progress. He says that if he had the funds he could find Christian homes for homeless children under five at the rate of one a week." Barnardo and Owen listened with deep interest. But no one in the room, even Kelso, seemed to worry that perhaps the Reverend Mr. Watch was embarked on a scheme for which he was not qualified, one that might be delivering children into great harm.

Even before Barnardo reached Toronto in August of that year, hundreds of former Barnardo boys had read of his forthcoming visit in their copies of *Ups and Downs*, a quarterly put out for many years by his homes in Canada. As the day of his arrival drew near, they came to the city from all across southern Ontario and were crammed into every possible space at 214 Farley Avenue, the home into which each one had been received as children. They were registered and given their accommodation and an enamelled button bearing the likeness of the man they had come to see, Thomas Barnardo. Several asked anxiously if he had already arrived: a few could be heard wondering—like young men who longed for a father who was vivid only in memory—if he would still recognize them after the years of separation. For an entire day, almost five hundred young men sat around on the lawns at Farley Avenue, a remarkably quiet, almost subdued group, whose only pranks were pillow fights and whose only departure from the grounds was a walk to a nearby candy store where they counted out pennies for bottles of pop. That evening, a stuffy and humid July twilight, they sat, row upon row, in the home, each one wearing his Barnardo button, each one among the only brothers he had, each one waiting for the only father he would ever know.

Many years later, when some journalists would begin to review the phenomenon of child immigration and the life of Barnardo, they would condemn the work and dismiss the man as a naive do-gooder. Such critics would never understand the feelings of the men in the dining room of 214 Farley Avenue in Toronto on that evening in 1900. Whatever the flaws that were inherent in the very principal of child immigration, Barnardo's commitment to children was genuine and their affections for him were deep and permanent. That evening, halfway through the meal, Barnardo suddenly appeared, standing all alone in the doorway. Among those in the dining room was one of Barnardo's most devoted Canadian supporters, a Methodist minister and journalist named Frank Vipond, who later described the moment of his arrival: "There was a second of absolute quiet and strange stillness, as if a rush of memories had paralyzed every tongue and every muscle. In the strained look on every face one could read the inward working of grateful hearts and could understand the emotions which the sight of the figure in the doorway had evoked. The spell lasted but a moment and then, as one man, all sprang to their feet and in the thundering cheers which rang out again and again, Doctor Barnardo learned, if he did not already know, that his hold on the hearts of his old boys was as firm as in the days of long ago and will continue to the end."

Next morning Alfred Owen told them at breakfast that on Wednesday and Thursday evenings, for those who could stay—some had to return to the farms that day—there would be an excursion on Toronto Harbour, with Dr. Barnardo aboard, on the steamer *Lincoln*. That evening, after an early dinner, Torontonians who were on the streets near the corner of Farley Avenue and Yonge Street could have seen a long line of two hundred young men walking two by two in military style to the harbourfront. They boarded the boat and spent the evening on the water, mostly listening as Barnardo told then how it was back home and moved among them speaking to each one, and with his incredible memory for facts and details recalling something from the life of every man on board. The next evening it was the same, with a different group on board, and this time it was a farewell voyage. Though he did not know it then, Barnardo made his last speech to old boys in Ontario. They spent two hours out beyond Toronto Harbour, sailing through mist and light, the sounds of their singing—"The Maple Leaf Forever", "The Boys of the Old Brigade", and "Way Down Upon the Swanee River" —drifting upon the gathering dusk. Then, as the boat began its return, the engines were silenced and all gathered on the forward deck to hear Barnardo say good-bye. He spoke very briefly. He told them that the ideal life was a life lived for others, that they should always look out for the welfare of the youngest children, those who lived near them. There was a prayer, his final good-bye, and, as the engines started up three cheers from the boys, "The influence upon others of a great man," said Frank Vipond, recalling the evening, "often survives the strain of separation, sometimes outliving the man; the influence of a great and good man always does."

He went, of course, to Peterborough, and just as he had in Toronto, he inspected the building, going through Hazelbrae from the basement floor to the attic timbers, and then examining its business records. Often he was in the office until midnight, his eyes straining over accounts, letters, and inspectors' reports, all compiled by his staff, which by then numbered fourteen.

But it was when he reached the West, and went from Winnipeg to the farm at Russell, that he appeared like a man who knew he was looking upon his obsessions for the last time. He seemed finally to have abandoned his endless fretting over detail. For days on end he was with his boys in the warm fields or else simply strolling alone, sometimes for miles, on the farm. He wrote to his wife back home in London saying that he was feeling a bit better now, and that the farm was a lift to him. "You would be charmed with the prospect here," he told her. "It is simply lovely from every point of view."

He could not have known it then, or even dreamed that of all his work in Canada the farm would be the first to die, its land sold in parcels by his trustees in 1908, just three years after his death, during a period when they were facing great financial stress. Much of it was sold to men who had first come to the West as Barnardo boys. But for more than a decade, well into the 1920s, the Home itself stood empty, its windows like sad eyes that had been witness to the passing of a great hope.

Seven
The Children

One morning in early December near the turn of the century, J.J. Kelso cleared his desk of its mountain of paper and for almost two weeks spent all of his days and many of his evenings alone in his office, putting on paper his view of the immigration of children from Britain. He was then thirty-three years old, still a young man, but with his record of achievement in humanitarian work—he had served for five years as Ontario's superintendent of neglected children and had organized the first Children's Aid Societies throughout the province—he was a figure of no small stature. As he sat at his desk in his shirtsleeves, his pen moving quickly across the broad foolscap, he knew that elsewhere in Toronto, in the rooms of politicians and the offices of newspaper publishers, everything he was writing would be taken seriously, not just as the vision of an idealist, but as the opinion of the most credible authority in Canada in the field of child welfare. He did not think of it then, of course, but the monograph that he was preparing would have a relevance beyond his own time, providing historians with a revelation of how child immigration was viewed in his day, not just by Thomas Barnardo or Annie Macpherson or Maria Rye, each of whom had a special reason for promoting it, or by the farmers of the country, who saw it as a source of cheap labour, but by a man who was an informed and independent witness to the work.

He began his lengthy statement by stating that during recent months he had personally inspected every organization bringing children to Canada. He then listed most of them, putting beside each one the number of children it had thus far brought out. He named nine organizations, plus a category called "other small agencies". Then he totalled the number of children who, under the auspices of such groups, had come to Ontario between 1870 and 1897, the year then ending during which he had conducted his inspection. The number came to 28,945. In addition, he calculated that there were 10,000 other children who had been placed in other parts of Canada. Thus there was a need, he said, as the government of Ontario recognized by its act of the legislature that year, to regulate such work, inspecting the organizations themselves, and seeing that they in turn inspected the children on the farms at least once a year. The need for such supervision was made all the more clear, he felt, by the fact that Ottawa's supervision, supposedly in place from the beginning, was only nominal, consisting merely of a superficial check of the children at their port of embarkation in Britain and their port of entry in Canada, and a suggestion that when federal immigration agents were not busy they drop in on the children, a practice that, even when followed, was invariably inadequate.

Kelso knew, of course, that it was not his outline and advocacy of the new Ontario act that was keenly awaited by the press and the public. It was his opinion of child immigration that they wanted. Were many of the children morally tainted and from the criminal class? Were they, even the decent ones, scandalously overworked and horribly abused? Were the homes that brought them to the country—Barnardo's, Macpherson's, Rye's, Fegan's, Quarrier's, Middlemore's, Stephenson's—not pocketing a tidy profit from their operations? Kelso, ever the journalist, with a journalist's impulses, knew that if his report was to be effective it must speak to such questions and do so in ways that were direct, clear, and candid.

He began by noting that the hostility to the children in Ontario was widespread, due largely to the extravagant treatment given in the papers to those children who got into trouble. Many of these stories, he insisted, were inaccurate. "Last year," he wrote, his eyes now and then lifting from the page to stare through his shadowy window, "a sensational article was printed in a country paper to the effect that a girl—an English waif—had tried to poison a whole family and had then disappeared, saying that she was going to drown herself This story was copied in a Toronto daily and was soon on its rounds through the province. Numerous editorials followed all denouncing child immigration on the strength of this article. On investigation I found that the girl was born in Toronto and lived for years in one of our charitable institutions and that there was no ground for referring to her as an English waif. About the same time another sensational article went the rounds of the papers to the effect that a farmer returning home found that an English youth in his employ had attempted to assault his wife and he unceremoniously kicked him off the premises. I immediately wrote the farmer for full particulars, and he replied that he did not know whether the lad was English or not, as he had been living in the neighbourhood for some years and had not been engaged from any of the homes. In other cases that I have investigated, the fault was with the employer, the children having been driven to desperation by constant ill treatment."

The publicity, Kelso argued, was doing great harm, not only to the homes engaged in the work, but to the children themselves trying to begin life in a new country. "In the case of young girls particularly, this constant reference to 'slum' and 'outcast' children has exposed them to the base designs of disreputable men, who readily believe the slanders that are so lightly scattered about. My observations lead me to believe that many of the old-country girls who go astray would have remained respectable if given half a chance to do so. Public opinion is so much against these children that all sorts of iniquities against them are prevalent..." They were not, he assured his readers, defective in character; they were not even "foreigners", being as Anglo Saxon as any native-born Canadian.

When he turned to the quality of the treatment given the children by their employers, the farmers of Ontario, Kelso was brief and to the point. His opinion—with its confidence in the efficacy of work and its trust that small children, some not even twelve years old, would fare well as farm workers so long as they were not abused—serves as a mirror of the attitude of even the most sympathetic Canadians toward the principle and practice of child immigration. "The charge is often made," he wrote, "that this species of immigration is child slavery pure and simple, but there is no legitimate reason why it should be so. Farm work should be healthful and enjoyable employment for young people, if the employers are reasonable and kindly disposed." He said the Ontario governments new act would ensure that representatives of the various homes visited the children in their new surroundings to detect any injustice. "Unfortunately," he concluded this short paragraph, "there have in the past been cases brought to light forcibly illustrating the need for vigilance in protecting children from cruel taskmasters, but there is hardly sufficient ground for the sweeping charge that this is the prevailing condition." Thus, the most respected philanthropist of the day in Canada gave his blessing, sincerely and with the best of motives, to the policy of providing the farmers of Ontario with children of tender age—most were between twelve and fourteen—who would be received not to be loved but to work.

"Notwithstanding all the complaints that have been made against child immigration, it is only reasonable to suppose that if the work were suddenly stopped many a farm home would be in a quandary to know how to get along." Nor did he accept for a moment the slander that the homes were profiteering on the children. He went beyond this to say that some of them, which in addition to supplying children for work were also now boarding a large number and paying the boarding costs, were thereby a financial boon to Ontario: "Few people in Canada realize how much Dr. Barnardo expends in this country on immigration work...The large amount of money paid out in the Muskoka District for the board of small boys is one of the principal sources of income in the district..."

Having expressed his belief in the work in general, Kelso became more specific, dealing with each of the organizations in turn, setting out its history and philosophy, and then explaining in a few paragraphs how it went about its work in Canada. He dealt at greater length with Dr. Barnardo's work, since it was so much larger than the others and therefore more of a target of controversy, but he went on to report briefly—except for one home—generously on all the institutions bringing children to Ontario: Dr. Stephenson's Home in Hamilton, Marchmont Home in Belleville, Annie Macpherson's Home in Stratford, William Quarrier's Home in Brockville; Southwark Catholic Emigration Society Home near Ottawa, Fegan Distributing Home in Toronto, and, of course, the questionable Maria Rye's Home in Niagara-on-the-Lake.

The work of Dr. Stephenson's Home (named after Bowman Stephenson, a Methodist minister who began his rescue work in London in 1870) had been conducted in Hamilton for twenty-five years, and the home had brought out almost fifteen hundred children, the majority being placed on farms in the Niagara area. "Children are frequently changed from one home to another," Kelso observed in a telling reference, "but this cannot be regarded as evidence of unfitness, as the arrangements are usually for one year, and the management believes in making changes if better terms or kinder treatment can be secured thereby." The Marchmont Home in Belleville (the institution opened by Annie Macpherson at the invitation of local citizens in 1870) had, he said, been run for many years now by Miss Macpherson's faithful worker Ellen Bilbrough, joined in the latter years by her husband, the Methodist minister Robert Wallace. "From 200 to 250 children have been received each year of both sexes," he said, "and from three years up to fifteen. Each party is disposed of almost immediately after arrival, and Mr. Wallace states that the demand for children is constantly in excess of supply."

Annie Macpherson's Home in Stratford (originally opened by her in Galt, Ontario, in 1871, then moved to Stratford in 1883) was a large, comfortable building, Kelso found, run for her by her nephew William Merry, a Baptist layman who had attended Kelso's famous child-saving conference a few years earlier. When he called in

Stratford, Kelso was told by Mr. Merry that it was Annie Macpherson's policy to come to Canada every summer and to visit each of her children personally, a task of enormous size, since each year more than two hundred children were brought over.

W. C. Fegan, the devout evangelical from London (who first came to Canada on the ship bearing Thomas Barnardo on his initial visit in 1884), had established his distributing home at 295 George Street in Toronto, a rambling dormitory given to him by William Gooderham, a Toronto churchman and philanthropist who dedicated his life to good works. Kelso noted that some of Fegan's children—he brought out only boys—were older, had been living on the streets of London for several years, and therefore seemed to have a hard time settling down to "the monotony of farm life". However, he expected this would improve as Fegan lengthened the period of time the boys were to spend in his home in London, learning better attitudes before leaving for Canada. "The outfit supplied to each child on leaving the old country." Kelso observed, "is a liberal one, as may be judged from the following list: two cloth suits, two suits of underclothing, three hats or taps, two pair of boots, three pair of socks or stockings, three handkerchiefs, one jersey, one overcoat, with a strong box to keep these articles in: the whole valued at a little over $25.00."

The Southwark Catholic Emigration Society (the single Roman Catholic agency sending children to Canada at the time) had begun its work the previous year, 1896, long after Rye, Macpherson, Barnardo, and the others, and sent only small groups of children to its distributing home in Ottawa on Richmond Road, with the intention of placing them on farms outside the city. One of the organization's founders, a man named the Reverend Edward St. John of Southwark, London, came to Canada, visited Kelso, explained the organization's program, and assured him it would comply with the new Ontario act to regulate child immigration. "Later," said Kelso, "I paid a visit to the receiving home. The home appears to be well adapted for a distributing centre, as nearly all the boys are located in the Ottawa district and it is the intention to concentrate the placing out in Eastern Canada."

William Quarrier's Home in Brockville (founded over twenty-five years earlier by Quarrier, a Scottish boot maker and friend of Annie Macpherson's who was moved to work with children after being appalled by the poverty of a boy selling matches on a Glasgow street) was known as Fairknowe, and, as Kelso would say through all of his career, was well run, with what he called a desirable class of boys and girls, all Scottish, all brought out from Quarrier's cottages in the countryside of Bridge of Weir, Scotland. But Quarrier was angry that year—with Kelso, with the government, and especially with Arthur Hardy, the Premier of Ontario—convinced that the new act, which the other organizations were accepting, albeit reluctantly, was an unjust intrusion upon the work that he had carried on so long and so well. He had even met with Kelso and Hardy, arguing with both of them that in view of his record he should not be burdened by the new legislation with all its closer scrutiny of his work and supervision of his children.

Hardy replied in writing to him and since his letter was an official statement of government policy—and was, of course, largely prepared by Kelso for the signature of the Premier—Kelso decided to include it in his lengthy report of that year. "In adopting the act regulating the immigration of children," Hardy wrote to Quarrier, "the Legislature of the Province had no desire or intention of unduly hampering a good work such as yours. The Scotch are well known as a most desirable class of settlers and from all we have heard of your good work, both in Scotland and in this country, we have confidence that you would only bring the best class of children into Ontario, even though no law existed on the subject. But with so many agencies engaged in the placing of British children in Ontario, it was felt to be imperative that some regulations be adopted whereby careless or mere money making work could be put a stop to. As you doubtless know, there is a strong public prejudice against the importation of children, owing partly to the work of placing and supervision not having been properly attended to by some of the agencies." But Quarrier—as stubborn as he was religious—replied that since the Premier admitted there was no fault in his work, he should not be penalized simply because of a few clamorous voices that didn't know the facts. He then ceased sending out his children, although, as Kelso observed correctly, he would probably resume his work once he understood "the spirit in which this supervision is entered upon".

It was, as always, Maria Rye, who ran Our Western Home for girls in Niagara-on-the-Lake, who gave J.J. Kelso his deepest doubts. She moved him to such indignation that he would almost lose his temper, not only because of her abrasive personality, but because of her careless policies, especially her refusal to have any supervision, by inspection or by visitation, of her children once she had gotten them off her hands in Canada. Despite slipshod methods, she had been permitted to bring more than four thousand girls to Ontario, most of them between twelve and sixteen years old, even after the report of Andrew Doyle condemned her. Now, twenty-five years later, Kelso made no effort to conceal his gratitude that upon her retirement her home was being transferred to the care of the Church of England Waifs and Strays Society of London: "As a result of my enquiries it appeared quite evident that the work had not been properly handled in the past and that some radical change would be necessary before it could be considered satisfactory from a Canadian standpoint. The arrangements—if there could be said to be any arrangements—for the supervision of the children after going to foster homes and situations were far from adequate. Miss Rye, during the long period in which she was engaged in this work, did not make any effort to have the children personally visited after leaving her care, and she is credited with the statement that the other homes were going to an unnecessary expense in maintaining a staff of visitors. No formal agreement has been entered into between the home and those receiving the children beyond signing the application form; no personal visitations were made after the child left the shelter, and the correspondence between the child and the home has always been of the most meagre character. The consequent danger is that the child soon realizes the lack of interest that is manifested in its welfare; and the foster parents see that they are not likely to be interfered with if they overwork and otherwise take advantage of their young charges."

Around the middle of December 1897, J.J. Kelso read over his long narrative to the Ontario government. He called it simply: "A Special Report on the Immigration of British Children". Then, the day before he submitted it he wrote a final paragraph, one in which he would reveal, as much as in his entire report, the spirit of his age. He said that he had hesitated to prepare the report, knowing as he did the strong feeling of hostility toward child immigration. Nevertheless, he went on, it was only right that after reviewing the work in all its aspects he should make public his conclusions. He said: "Those conclusions are, briefly, that child immigration, if carried on with care and discretion, need not be injurious to the best interests of this country." It was as if Kelso, Canada's most humane worker in child care, was in the end somehow defensive, somehow reduced to pleading that innocent children, so often frightened and heart-broken, would not get in the way of the powerful ambitions of the emerging Canada.

Elmvale, Ontario: a small village a bit north of the town of Barrie. It was a morning in April, silent and shining in the cool air of the early spring, one year past the turn of the century.

Shortly before noon, men glanced at clocks, and women removed aprons and there was, over the tranquil main street, a faint stirring of expectancy. It was train time. Men in shirtsleeves, the women beside them, gathered on the grey platform of Elmvale station. The train came in, doors opened, sacks were unloaded, and from the coach a man stepped down with a suitcase. Two ladies, baskets over their arms, were whisked away in a carriage of suitable comfort. Then there was a shout of "All clear", a slamming of doors, and the train was gone. No one noticed, among the passengers and baggage, a small boy who stood alone almost where the conductor left him, just outside the station door. Thirteen-year-old Fred Treacher, a slight, nervous boy with grey eyes, sat on the small metal trunk that contained all he owned. He was wearing a wool suit, dark and rough, and on his left lapel was pinned a tag bearing his name and his destination, "Frederick Treacher, Elmvale, Ontario".

He sat there in silence. Sometimes, when he lifted his eyes from the station platform, he gazed at a broad meadow beyond the station and thought of the fields around the home his mother had put him in a few months earlier. He recalled the small town of Stony Stratford, near London, and a beautiful stone building run by a very religious man, J. W. C. Fegan, who, just like Dr. Barnardo and Annie Macpherson, was taking children in and sending so many of them, like himself, to the farms of Ontario. Fred wished that it had never happened as it did, that his father had not died, that his mother had not placed him in Mr. Fegan's Home. But she had. There were, after all, many children in the family. Even when his father, a shoemaker, was alive they were all extremely poor. Once he remembered his father coming home from work with only a crown to show for a whole week's work. Then one day he took very sick, and in a few days he was gone. Fred's mother seemed very confused after that, and in a couple of weeks all of her children, the girls as well as the boys, were placed in orphanages. Fred and his younger brother Bert were delivered to Mr. Fegan's Home. He spent several months in the home, the massive stone residence that Mr. Fegan had bought just a few years earlier, in 1900, playing games on the green, unwashed lawns and learning to sing in the boys choir. Often, he would spend time talking to the lady who was Mr. Fegan's helper, a kind and understanding woman who would listen to his fears and teach him games and new songs, so that in time he came to feel that she was actually his mother. In fact, one day in the fields, a bright, warm day when he was happier than he had been for a long time, he told another boy that she was his mother. But then, one chilly afternoon in March, a day he would always remember, she took him aside and told him that he would be leaving her soon, along with the other boys, for a life in Canada, a country with so many more opportunities than he could ever have in England. Thus, on a wet, windy day in April, on board the *Empress of Britain* with forty other boys, he landed in Montreal, came by train to Mr. Fegan's Distributing Home in Toronto, and, within a week, in response to a letter to Fegan's asking for a boy to do farm chores, was bundled aboard a train in the care of the conductor. Now he sat on his trunk at the Elmvale station, waiting for the man who had sent for him.

An hour passed. He worried that the conductor had made a mistake, that he had been put off in the wrong place, that there was no one at all to meet him, that he had been left and forgotten. Then suddenly, like the crack of a rifle, he heard his name: "Fred!" He turned, and there, standing beside a buggy, its paint peeled and its seat in tatters, was the man who had come to take him home. For a moment Fred said nothing, as if he sensed that the man's voice, which was cold and sharp, was not speaking to him so much as silencing him. The man walked slowly toward him, a man with hair as black as boot polish, eyes the colour of sand, and a face that had once been strong and hopeful but now seemed only a mask behind which were hidden dreams that had long since died.

"Okay, Fred," he said, "bring that trunk here."

Without a word the boy hauled the big, oblong box thumping across the boards to the end of the platform. The man took one end and with the boy heaved the trunk into the back of the buggy, then climbed up onto the seat. He picked up the reins and, looking at the boy still standing on the platform—as if some new and ominous sense was stirring within him—he murmured, "You coming?" The boy quickly jumped up beside him. Thus began Fred Treacher's life as a home boy in Canada.

The farm was a long way from Elmvale, standing small and sad upon the cold fields of April, a place to which, years earlier, a man and a woman had come with high hopes that had been vanquished in a losing struggle against the land. They did not have many children, only two, but even these seemed to be burdens that overwhelmed their spirits, so that at times the woman—a weary wife who despite her failures ruled the life of her husband—was driven into dark and terrifying fits of temper. When Fred arrived on that first day, no one asked where he came from or who his parents were or what his hopes were for life in Canada. Instead, he was given a place at the table in the kitchen and there, in a silent loneliness that he would know all his childhood, he ate his potatoes and bread by himself. Sometimes, as he heard the clatter of plates and the passing of food in a room beyond the kitchen, he wondered why he was eating alone and worried that already he had done something wrong. But in time he would understand that in this house he would always eat alone. His room, to which the man took him when he finished his food, was small and square, and in the corner stood a rickety bed upon which was laid a straw tick. On the opposite side was a chest of drawers and a straight-back chair. Most of all he noticed that the room was cold, so cold that later, on winter mornings, he would find his moccasins frozen. On that first night in his new home he remained awake in the dark, and from his bed, through the narrow window, he watched for the first time the moon rising in Canada. It was, he thought to himself, the same moon that was in the sky over England, the same moon his brothers and sisters would see if they looked.

Fred found the work on the farm not only hard and long—beginning before dawn and ending after dark—but very strange, for he had never seen a cow until he arrived there. For several days the farmer tried to teach him to milk, but he could not do it, and, though the man said little, Fred knew that he was growing impatient. One night in May, while he was eating alone at the kitchen table, he heard the man telling his wife that the boy was not working out, that he was nothing but "a green Englishman", and he felt for the first time the sense of abandonment that would haunt him for years thereafter. Then, one evening, after he had failed again, he heard the man's wife— who rarely spoke to him and then only when she was putting his food before him—say that the best thing for the boy would be a good whipping. For many hours he stayed awake, his loneliness now turned to terror, hearing over and over again the woman's voice, high and strange, urging her husband to take him and thrash him.

In the morning, his throat raw from crying, he did not eat. He was led, silent and trembling, to the barn. The man kicked the stool toward him and, without a word, motioned to him to begin milking. He tried for almost a minute, but there was nothing. He stared at the floor and, suddenly, uncontrollably, began to weep. The man reached out and tapped him on the shoulder in a way that was almost kind. He beckoned the boy toward the yard. As the man followed the boy outside, he reached over the door and took down a glistening black snake whip.

At first the boy was not sure what was happening. He heard a shout from behind, but he did not understand. Then he heard it again and clearly: "You cockney bastard!" He turned and saw the whip raised above him like a blade cutting the sky. He ran, pleading, crying, screaming. Suddenly the door of the house opened and he saw the woman standing waiting. He ran toward her, but she quickly blocked the doorway. Fred Treacher fell sobbing upon the hard, brown grass, and over him stood the man, lashing him again and again and again.

For days the boy was like a frightened animal, coming out of hiding furtively, only to eat and to work, but then quickly retreating to the comforting loneliness of his room or, as the spring became warmer, to the quiet of the hayloft, where he found the pigeons to be his friends. He knew that, according to the agreement, he was to be sent to school, and he asked when he was to begin, but the man said there would be no school, not this term anyway, because he needed him for work. He knew that he was to receive an allowance for clothes and a wage, though only a pittance, but the man said that he did not have it, that he would pay it when he could, for money was very scarce. One Sunday morning, after milking, he walked the long distance to Elmvale, to the church, and there, surrounded by the singing of hymns and the certitudes of the sermon, he found something in Canada that was familiar and reassuring, and he began a custom that would be part of his youth, as if, in the practice of worship, he was able for a time to leave his pain behind him. He would go to church each Sunday, by himself, though often when he returned he was rebuked, and once or twice whipped for having left the milk separator unwashed. Once, after he had been beaten repeatedly, he told a neighbour, a farmer who had had many home boys during the years and treated them decently, almost as though they were his own sons—and the man's eyes narrowed as he said something that shocked Fred Treacher: "If he tries that again you run the pitchfork through him." From that day on, the boy did not take abuse without protest. He began to talk back, and once he fought back.

Then, on a cold and rainy day in late November, after he had been there for almost eight months, Fred was called from the barn into the house. Standing in the kitchen was a man—tall, well dressed, and wearing glasses—the inspector from Toronto who had come to visit him. The inspector looked down from his great height, slowly removed his glasses, and, as he wiped them on his linen handkerchief, spoke to the boy: "Fred, I think it's time we had a little talk. Privately."

Together they went into the front room, a chilly place off the hallway where Fred had never been. There, sitting upon maroon settee, the boy summoned his courage to tell the man the truth—about the beatings and the whippings—even though he had heard from other home boys he met at church that telling the truth could make things worse. The inspector sat across from him, and for what seemed a very long time he said nothing, Finally he looked directly at Fred and in a very low voice he began: "I've just had a talk with these people. Goodness me, boy, who do you think you are? Do you realize how bad you are?" For a half-hour he went on, scolding the boy for his slowness, for his conduct, for his personality. It was clear that whatever he had been told by the farmer about Fred Treacher, he had believed it all. In answer to the boy's complaint that he had been beaten and whipped, the man replied he had no doubt that a boy as badly behaved as he, would be beaten. Then he wagged his finger at Fred Treacher, and, in a voice rising and threatening, he said: "If I had my way, I'd take you right now and give you my own beating!"

There followed threats that he would be sent back to England as unfit, a failure, a disgrace. The boy broke down and cried uncontrollably, but the inspector said nothing. He got up and left.

The following spring, when he was fourteen years old, Fred Treacher received a letter from Mr. Fegan's Home in England, a warm and friendly letter telling him that his younger brother Bert, who had been placed in the home with him, would now like to come to Canada, and if possible live on a farm near his brother. Bert was nine. The next day, the letter tucked in his jacket pocket, Fred crossed the fields to the nearest farm, to the house of the man who, in the months he had been in Canada, had been the only person to treat him with ordinary understanding. He asked if perhaps Bert might stay there; over the years so many boys from England had come and been happy in his care. The man, a slight, ruddy-faced farmer with warm grey eyes, read the letter and said simply, "Why not?" A few days later he wrote the home in Toronto, and that summer Bert Treacher was reunited with his older brother Fred.

For Bert, who was a bright boy with blond hair and a mouth that smiled easily and often, it was as if he had been chosen as a son, surrounded by the affections of a kind man and woman and provided with the sense of belonging to a good and caring family. He did light chores—learning to separate the milk and wash out the buckets—but while he was expected to work, he was not expected to slave, and in the very first week he was there he was told that as soon as fall came he would begin school. Often on summer evenings when he could get away, Fred crossed the fields to the farm, and there in the large kitchen he sat at the table with Bert and his new parents, saying little but somehow feeling that life was easier just knowing that his younger brother had done so well.

That August, on a very hot afternoon when the air was sweet with the smell of hay, Fred Treacher, who was going on fifteen, set out once again to cross the fields to find his brother and, he hoped, give him a hand with the late chores. He reached the house and, finding it empty. climbed to the top of a hill overlooking a lake where Bert liked to feed the ducks. He looked down and saw standing there four people: the farmer—who seemed to be stirring the water with a long pike-pole—his wife, and two men he did not know. He called out, asking simply where Bert was. Only the woman looked up. Slowly she said that Fred should stay where he was and not come down. Then she began to climb the hill toward him. But before she reached him, he saw. The long pike-pole emerged from the water and at the end of it, hanging on its hook, was a boy's cap, a peaked cap, the kind worn by boys of the Fegan Home. It would take time, for the water was muddy, but they found Bert's body beneath the raft on which he was playing.

That winter, Fred Treacher, still abused and beaten, got up very early one morning, his only possessions the clothes he wore, and, like so many boys of his kind and his time, ran away. He crossed the south of Ontario to a farm near Belleville and there too he found only pain. It would be only the First World War that would rescue him from despair and give him the dignity that his childhood did not have. He went overseas, and when he returned he settled in Toronto, becoming an electrician, an elder in his church, and in time a man to whom other men gave their respect. Through the years he would go back to Elmvale and into the country beyond it, as if in search of a youth he did not remember. Once, more than sixty years after it all had happened, he returned to the cemetery, the small grave, and the headstone he remembered from his boyhood. It said that Bert Treacher, a home boy, was buried there. But what touched Fred in a way he never forgot were the words that were placed beneath the name: "Dearly loved, Dearly missed".

One day in the spring of 1909, a man and a woman in Montreal, Mr. and Mrs. Godbee Brown, sat in the living room of their comfortable home on Maisonneuve Street and for most of an hour studied the pages of the recently published yearbook of McGill University. There, among the many serious likenesses of young men on their way into the professions of law, medicine, and the ministry, was the photograph of a young woman, a striking-looking girl, around whom centred all their affections and ambitions. This was Theodora, their daughter, their only child, a girl whose gifts of mind and personality they had nurtured with devotion from the first day she entered their lives. Godbee Brown, a prosperous and cultured man, thumbed through the yearbook, nodding at the several photos of teams and clubs that included his daughter. Once more he turned back to her graduation photograph, reading aloud the brief biographical sketch that appeared beneath the picture of Theodora W. Brown. "Miss Brown entered Royal Victoria College

(McGill) in '05 and graduates this year, taking second-rank honors in History and English, and receiving the degree of B.A. from the faculty of Arts....That Miss Brown was an ardent student will be shown by the honors taken, and Miss Brown's popularity is revealed through the fact that the '09 class of McGill elected her their vice-president."

The outline of Theodora Brown's career at McGill made no reference to her early life, but even if the editors had asked her about it and even if she had agreed to explain it, there was little she could have done to provide it. For her birth and her infancy were a mystery, hidden in one of the brief scribbled notes, made long ago, when she was given over to the care of one of the child care organizations in England. In the spring of 1890, when she was five years old, she was put aboard the steamer *Vancouver* and sent to Canada, along with thirty other children, all destined for the Marchmont Home in Belleville, Ontario. When she arrived on that May day, Theodora Brown was taken into the care of Marchmont's superintendent, Ellen Bilbrough, the dedicated, motherly woman who had come from England with Annie Macpherson and had stayed in Canada, at Belleville, to oversee the work her friend had established. By the time Theodora had arrived, Ellen Bilbrough had married the Reverend Robert Wallace, who, like his wife, would dedicate his life to receiving destitute British children and placing them in Canadian homes.

Ellen and Robert Wallace were very taken with Theodora—whose name then was Theodora Wood—in particular her lively, curious mind and cheerful personality, which were mirrored in her large, bright eyes. At five years of age, she was one of the youngest children to come to the Marchmont Home and thus was destined not to be placed out for wages, but to be adopted. For a time the Wallaces wondered if they might adopt her themselves. But in the fall of the year in which she had arrived they received an inquiry from Mr. and Mrs. Godbee Brown, a couple in Montreal who were, like the Wallaces, devoted Methodists, and leading members of the congregation of St. James Methodist Church in Montreal. They were also, despite all their hopes, childless. Thus, in October of 1890, Theodora Wood was chosen by one of the leading families of church and society in Protestant Montreal, a couple whose home included a library and conservatory, where her father would read her the classics. In 1895 when she was ten years old, her mother would take her to Europe for a year and provide her with lessons in German. Her life would be surrounded with the advantages of an affluent family and the affections of a man and a woman whose joy at her arrival led them to call her Theodora Wallace Brown in gratitude for the gift of Robert and Ellen Wallace of Marchmont Home.

One day in the winter, a year or two after she had come to the Browns, she came home from school one afternoon to see some children in a nearby yard rolling a huge snowball. She ran toward them, her spirits, as always, buoyant and expectant, hoping to join in the play. Suddenly one of the children moved in front of her and made a comment that was to ring in Theodora's memory for the rest of her life: "You know what? You're not really Theodora Brown. You're a home girl. You came from the home." Theodora said nothing, but turned and ran home in bewildered silence. Once there, she threw herself in tears into the arms of Charlotte Brown and told her what had been said. Mrs. Brown did her best to explain, of course, but it was hard, very hard, especially when she knew so little of Theodora's past, of her parents, of how she came to be placed in the home or why. She would never know; nor would Theodora. On that cold day, early in the 1890s, Theodora Brown learned that, contrary to what she had come to believe, all children did not come to Canada on ships across the sea, and that in her case there was a mother and father she would never know, and a decision she would never understand.

When she was in her teens, a girl of promise at school and in her private studies (music and art), her father decided that she should go on to private school to Stanstead, a college of the Methodist Church, located in the town of Stanstead on the border between Quebec and Vermont, where successive generations of children of Quebec Protestants would take their early education on their way to business and the professions. She remained there for three years and then finished her matriculation at another private institution, the Montreal Girls' High School; in 1905 she began her remembered passage through McGill University. For the most part she was a pleasant and friendly woman with a keen intellect, and when she completed McGill she married a fellow scholar, an academic named Irving Vincent, who was destined to rise quickly in the system of education in Protestant Quebec. But despite all of this—her intelligence, her achievement, her maturing style—there was a deep yearning for the past in her life, as if she was seeking to find out who she was, not out of curiosity or even bewilderment, but out of a desire to fill a void within her spirit. She became, in her adult years, a member of the Anglican Church, not to fulfil a religious conviction, but to draw closer to the land of her birth and her past, and when she had a daughter of her own, Phyllis, she would remind her over and over again that she was special, since she was her mother's own "flesh and blood".

In 1948 Phyllis, who had married and had her own first child, returned to Montreal, to bring to Theodora Brown her granddaughter.

Her joy on seeing her grandchild was of a unique kind. Then, in 1956, when she was barely into her seventies, she died and became for all who knew her part of fond and lasting remembrance. In time, her daughter would become a student of genealogy and would spend years trying to penetrate the riddle of her mother's childhood in Britain. But beyond her experience in Canada, Theodora Brown's life would remain the mystery of an abandoned child, a journey across the sea, and a destiny that was fortunate.

Charles Elliott was sure on that day long ago in London, when he was a very small boy, that his father was telling him the truth when he said he was taking him to visit some relatives, where he would stay awhile and then—when his father was well again and working once more—be brought back to be with his parents. It was only when they arrived at their destination, a rambling set of buildings in Stepney in London's East End, that Charles began to wonder if something far more serious was happening to him. A woman came to the door, a large, stern woman, who looked at Charles warily; then, suddenly, his father broke down and began to weep. He promised his son that it would only be gone for a little while, that soon, when he got work, he would come and take him back. Of course he never did. Charles Elliott became a ward of Dr. Barnardo's Homes.

He did not care much for life in the home at Stepney, with its military atmosphere, in which boys were severely regimented, marching to the blast of a whistle, to their meals, to their work, even to their prayers. He ate with crowds of other boys, all of them strange to each other, in a dark, plain dining hall. There was never enough to eat; at night, in his bed, he would lie awake for hours wanting nothing in the world so much as a slice of bread. In a few weeks he was moved to one of Barnardo's branch homes, and then to another, at Woodford Bridge, a short distance from London. He would find life there not just harsh but, because of the matron at the time, an experience of unforgettable cruelty. Often, if a boy did not make his bed properly, or left a sock dangling, he was beaten with a broomstick. Sometimes she would tally a boy's faults and then on Saturday night he would be made to wash the dishes for forty others, and to do so in ice-cold water. But her most malevolent punishment, Charles thought, was reserved for boys whose manners at the table did not suit her.

They were always hungry. On Saturday evenings they were treated, not just to their regular fare—usually three sandwiches—but to one piece of cake as well. For every boy there, the moment of the cake's arrival at his table was a moment of unsurpassed joy. They could barely restrain themselves long enough to eat the dull sandwiches before they tasted the delicious cake. For some, the hunger and the temptation were too great and they reached for the cake first. Invariably she caught them, and when she did, she denied them not just the cake but the bread as well.

A few months later, in June, Charles's mother came to the docks in Liverpool, gave him a hug, and watched as he boarded the *Corinthian* for Canada. There were over a hundred boys on board for the crossing, which would take almost two weeks, all of them caught up in the excitement, so that the sadness of their parting was swept aside by the anticipation of the adventure that awaited in Canada. They ate and slept in steerage, and while the air was sometimes bad, and the food was generally plain, they were supervised and taken care of. Alfred Owen, Barnardo's Canadian superintendent, was in charge of them, and often they were brought up to the deck for games and visited regularly by the captain, who, like many other steamship men of his time, took an interest in the immigrant children that was professional and sometimes even fatherly.

Occasionally, Charles would stroll the deck with a boy he had met on board, a youngster his own age who came from one of Dr. Barnardo's other homes around London. This boy's parents, in an arrangement that was possible in those years, had put him in the Home, come out to Canada themselves, found work on a farm, and now, almost two years later, were awaiting their son's arrival in Canada. He was an adventurous boy and one day, after the ship had been in rough water for two days, he came on deck to the enclosed area from where the children were allowed to watch the sea. He spied a bit of flotsam in a wave washing the deck. He ran to catch it, whereupon the wave, then receding, pulled him with it, so that he crashed into the iron railing. He was knocked unconscious and that night he died. In the morning, the boys lined up on deck, and above them, on the upper level, hundreds of other passengers stood in silence at the rail. The ship's engines were stilled. The ocean, which had been heaving for three days, was as blue and calm as a millpond. On the lower deck, the chute was placed over the side and tipped toward the sea. The small wooden coffin, built by the ship's carpenters and covered by the Union Jack, was secured at the top of the chute. The ship's padre read a few verses, the boys sang "Nearer, My God, to Thee", and the minister intoned the words of the Burial at Sea: "We therefore commit his body to the deep...." Then they slid the coffin into the quiet, waiting water.

Before the ship reached Canada, Charles was told by Alfred Owen that he was going to Fenwick, Ontario, to work on the farm of a man named Cyrus Nunn. In the last week of June, in the company of a Mr. Jones, a representative of Dr. Barnardo's Home in Toronto who was placing several boys in that area, Charles Elliott arrived in Fenwick. More than anything that ever happened to him, he would remember the conversation that took place that day. Mr. Jones knocked at the door. It was answered by Cyrus Nunn, a Scot of great moral virtue, but a man whose gentler side was shielded by his Celtic exterior.

"Well, sir," said Mr. Jones, "here's your boy."

Cyrus Nunn looked down at the sparrow of a boy standing in his front yard. Then he shook his head. "He's no good to me," he said, "he's too small. I wanted a working boy."

"I know he's small," sighed Mr. Jones. "But I can't do a thing about it. They're all small this time, the whole lot of them."

Cyrus Nunn said that he was sorry but, really, he needed a working boy and Mr. Jones should take this little fellow back.

"I can't," said Mr. Jones. "I tell you what. You keep him a month. I'll see if I can find a place where they want a little fellow. And in a month, I'll come back and take him somewhere else."

Charles Elliott stayed the month, and, since he was so small, he did not work on the farm but around the house helping Mrs. Nunn with the washing, the baking, and the cleaning. Then, true to his word, one day in the first week of August Mr. Jones, Barnardo's man, showed up at the house. Mr. and Mrs. Nunn were waiting for him. So was Charles.

"Well," said Mr. Jones, "I've come to take him back."

There was a moment when no one seemed to know what to say. Then Mrs. Nunn stepped toward Charles and put her hand on his shoulder. "You can't have him, Mr. Jones," she said. "He's our boy."

Charles Elliott stayed with Mr. and Mrs. Cyrus Nunn. Aided by all they meant to him, he went through school, took numerous other courses, graduated from Queen's University, and spent much of his career as a high school teacher in Welland, Ontario. When he retired, he returned to live the remainder of his life in Fenwick, not far from the farm where the man from Dr. Barnardo's Home had placed him so many years earlier.

In the year 1901, the man who was the chief benefactor of child immigrants such as Charles Elliott, Thomas John Barnardo, was back in London, England, facing a crisis in his health that would turn the waning years of his life into a desperate struggle against lengthening odds. He was not yet an old man, only fifty-six, but the years of unremitting effort and turbulent controversies had worn him out too early. His body could no longer respond to the demands his ambitions would place upon it. He suffered from bronchial illness and insomnia, and his recurring bouts with depression were more frequent and more devastating, so that for days he would be forced to his bed, struggling to rouse himself to write numerous letters to supporters and memos to his staff. But it was his heart, which had begun to present problems even before he turned fifty, that now showed signs of serious strain.

Early that spring, in April, he suffered an attack of angina pectoris so severe that his physician ordered him to take the first of a long series of rests at the health resort in Germany known as Nauheim. At first the news dejected him, but then, as he prepared to leave, he filled his suitcase with letters—he would never have a filing system—and told his secretary to prepare for work at the resort. "After careful examination," he told his wife, "he [the physician] informed me that if I was to submit myself absolutely to the treatment which he prescribes, then in two months time there is no reason why I shall not recover a great deal of my former strength and vigour." The treatments, which he underwent several times between 1901 and 1905, consisted mainly of mineral baths and prolonged periods of rest, after which he would summon his secretary and spend the rest of the day and night dictating letters at an incredible rate. With his passion for correspondence, he was sending out from Nauheim hundreds of letters every week. Then he would return to London, to his office at Stepney, and for the next several months he would drive himself with such reckless compulsion that his numerous breakdowns were virtually fore-ordained.

His superb gifts as an entrepreneur and as an administrator were at the same time his undoing, for his fascination with detail meant that he could not delegate responsibilities to his staff; instead he forced himself to work, even if he could barely walk, from dawn to dark. The most obscure details of the work of his subordinates took up his attention. Once, that same year, when he drew up a directive on the approach his inspectors should take when examining some of his branch homes in England ("A bed should be unexpectedly opened in each bedroom so as to see if the sheets are kept too long on the beds"), he even prescribed the paper their inspection reports should use: "Needless to say, all such reports should be on one side of the paper only; that as far as possible the paper used should be ruled quarto; that each new item should have its underlined heading at the left hand corner of the paragraph..."

Then, in the face of his declining health and his financial struggles, he decided one day to run for public office, as a member of the council in his borough, which was Essex. He lost by one vote, was given three recounts, and, in the end, presented a petition demanding a scrutiny, which was rejected. One of his daughters (Queenie, who was to become in later life the wife of Somerset Maugham) demanded that her father work shorter hours, but, of course, he could not let up. He told her that it was impossible for him to get home in time for dinner with the family at eight in the evening. "I tried it for a night or two," he told her one morning; "and I will tell you what it meant. It meant that to get home for dinner, even if dinner were at eight o'clock, I had to leave my office at six, just the time when our business was beginning most actively. I have so many visitors in the day and so many appointments to make that I can only settle steadily down to correspondence after six o'clock when the front office is closed. Then I can get through a splendid batch of work between then and eleven, and gradually it has come back to my leaving the office as I used to do at a quarter past eleven, by which I am able to catch the ten to twelve train at Waterloo and get into the house by twenty to one." In fact, it was often past midnight before he even left the office, running down the ten steps to the pavement and jumping into a cab for the race to catch the last train home, arriving well past one in the morning.

In the morning he rose before seven, drew a cold bath, kneeling in prayer as the tub filled, ate breakfast with the family, led the servants in daily devotions, and promptly at 8:30 left once again, not returning until the small hours of the next day. During most of that punishing schedule, Barnardo was not merely supervising the work of his many homes or accompanying his numerous workers on their nightly vigils, but expanding all over Britain, opening new reception homes, child orphanages, and training institutes, until he had, all told, thirty-five homes and eighty centres for child care of various kinds. He even took a derelict school near Norfolk and with the help of a wealthy benefactor—a shipowner and evangelical named E. F. Watts—turned it into a "ship on land" to train boys in seamanship for the Royal Navy. By then, just over thirty years from the time he opened his home in Stepney, Barnardo had taken into his care almost 60,000 children, had sent another 20,000 to Canada, and had given assistance in the form of food, clothing, or training to more than 250,000. In a single year, 1905, he had, throughout his organization, 8,500 children.

Early in February of that year, after suffering an attack just a month earlier—he had by then visited Nauheim four times—Thomas

Barnardo, his health so bad people spoke quietly of him as a dying man, was invited to attend a meeting called by the Lord Mayor of London. The purpose of the gathering was to discuss a new emigration scheme for children, one proposed by a woman named Mrs. Close, who planned to send children to New Brunswick. Barnardo decided to go to the meeting, for after all, he reasoned, he was the most senior figure in the work, a personality around whom the years had woven a mystique until now, he was a man of great fame and authority. Among those present, listening to the arguments for and against the scheme conceived by the newcomer, Mrs. Close was an anonymous reporter from Canada, a representative of the *Globe*. His account of the meeting, carried in his paper in February 1905, would remain one of the last descriptions of a public appearance by the man who, in his lifetime, chose Canada as the home for tens of thousands of British children:

> All the time another gentleman was speaking, a small, dapper man with a certain suggestion of the foreigner about him was standing close to the platform, armed with a very long ear-trumpet, which was upturned to catch every word which might fall from the speaker's lips, who was warmly advocating the utilising of "existing agencies instead of the establishment of a giant scheme such as proposed. The small gentleman, clad in the most irreproachable of frock coats, his moustache brushed upwards a la the German Emperor, immaculate linen, his collar of a new and remarkable pattern, his rather scant hair parted and smoothed with infinite care, pince-nez on the bridge of his rather *retroussé* nose, was evidently deeply interested almost before the closing sentence of the speaker to whom he listened with such attention was completed, he was on the platform, and with a courteous bow handed his card to the Lord Mayor, and when the din of the myriad of voices claiming to be heard was stilled by the autocratic ruling of the Chairman. Dr. Barnardo's name was announced. So here was the indefatigable labourer who has placed thousands of children in every portion of Canada. It was inconceivable. No words can describe the enthusiasm of that man, no pen could picture the marvellous way in which he managed to ridicule the scheme proposed. The speaker filled one with amazement. With his coat sleeves

pulled up, showing a large expanse of white cuff, his ear-trumpet either tucked under one arm or flourished as a mark of accentuation, a sheaf of notes from which he quoted figures, holding the papers close to the eyes, being evidently terribly nearsighted, one marvelled all the more that with two such disabilities this intrepid little man had accomplished thirty-seven years of the most arduous and heart-breaking work a man could attempt.

In late summer his condition grew worse, until his doctor ordered him, for the fifth time, to take another period of rest and treatment at Nauheim. He set out, all alone, on the last day of August. Then, on September 9, his wife received a telegram that he had suffered another attack, that he was too weak to take the treatment, and that the doctors were sending him back. He arrived home in London on the train on September 14. By the weekend he seemed to rally, so that by Monday he was able to dictate a few letters, including one the next day, Tuesday, September 19, to a nephew, promising his help in getting the boy free passage to Canada. That evening, just before six o'clock, his wife went to his room carrying a tray of light food. She put the food before him, and sat beside him as he began to eat. He whispered that he felt very tired and asked if could rest his face upon hers. But before she reached him, his head dropped forward and he was gone.

Newspapers throughout Britain carried long columns on his work and editorials on his life. "It is impossible," said the most influential of them all, The Times, "to take a general view of Dr. Barnardo's life-work without being astonished alike by its magnitude and by its diversity, and by the enormous amount of otherwise hopeless misery against which he has contended single-handed with success. He may be justly ranked among the greatest public benefactors whom England has in recent years numbered among her citizens." The Queen made a public statement acknowledging him as a great philanthropist whose death was a loss not only to all of his children but to all of his countrymen. His body was removed to the large hall in which he had preached so often, at Edinburgh Castle, where for the rest of that week thousands of Londoners passed by in silence and where small children could be seen putting pennies together to buy a single flower to lay near the casket. "He takes his place," an Anglican leader said, "at the side of John Howard, the friend of the prisoner, at the side of Elizabeth Fry, the friend of the fallen, at the side of William Wilberforce, the friend of the slave..." Then, on September 27, a Wednesday, his body was borne through the East End, along streets packed with tens of thousands of Londoners, in one of the largest funeral processions in British memory. Behind the hearse came his cab, empty save for his faithful driver of twenty-five years, then the Boys' Band with muffled drums, then scores of his workers and supporters, and finally, stretching for miles, fifteen hundred Barnardo children, ninety-one of them ready to leave for Canada the following day. He was buried in Barkingside, in the borough of Essex, on the land of the Girls' Village Home that he established in 1875 and where today, so many years after his death, the houses still stand and the children still go through the doors to the humane care of the organization he founded.

Eight
Life Beyond the Golden Gate

In the last week of August in the year 1905, as Thomas Barnardo was entering the final days of his life, the steamer, *Dominion*, bearing yet another cargo of his children, broke through the fog of the St. Lawrence River and into the warm air of Quebec harbour. In time, after the passengers had disembarked and left the wharf, and after the freight had been removed and sent on its way, the agent for the immigration department came out of the shed, and with a wave of his hand signalled that they could now bring off the children.

The society in which these youngsters were about to begin their lives as Canadians did not dislike children, but in its treatment of them—especially those who were the offspring of unknown and distant parents—it seemed bent on thwarting any sense of self they may have had, any tendency to feel special worth. It did this, not so much out of villainy as out of morality, convinced that the dampening of a child's spirit and the curbing of a child's will by discipline were the obligations laid upon it by a religious tradition as old as the ancient proverb of its pulpits: "Withhold not correction from the child: for if thou beatest him with the rod, he shall not die." The most progressive view of the age, one that drew strong criticism, was advanced by the *Ladies' Home Journal*, which near the turn of the century ran a series of articles maintaining that children were not depraved. But the notion that the raising of children was a serious and involving task, a notion that thirty years later would evolve into the field of child psychology, with its scrutiny of parental influence by men such as William E. Blatz of Toronto and its examination of the impact on children of rejection, dominance, and hostility, was a world away from all but a few children, and especially distant from the world of the immigrant children. Indeed, it was around that same time when the most eminent psychiatrist in the country, Dr. C. K. Clarke, had seen a group of immigrant boys aboard a train and afterward denounced them all as degenerates who were contaminating the country. "The ear marks of degeneracy were everywhere; symmetrical heads, stunted forms—the whole type bad."

On that day in August 1905 there were just over a hundred of them on board the *Dominion* as she docked at Quebec, all wearing the same dark wool suits, tight wool coats on top and dark short pants below. They came down the gangway quietly and were taken to the immigration shed, where two doctors, working side by side, examined each one of them and then directed them to a far corner of the shed, where they stood, vague and uncertain, until the last boy had been checked. The man from Dr. Barnardo's Homes who had accompanied them from London—and who had come off the ship early to see that each of their small metal trunks was put aboard the train—entered the shed and said it was now time to climb aboard for the journey west. They followed him in single file, and with hardly a word from any one of them they filled three of the plain, bare cars of the Canadian Pacific Railway. At the back of the third car, sitting beside an older boy who had helped him climb the high step to the coach, was one of the youngest children of the group, a thin, wispy boy, eight years old and small for his age. His name was John Dove. He did not know where he was heading, only that his destination was a farm somewhere in Canada.

Often in the nights when he stretched out on the floor beside his seat and tried to sleep, he would remember the morning over a year before when he came home and saw his mother sitting at the table in the kitchen talking with a man he had never seen before, a small man with a trim moustache, tiny glasses, and a grey suit that seemed as if it were brand new. "Here, my boy," he had said, "here's a penny. You go fetch some plums, enough for us all." John went off and bought the plums, but when he returned the stranger had left. His mother told him that the man's name was Dr. Barnardo and that in a few days he would be going to live with him, just for a while. At first, after they had taken him to the home, he was terribly unhappy, for he did not want to leave his mother. The home was very strict and the food was scarce, hardly more than he had had at home—a mug of cocoa for supper, a slice of bread, bit of butter, and a single plum. But within a month or so he seemed to settle down, and while some of the women treated him roughly, Dr. Barnardo, then in the last year of his life, was unfailingly kind, stopping him in the yard to ask how he was feeling, listening to his worries, and telling him over and over again that his mother loved him and that everything would work for the best. Then one day he and some boys were called to a room on the top floor, given a medical examination, and told that in two weeks they were leaving for Canada.

Most of the boys who came with him in that summer of 1905 left the train in Ontario, but for reasons no one ever explained to them, the car in which John Dove was riding was hitched to others and kept on to the West, to Winnipeg, where to in the first week of September, they were met by Dr. Barnardo's superintendent for western Canada, E.A. Struthers and taken to the distributing home at 115 Pacific Avenue. Within in a week, all of them—except John Dove, who was so young and small—had been scattered all over the prairies, placed with the farmers who had written in answer to ads in the newspapers saying a new shipment of boys had arrived. For two weeks he was the only child in the home, spending his days scrubbing floors and peeling potatoes for staff meals and wondering why he was left behind. Then one day toward the end of the month, a letter came from a woman in the lands beyond Silver Plains, Manitoba, saying that the boy the home had sent her was not working out—he was sick, and she needed a new one. Mr. Struthers told John that he need not pack, since the sick boy was not that much bigger and would leave his trunk at the farm so that John could use the clothes and shoes that were already there. On September 27, 1905, eight-year-old John Dove left for Silver Plains.

He was met at the train station in Silver Plains by a middle-aged woman, a spinster, who lived with her sister and her father on a farm a long way from the town. When they arrived at the house, a small frame dwelling that was grey with age, she did not introduce him but took him instead to the attic, where in the corner was the small trunk with the other boy's clothes and a straw tick. There was no window. This was his room, where, in the winter, the snow would drift through the roof, to settle in a white powdery mass beside his mattress. The day after he arrived he ate breakfast alone, and then the woman took him to the back field, where he saw for the first time in his life a herd of a hundred cattle, which he was told would be his to look after from that day on. He must also learn to milk the cows, the woman said, cut the wood with the bucksaw, draw the water for the family and the cattle, and see to the chores around the house. For this he would receive his board and one dollar a month.

He learned to milk the cows, and fell into the routine of setting off alone, with a bit of meat in his pocket and over a hundred cattle before him, heading toward the great pastures of the prairie, there to stay all day with no one to guide him and no one to speak to. After he had been there only a month, the animals strayed to the river and ten of them went in to drink and sank in the mud, leaving him standing terrified as the water rose around them. He went home, crying hysterically, and when he explained, he was taken outside, lashed with a switch, then told to milk the cows, cut the wood, and go to bed. When the Manitoba winter came with its punishing cold, he could hardly bear it, rising alone at five in the morning to put on the clothes the home had given him, too light and too few for the bitter Canadian winter. When spring came—a wet, gentle spring that seemed to bring with it a promise of better days—an event took place that was to leave a mark on John Dove deeper than that made by the floggings and more permanent than that left by the loneliness of the empty prairie.

One of the sisters began to prepare for her marriage, baking breads, making cakes, and laying plans for a day that would be a high festive occasion for the household and the community. For many days there was a mood of great expectancy in the modest house, which lifted the spirits of all who lived there, including the small boy in the room in the attic. On the day of the wedding he rose especially early, finishing his chores in record time so that he might be prepared for the ceremony and the party and especially for the cakes that had delighted his eye when he saw them made. By noon he was ready, even to having shined his shoes the way the boys in England shone the shoes of gentlemen. He was sitting alone in the kitchen when one of the sisters, the bridesmaid at the wedding that afternoon, came downstairs. She looked at John and then turning, as if she did not want to face him as she spoke, she looked into the mirror on the wall. Then, coldly, she asked him why he was all dressed up.

"Because today's the wedding. And I always get dressed up for church anyway."

"What concern of yours is the wedding? You'd be better off if you worried more for the work of this place. You get into the work clothes and you get out there where you belong."

He did not go to the wedding, nor was he permitted in the house at the reception. And when he finally did come in, neither the sisters nor their father had thought to save a piece of the wedding cake for the boy in their care.

In the fall, after he had been there only a year, he was taken away, back to Winnipeg, to the home on Pacific Avenue. There he stayed all winter, the only boy in the place, sweeping the offices, emptying the garbage, and peeling the potatoes for the family meals of the superintendent, Mr. Struthers, who lived in the building. Often, when he had finished his work, he would go to his bunk in the dormitory and there try to teach himself to write by copying letters in the newspaper.

It was late in March, in the midst of a cold snap, when Struthers told John, who was then going on ten years of age, that he was to be put on the train once more for another farm, this one more distant from Winnipeg than the last, thirty miles north and west of Brandon. The agreement had been made with the farmer, Struthers explained, and John would be signed over to him for six years, until he was sixteen, and for this he would receive his board, his clothes, and at the end of the six years, the sum of $110. As usual, the man would be obligated to send him to school, at least when he was not needed to help around the house as chore boy; he was not to work in the fields as a labourer since he was so young and so small.

He arrived at his new home on a Saturday, a bright, still day on which the fields that surrounded the farm seemed to sparkle in the hard light. He was, the farmer explained, to help his wife, a generous, sympathetic woman John came to love, who, it turned out, would have a child every year he was there. She needed John as a helper, with the washing, with the cleaning, with the feeding and bathing of her many children. She treated him as if he were her oldest boy, so that he found, for the first time in Canada, an attitude of kindness.

When he had been there about two months, the farmer, a big, rough man with thick shoulders, told him that despite the agreement that John would only work around the house, he needed him in the fields. Thereafter John's day began before dawn, when he rose, lit the fire, prepared the breakfast, woke the others, ate himself, then went to the barn for milking and returned to do dishes, bathe the baby, and tend to the chores around the house. He would help with the noon meal, and in the afternoon he would go to the fields with the hired man, returning after dark, and then, after he had eaten supper, he would milk the cows again. Usually the hired man had gone to bed by the time he carried the pails of milk to the house. Once, overcome with weariness, he set the two pails on the grass and stretched out between them for a moment to rest. He awoke five hours later, the farmer towering over him, glaring at him and yelling that he was a lazy son of a bitch. He grabbed John by the neck and shook him, then dragged him to the barn and there gave him such a beating that his arms, his chest, and his throat were left bruised and aching. When he went in to the house, crying pitifully, the man's wife put her arms around him and they both wept.

It was, John would learn, only the beginning. He stayed there six years, working so hard and long and losing so much weight that even when they sent him to school—a few months here and there in 1908 and 1909 and 1910—he was so sickly and so sad that his teachers came to regard him as a small creature overwhelmed by his fears.

In all his years on the farm in Manitoba, he was never visited by anyone from the home that had placed him in such uncertain and painful circumstances. Each year, he knew, the inspector came, but John was never there—he was in the fields or in the barns, and the man did not wait to see him. He simply dropped in at the house and had a chat with the farmer, who told him that all was well. He took the man's word, John said years later, because, after all, the farmer was a pillar of the local church, the kind of man who, every morning without fail, would lead the household in devotions, reading a chapter of the New Testament at the table, and then, kneeling beside his chair, pray that God would bless his home and all who lived therein. Who would doubt such a godly man?

When he finished his sixth year on the farm, John Dove had come to the end of the contract the home had made with the farmer and was, as he chose to put it, a free man. He explained that he was leaving, that he was going on his own, that he would like his salary that had been held for him the entire six years and came to $110. He received all of it, plus $1.75 in pennies, nickels, and dimes which various friends had given to him over the years and which he, in turn, had placed in the keeping of his employer. That spring, 1911, he left the farm and in time he left Manitoba. But he would go back, time after time, drawn it seemed by some paradox within himself, to stand gazing at the old house where as a child he had felt the first touch of tenderness and the lasting wound of a painful boyhood.

In the autumn, when the hay was in and the first frost dusted the fields, the children, according to the agreement entered into by most of the homes, were to be sent to school, almost always a small one-room building beyond the crossroads, in a bare field bordered by a stand of spruce and maple. In almost every one of them in those years, particularly in Ontario and on the prairies, there was a child who was different from the rest—dressed differently, speaking differently—facing not only the struggle to understand farming, but a road to learning made painful by loneliness and the slur of inferiority cast upon him by teachers and children alike. The boys almost always would be wearing the same clothes they came out in, the short pants, the short jacket, the thin socks, and, until they wore out, a pair of high black shoes. Only a few, those whose employers sensed something of their need to be clothed warmly or to be dressed like other children, wore something other than the plain suit given them by the home or the pants and shirt that had been put in their small metal trunks. More often than not they were shy, wary youngsters, always at the edge of the class unsure of themselves and uncertain of their place. For a great many, the path to education was strewn with almost insurmountable obstacles. Only a few, usually through a combination of their own persistence and a dash of luck, went beyond grade eight.

In the years near the turn of the century, a boy from Dr. Barnardo's Home in Toronto, Herbert Cobb, who had been placed in care of an elderly woman in the Muskoka district, was discovered to be attending school in the winter with no shoes. He was removed from her care and sent to another home near Port Perry, Ontario, where he fared little better, having to work from five in the morning until ten at night and being so poorly clad in winter that once, when he managed to go to school for a few weeks, he arrived with his feet almost frozen. A neighbour who knew of his misery wrote Barnardo's Home, and after long negotiation won permission to adopt him, subsequently sending him to a private school and to Victoria College in Toronto, after which he became a minister of the United Church. Elsewhere in Ontario, another boy, Arthur Payton, was struggling against the same long odds on a farm near Lake Erie. When he was fifteen and attending school only when his employer permitted, he decided that he wanted to become a minister, even though his boss never went near a church and ridiculed his ambition. By the time Arthur was able to leave the farm at the age of eighteen, his schooling was far from completed, but some friends and the local minister helped him get to Montreal to Wesleyan College, where he finished his matriculation in two years and then entered McGill University. He received an arts degree in 1928 and his divinity degree in 1931, becoming for Barnardo's a source of such pride that his photograph was widely circulated as a symbol of what a Barnardo boy could achieve. He was minister of a number of United churches mostly in Quebec and Ontario, and in 1969 he was elected president of the church's Bay of Quinte Conference.[3]

For most immigrant children the school was a world away, and if they entered it at all, it was for a brief and fleeting time, too brief to learn much, but long enough to feel the hurt of being looked upon as a ragamuffin with a funny accent. In fact, the numbers of children being denied the education that had been promised became so great that in Toronto the men at the Barnardo headquarters grew concerned. In a 1904 issue of *Ups and Downs*, the magazine sent to so many of the boys and girls in Canada, an editorial bearing the unmistakable imprint of the faithful Barnardo champion Frank Vipond expressed its disapproval, albeit gently, of the farmers' neglect of the education of the children: "There is no doubt that the natural mind of the average Canadian farmer inclineth not to the sending of his hired boy to school, especially when there is a large quantity of stock to be tended to and otherwise a considerable amount of winter choring. The admirable Education Acts of the Provinces of Ontario and Manitoba find, we are sorry to say, a good many 'passive resisters' to their enforcement. Moreover our experience amongst boys has long since convinced us that the craving for book learning is an acquired taste, and a taste that very few boys are at all eager to acquire. Manifold and ingenious are the excuses and pretexts for boys remaining at home during the months when the agreement requires that they attend school; the roads are drifted, the weather is so cold, there is such a poor teacher in charge of the school just now that the boy would learn nothing; there are several bad boys going to the school, and their influence might have a bad effect on him; the other children tease him on account of his English accent; he needs new clothes, and there has been no time to get into town to buy them for him....It is an up-hill fight we know, for most of these young aspirants, living on next to nothing, and eking out their resources by all sorts of shifts and expedients; but they have the encouragement of seeing all about them examples among the most successful and highly placed men in Canada, of those who were self-made, and who have risen from the ranks by their own enterprise and exertion. So let them struggle on, and they will find that in things temporal, as in things spiritual, 'in due season ye shall reap if ye faint not.'"

The men and women who tried, so often in vain, to see that the children did in fact get to school when the farmers would permit them were "the visitors", a tiny band of devoted workers, invariably church elders and deacons or else zealous supporters of the YMCA, who saw their work with the homes as an almost religious vocation. One of them, a man named Ernest Nunn, who spent all of his adult life as a worker for Barnardo's, first in London and then in Canada, was himself an orphan. As a young man in Dublin, he worked for a child-rescue organization, and in 1893, pursuing a lifelong ambition, he was granted a job interview with Thomas John Barnardo. He went to London, to the headquarters at Steeply Causeway, where Barnardo let him cool his heels for a whole day and then, apparently to test his sincerity, offered him a job as night watchman. He was so anxious to work for Barnardo that he accepted, becoming in time a superintendent in various hostels and reception homes that Barnardo then had throughout East End London. Later, in 1903, he made his first trip to Canada, bringing out with him one of the groups destined for Barnardo's farm in the sprawling lands of Manitoba. After working in the homes in

London for over twenty-five years, he came in 1920 to work permanently in Canada, at the home in Toronto, bringing out shipments of children usually three times a year until organized child immigration ended in the late twenties. Between trips, he crossed and recrossed Ontario in the immense task of trying to visit, once a year, the thousands of children placed on farms by Dr. Barnardo's Homes. Usually, like Barnardo himself years before, Nunn would take the train to a small town, one in the heart of a farming area where there might be dozens of boys. Hiring a horse and buggy, he would set out on his rounds, hoping to visit every boy in the area, interviewing him privately, meeting the farmer separately, and then chatting with both together. There were, throughout the entire history of child immigration and for years afterward, grave reservations over the inspection system— whether it was done at all and whether, when done, it was thorough—but in the case of Ernest Nunn, hundreds of Barnardo children would grow old remembering him as a quiet, decent man who did his best working in a system that had inherent imperfections.

By the time that Ernest Nunn came to Canada, Barnardo's had a new Canadian head, Alfred Owen having retired to be replaced in 1919 by a slender former YMCA worker in Britain, John W. Hobday. When Hobday arrived, he was in effect re-establishing Barnardo's immigration work, which had ceased during the First World War after two of the ships bearing children to Canada were detained by enemy destroyers in the Atlantic. The Barnardo headquarters, the spacious, impressive building at 214 Farley Avenue, stood idle throughout the war and eventually was sold. One of Hobday's first jobs was to find new facilities. In the meantime he set up a temporary office in a dingy part of the downtown area on Peter Street, not far from the factories and warehouses of industry. He had a staff consisting of his wife, who was called Lady Superintendent, an assistant superintendent, the Reverend W. R. Johnston, an accountant, a medical officer, a house-master and matron, and four inspectors: Robert Bruce, whom the boys called "Daddy" Bruce, John Kidner, John Stanners, and Ernest Nunn. In one of his first acts after becoming Canadian manager, Hobday reported that during the war, 6,211 Barnardo boys from Canada had joined the services, of whom 514 had been killed in action. He also said that in the first twelve months of his work in Canada, the inspectors made, in Ontario and on the prairies, the incredible number of 13,215 visits.

Hobday was by then in his mid-forties, a man of twinkling eyes and warm spirit, whose attitude toward children, a liberal humanitarianism, had been shaped by his years with the British YMCA, where he had risen to become assistant general secretary of London's Central Y. He was an Anglican, and if his attitudes were in some instances a bit elitist, he was a man of endless patience and unfailing kindness who became almost a father to thousands of children, many of whom he would bring out personally.

Once, in 1926, a lonely boy of thirteen, Albert Wayling, who had been placed on an Ontario farm, was rejected as unsatisfactory and returned to the home in Toronto. He arrived in the autumn of that year feeling that his world, poor as it was, had fallen apart. He was met at Union Station and taken to the home, fearing a severe reprimand or something even worse. Over fifty years later, after Albert Wayling had retired from a useful and successful career, he described his experience after that long trip back to Toronto: "I was given a room, and left to my own devices, with the exception of meals. I was there for about three days when I was interviewed by Mr. Hobday. To me, he was the epitome of kindness and understanding of youngsters in my circumstances and I think he carried the load of all of us on his shoulders. We visited, I think for two or three hours, during which time he asked me all about my family. This was my undoing as it was the first time anyone had shown any interest in my background and it touched me deeply. Never once was there a word of rebuke or any hint of punitive measures. He finally wound up the visit with a short comparison which I never forgot. He likened Dr. Barnardo's Homes, the Canadian farmer, and myself, to a brick archway. On one side was the Barnardo organization, on the opposite side was the farmer to whom I was assigned, and in the centre, the keystone, which was me. If I didn't maintain my position, the whole arrangement failed. This impressed me greatly and gave me the feeling of importance that I evidently needed. He wished me luck and assured me that if I had any problems to be sure and contact him and he would always be there to help. I left him with a feeling of confidence, and a vow to keep my end of the bargain. I never saw him again, but I never forgot him."

The room in which Albert Wayling met John Hobday on that day was in a stately mansion on Jarvis Street just north of Carlton, number 538, which Hobday acquired in the spring of 1923 as the permanent headquarters for Dr. Barnardo's Homes in Canada. It had been for many years the residence of Sir William Mulock, a man of means, a former minister in the Laurier Cabinet, and a justice of the Ontario Supreme Court. Mulock was also an Anglican, and through the Church became not only a friend of Hobday's but a sympathetic supporter of the work of child immigration, particularly Barnardo's. When Mulock found his mansion too much to care for in his declining years, Hobday—through the contributions of supporters, some assistance from London, and above all the several thousands of dollars donated by former Barnardo boys and girls then working in Canada—was able to buy it. The home was a massive, striking building with three floors, room for offices on the ground floor, a dormitory on the second, and Hobday's family quarters on the third. It remained in service all through the twenties until child immigration ceased, so that today men and women who came to Canada under the guiding hand of Dr. Barnardo's Homes remember it with both fondness and sadness as the first place in Canada in which they ate a meal or slept in a room, but also as the refuge to which so many returned, broken in spirit, after one of the inspectors removed them or after a farmer somewhere decided that he no longer wanted them.

On a high and sloping hill beyond the city of Halifax in Nova Scotia, looking down upon the steel-grey water of Bedford Basin, stood an old house—aged by the weather but with a sturdy look to its plain exterior—which for many years served as the Canadian branch of the Middlemore Home, an institution founded in Birmingham, England, and conducted by members of the Quaker religious movement. Each spring and autumn, in the harbour that was almost within sight of the home, the ships would arrive from Liverpool and on board in the steerage were small groups of children, never numbering over thirty, who were destined by some misfortune to become wards of Middlemore Home and then, through the choice of someone else, the child servants of the Maritime provinces. They were met at the ship by the home's superintendent, William Ray, himself from Birmingham, a former insurance agent who, from 1914 on, ran the home, placed the children, and did his best to visit them once a year. His wife, Ellen, whom he had met when he was a young immigrant in Stanley, New Brunswick, worked with him, and served as the home's matron. Together they would load the children into horse-drawn wagons and take them to the home in Fairview outside the city, where they would stay, sometimes as long as three months, while William and Ellen Ray waited for the applications to come in, in response to their newspaper ads. Then, one by one they placed them, the boys being put on trains alone, the girls being taken to their destinations by Ellen Ray.

All through the years of its work, from the 1890s to the 1930s (when the building was sold and became a tourist home), there were people throughout the Maritimes, clergymen, politicians, and others, who had serious doubts about the Middlemore Home—about its care in selecting good homes, and its interest in the children once they were placed out. As early as 1894, when the founder of the home in Birmingham, John Middlemore, arrived with a group of children himself, the immigration agent in Halifax complained that he simply distributed the children without even providing a list of them or their whereabouts. "He told me," complained Edwin Clay, the Dominion immigration agent, "some of these were workhouse children and he promised to give me a list of them with their location but he has not done so. Some of these children were placed in Nova Scotia and some in New Brunswick but more than this I cannot say. Mr. Middlemore has no homes here and I trusted to his honesty to supply me with the information asked for, but he failed to do so."

Over thirty years later, in 1927, after child immigration had come under serious scrutiny both in Britain and in Canada, the vice-chairman of the Middlemore Home in Birmingham, Paul S. Cadbury, wrote to the Premier of Nova Scotia, Edgar Rhodes, arguing strongly against, closer supervision of the Middlemore Homes' work in Nova Scotia or (as was being recommended by the Children's Aid Society of Cape Breton) the transfer of child-importing from the Department of Natural Resources to the province's director of child welfare, where it obviously belonged. In a letter to the Minister of Natural Resources in February 1927, in which he threatened to transfer the work of the Middlemore Homes elsewhere, Cadbury said he saw no reason for any change in the regulations. "I do not think," he wrote, "the work of bringing child immigrants into the province should be under the Director of Child Welfare." If, however, the government insisted on this change, he argued that it apply only to children under ten years of age. "Over this age," he wrote, "both boys and girls are of some use in the farms on which they are placed and should rightly come under the department of natural resources."

When Cadbury wrote his letter, one of the children in the Middlemore Home just outside Birmingham was a girl of thirteen named Annie Smith. Annie was small for her age, with a quick mind and a personality that was surprisingly cheerful in light of a sad early childhood. She was twelve when her parents divorced, and on the advice of a lay missionary she entered the Middlemore Home and found it to be the happiest place she had ever known, where she could attend school, which she loved, and where, on rainy days when the children could not go out, Mrs. Cadbury would gather the girls together and teach them to embroider. She stayed there two years, until she was fourteen, which at that time in Britain meant that she was old enough to go to work. She would have preferred to stay in school longer, but that was not to be. The people who ran the home told her that since she was now of "leaving age", she would be going to Canada, to Halifax, and then to a family that needed a girl to help around the house. Annie did not fear this, in fact she looked forward to it, having read that very year L. M. Montgomery's celebrated book *Anne of Green Gables* and believing that the life to which she was going was one of beautiful farms and lovely people.

In July 1928 she arrived aboard a ship in Halifax harbour along with twelve boys and eleven girls, all of them met by William and Ellen Ray and taken to the old distributing home on the sloping fields of Fairview. After the happy days of the Middlemore Home in Birmingham, the Rays' home seemed dull and drab, as if it were simply a storage depot where they were put until a farmer came along who wanted them. Annie was there for the rest of that summer, helping with the washing and the cleaning, but mostly spending the long days simply waiting, from time to time saying goodbye to one of the girls who was being sent off.

Then, late in September, Mrs. Ray came to say that her time had come, that very early the next morning they would be getting on the train and leaving for her new home in New Brunswick. Mrs. Ray did not tell Annie the name of the family or whether she and her husband knew them and felt they were good people who deserved to have a child in their home. Nor did she actually take Annie to the farm and introduce her to the people, telling them who she was and where she was from. Instead, she travelled with her, sharing some sandwiches from a shoebox, and then, after the train had left Moncton and head-ed toward the village of Petitcodiac, she gave Annie a note, explaining who she was and reminding the family of the amount they agreed to pay the home, a fund which would be held for Annie; then she put her off at Petitcodiac station and simply waved goodbye. There was no one to meet Annie Smith.

She was there about half an hour when the farmer came, took her note, and without a word led her to his old car, where his wife and a neighbour couple along for the ride were already sitting. They drove off down dirt roads and over small, scrubby hills until, in the back acres of New Brunswick. They arrived at her new home. It was not, as Annie had dreamed it would be, the green and stately setting of *Anne of Green Gables*. The house, which was tiny and square, was unpainted and stood in a small dirt yard. There were no curtains in the windows and over all there hung an aura of grim despair. Living within its thin walls were the husband and wife, four children, and a hired teenager from one of the other organizations placing boys, Dr. Cossar's Training Farms. For all of them Annie Smith lit the fires, got breakfast, washed the dishes, made the beds, scrubbed the floors, arranged the lunches, cleaned the barns, prepared the dinner, and then, if there was still light in the sky, went back to the fields with hired boy to pick potatoes until night fell. Once, after she had been there for a year, someone woke her out of a deep sleep, for she was crawling on top of her bed, reaching and reaching as if she were still picking potatoes. For her work it was agreed that she would be paid eight dollars a month, four dollars of which would be put in the bank until she was on her own and could claim it, three dollars sent to the home as its share, and one dollar given to Annie as her spending money. In the end, however, when she was leaving the farm and asked for the money that was hers, she received nothing, for the woman blamed her for breaking dishes, cracking lamp chimneys, and wasting food; she even blamed her for wasting a cord of wood by leaving the drafts open too long. Adding all this up, the woman deducted it from the money owing Annie and told her there was nothing coming to her.

She was on the farm three years, and though the work was terribly hard, and she was not sent to school, nor was she given the money that was rightfully hers, Annie's deepest hurts came from none of these but from the loneliness of her life and the unkindness, which at that time in her childhood filled her with overwhelming sadness. Once, when the farmer's wife took her to Moncton to buy her overshoes—it was then January and she had nothing but her shoes—she was hitching the horse to a post when a man standing nearby asked if the girl was a home child. "Yes," the woman replied. Whereupon the man said that such children were trash. And the woman, who was the only woman Annie Smith knew, replied: "Yes, they are, and poor trash at that." Often, when she was in bed at night and still awake, she could hear the woman telling visitors that British people were dirty, that Annie was lazy, careless, and stupid. Night after night she would kneel by her bed and pray that God would take her away. In time, another woman who learned of her anguish had her removed from the farm and she went her own way, until, when she was an adult, she left that part of New Brunswick and built a new and better life in Fredericton. Years after she had left, the man of the house was asked what he remembered about Annie. He replied that she was a good girl. "One thing about Annie," he said, "Annie never got tired."

On the last day of April in 1924, the *Globe* carried a brief note that, unknown to most of the people who read it that day, was presaging the last chapter of child immigration: "The Canadian system for the placing and supervision of children brought to this Dominion from the United Kingdom under the Overseas Settlement Committee, will be inspected this summer by a delegation to be named by the British government...." Thus, that autumn, on September 20, a commission of four people, two men and two women, headed by Margaret Bondfield, a member of the British Parliament and the Parliamentary Secretary to the Minister of Labour, landed in Montreal and began a tedious journey to every province, talking to immigration officials, to the men and women of the homes, and, as often as possible, to the children on the farms. It was, however, the atmosphere surrounding the commission, both in Britain and in Canada, that was to be as influential as its findings in hastening an end to the importing of homeless children as hired help.

In London, more and more people, particularly those in the Labour government, began to have the same doubts that half a century earlier had troubled the conscience of Andrew Doyle. The National Conference of Labour Women, worrying over the care the children received, urged that it be stopped. And when officials of Canada's two railways, Canadian National and Canadian Pacific, went to Britain in April of that year and proposed their own plans to bring out boys—by bypassing the child organizations altogether and taking children out directly from the families—the government gave them a flat rejection on the grounds they were splitting youngsters from their parents.

In Canada it was as if the country was wrestling within itself, trying to make up its own mind between the arguments of the farmers and the railwaymen, who wanted the children for the benefits they brought, and those of the growing numbers of people—politicians, union leaders, and social workers—who would end juvenile immigration altogether, out of either hostility, or compassion, or more often a cunning combination of both. For example, one sweltering day in the summer of 1924, just a couple of months before the British delegation began its tour, over a thousand women, members of the IODE, gathered for their national convention in Toronto at the King Edward Hotel.

One of the speakers that day, their convener of child welfare, was a sturdy woman with a metallic voice, a social worker from Ottawa who was director of the Canadian Welfare Council, Charlotte Whitton. Her speech, delivered in her familiar resonant style echoed the attitude then forming among those Canadians—in the churches, in the national councils of women, and in Parliament—who saw themselves as the pioneers of more enlightened social policy. She began by expressing the old, historic fear for the health of the country, facing hordes of children from Britain who were deficient, mentally and morally. "If the encouragement

of juvenile immigration, which must be recruited largely from the under-
privileged groups of the Old Land, is to continue," she said, "Canada
cannot insist too strongly and emphatically on the most stringent, pre-
cautionary measures to guard the mental, moral and physical fibre of her
own being." She then repeated the opinion of psychiatrist Eric Clarke—
whose opposition to child immigration was almost a public campaign—
who claimed, so she said, that a huge proportion of the mental defectives
of Canada were child immigrants or their offspring.[4] But then, moving to
a more emotional ground, she began to claim that the schemes were a
form of child labour, unworthy of a humane society: "Why are so many
children being brought to Canada? The only fair inference is that juvenile immigrants are being sought for placements in homes and conditions which the Canadian authorities will not accept for our own children. It does not redound to the credit of Canada that in an official publication of the Dominion Government we should speak of getting farm
helpers from ten to thirteen years of age. Do not these facts bear out a
contention of a cheap labour demand, a cheap labour that approaches
perilously near a form of slavery?" Or as J. S. Woodsworth, the esteemed
labour MP, who was to become the founding leader of the CCF, put it in
a debate in the House of Commons: "We were bringing children into
Canada in the guise of philanthropy and turning them into cheap
labourers." Moreover, the moral arguments were made thornier by con-
flict between Ottawa and the provinces over Ottawa's insistence that
child immigration remain under its wing, while it left the paying of the
bills for children who became wards in the lap of the provinces. In
Winnipeg, after several impassioned speeches at a meeting of the
Canadian Council on Child Welfare, the delegates asked that the two
levels of government begin to cooperate so that the children might be
adequately supervised. Andrew Doyle, the zealous British immigration
inspector, by then dead for several generations, would have been
intrigued, had he been in Winnipeg, to hear Canadians so many years
after his report still passing resolutions urging that "immigrant children
be properly inspected, homes properly selected and children cared for."

In 1924, the year in which Charlotte Whitton made her moving,
yet shrewd plea to the IODE, several groups—the IODE, the National
Council of Women, the Council for Social Service of the Church of
England, the Association of Child Welfare Officers—filled the air with
ringing calls for action, some kind of action, to limit the schemes, to
eliminate the schemes, or to scrutinize them more carefully. It was as if
the nation was more worried than ever, partly for itself, but partly for
the children as well. Perhaps it had been affected by separate and trag-

ic incidents in the early months of that year. Two of the children took their own lives. "Both Canada and Britain," said the publication *Social Welfare,* "were stirred by the suicides of two 'Home boys' upon Ontario farms. The lonely figures of these two waifs, far from kindred and birthplace, impelled to a bitterness of spirit which sought relief in death, kindled the pity of both lands."

Thus, in a country in which the immigration of children had become surrounded with confusion and touched by pangs of conscience, the Bondfield Commission from Britain arrived on September 20. The members stayed in Canada for ten weeks, beginning their inquiry in Ottawa with senior men in the Department of Immigration and then—through the offices of G. Bogue Smart, a man of great energy who, as the official closest to child immigration, was also a faithful supporter of it—were given the names and locations of children in every province. Shortly after the middle of November, back in London, the committee presented its findings the most crucial of which came after a long and, in a few instances, somewhat rose-coloured assessment of the conditions children were enduring.[5] "We feel," the commissioners concluded, "that however excellent the placings, the migration of young children is open to objection in principle. In the first place the comparative helplessness of the child makes this form of migration the most liable to abuse. There is the possibility of the loss of certain educational advantages. There is the danger of overworking. There is the further drawback that the placing of children under fourteen has in the case of one society resulted in an arrangement by which persons who have taken such children are allowed to employ them without paying any wages, till they reach the age of eighteen. After careful consideration of the whole position, we have come to the conclusion that the best age at which children should go to Canada is the statutory school leaving age in the United Kingdom." In other words, only those fourteen years old. In a matter of weeks the government of Britain acted in accordance with the recommendation. In August, Canada followed. That fall the last shipload of small children, mostly twelve and thirteen, touched shore and were quietly, quickly dispersed.

And yet, for all the beating of the air and the drafting of resolutions, and even the passing of laws, the emigration from Britain of young people of fourteen, fifteen, and sixteen was far from finished. As for the homes, in particular Barnardo's (which that year took over the work of Annie Macpherson's old Marchmont Home in Belleville, including oversight of six hundred of the children still under its supervision), Canadian manager, John Hobday, frustrated by the years of criticism and accusation and now bitter at the new regulations, threatened that Dr. Barnardo's Homes would cease work in Canada. "Influenced by the constant criticisms of irresponsible persons," he complained one day that August, "the Dominion Government, without any investigation whatever, has refused to allow immigration of young children. Our people have decided to stop bringing out children altogether." But two days later, after the *Toronto Star* carried a piece from London reporting that Barnardo's British officials said they would continue their work—by sending out children over fourteen—John Hobday allowed that he too would work within the policy.

For the next three years, therefore, the number of young migrants did not greatly diminish; the various homes simply kept children in their British institutions longer, until they reached the mandatory age. In fact, the established homes were now joined by new groups, each one bringing older teenage boys and intending to train them in various ways inside Canada for work on the farms. There were, for example, the Dakeyne Boys' Farm near Windsor, Nova Scotia, the United Church Boys' Training Farm in Norval, Ontario, and one of the most unique of all the programs, the Fairbridge Society, founded by Kingsley Fairbridge, which had a village home in the serene setting of Duncan on Vancouver Island in British Columbia.

The Dakeyne Farm—named after a boys' club in Nottingham, England, through which most of the boys came— was set in the lush fields of Nova Scotia's Annapolis Valley. Here, in a rustic, comfortable house, passed a stream of boys, usually fifteen to eighteen years old, who, on their own and with the consent of their parents, volunteered to come to Canada to learn the ways of farming on property which was owned by their club's founder, a British officer and youth worker named Captain Oliver Hind. For most of them, the one- or two-year stay at the farm was a tough experience, each boy being listed in a ledger in which all his expenses—for things such as passage out and his clothing while on the farm—were noted. Then, once he was hired by a farmer, usually in the springtime, he was honour-bound to reimburse his benefactor. Nevertheless, the Dakeyne Farm, which closed in the early thirties, left most of its boys with generous memories and a decent start in life. "Too many of the early schemes," says Roy Grant of Moncton, N.B., who was superintendent of the farm several years, "were a bit casual and too large to provide young children with the kind of atmosphere they needed to adapt to new work and a new country." Once, in 1931, not long before the farm closed, Grant helped one of the boys, a teenage youth named Robert Strachan, get his first job on a farm in New Brunswick. He noticed in Strachan a resourcefulness that struck him as special. Four years later, packing a saw and a hammer, Strachan said he was going to migrate to British Columbia and become a carpenter. He also became a member of the British Columbia Legislature, the leader of the Official Opposition from 1956 to 1969, and then, under Premier David Barrett, the Minister of Highways and later Minister of Transport.

The United Church of Canada's work in youth immigration was born amid one of the darkest hours of the twentieth century—the massacre, in 1915, of over one million Armenian Christians by the Turks. In time, seventy thousand homeless children were simply exiled to wander as nomads. A number of relief agencies were set up, one of them the summer of 1923, on a two-hundred-acre farm in Georgetown, Ontario, fifty small boys arrived, most of them between eight and twelve, many of them burdened with the memory of the murder of their fathers. The next year forty more came, so filled with terror that one man who was there would remember all his life how they shook for fear that they were simply being led, like their fathers before them, to some field of slaughter. The work of feeding, clothing, and educating the children was supervised by a group of volunteers from the churches—the Armenian Relief Association of Canada—but their training on the farm was the job of Alex Maclaren, a sturdily built Scot, a Methodist layman, and a graduate of the Ontario Agricultural College. Over the few years he was with the boys, Maclaren's rugged compassion and example (he had worked in rural teaching with the YMCA) helped to heal the wounds, so that eventually one of the boys, whose name was J. Apramian, would write of those years in Georgetown: "What wonderfully happy times those were for us. We had almost all the food we wanted, enough clothes to wear, freedom to roam on a 200 acre farm and just enough strappings administered to the open palm to spice it all!" Gradually the older boys were placed on farms until by the late twenties they had all gone, most of them to stay on the farms for only a few years before making their way into businesses of many kinds in Canada and the United States. When they were gone, Alex Maclaren won the backing of the United Church to bring in British boys, all in their late teens, and all experienced to some degree in farming, to learn better skills and earn better money on the farms of Ontario. Maclaren—who worked hand in hand with a British group called the Overseas League—insisted that the boys be older and that all of them have had at least a modest background on a British farm. Before the Depression ended his work in 1932, he brought to Ontario over sixteen hundred boys who, because of his realistic expectations

and his careful placement, were introduced to Canada in comparatively happy circumstances.

In many ways, the most imaginative scheme of all was the one conceived in the early years of this century by Kingsley Fairbridge of
Rhodesia, who even as a boy, impressed by the opportunities for settlement in his own country and dreaming of similar opportunities that
existed in Canada, decided to give his life to the emigration of poor children from Britain. Fairbridge was a brilliant boy himself—he became his
country's first Rhodes scholar—and during a visit to London while still a
teenager, he hit upon the methods he would use to help the children he
had in mind. "Train the children," he said, "to be farmers. Not in
England. Teach them their farming in the land where they will farm.
Give them gentle men and women for their mentors and guides, and give
them a farm of their own where they may grow up among the gentle farm
animals; proud of the former, understanding the latter." Fairbridge, clearly an exceptionally mature youth, set his sights on a Rhodes scholarship
so that he might further his dream of child emigration while studying at
Oxford. There, in October 1909, he explained his plan for what he
called "schools of agriculture" in whatever colonies would cooperate. His
children, he explained, would live in a common community, attend a
common school, and train on a common farm. That autumn he met in
London with the Governor of Newfoundland, Edward Morris, and was
promised fifty thousand acres of that cold, harsh colony on which to
establish his first school.

In the end he did not choose Newfoundland but went instead to the
warmer climates of Australia, where in 1912, he and his wife, both
almost penniless, established what became the first Fairbridge Farm
School on one hundred and sixty acres not far from Pinjarra in the western part of the country. It was not until twenty-three years later—well
after Fairbridge died prematurely in 1924 of broken health—that his followers finally realized his dream of a farm school in Canada, situated on
a thousand acres of rich, beautiful land about forty miles north of
Victoria, British Columbia. There, in September of 1935, the first group
of Fairbridge children, all taken from British orphanages, arrived to begin
life at an institution that would continue into the late 1940s. In time the
farm colony grew from the three modest buildings that greeted the first
group to over a dozen cottages for children, several staff houses, a chapel,
a hospital, a dining-hall, and a large modestly elegant home for the
Principal, a former classics professor at the University of British
Columbia and a friend and supporter of Kingsley Fairbridge during student days at Oxford, H. T. Logan. For most of its life the community con-

sisted of about one hundred and sixty people, of whom roughly forty were staff members—teachers in the school, mothers in the cottages, helpers on the farm—and the rest children, ranging in age from six to sixteen. All of them lived, studied, and worked in an atmosphere that was highly organized, rather rigorous, but, under the hand of Logan, a stern, fair man—also sincere in its moral idealism. The occupational goals it had in mind for the children were modest. The boys went to school and trained on the farm with a view to becoming farm workers; the girls took lessons in cooking and sewing so as to become farm wives. In time, after they had taken their first jobs at age eighteen many of the boys set their lives in other directions. Richard Todd, one of the children who came to Canada in the very first group in 1935, became a farm worker, and then for most of his life was a member of the armed services. He would always remember Fairbridge, and his memories would invariably be generous. It was a strict place, he would say, strict but fair. "The place had its limitations," he said. "For those ten years of my childhood I never used a telephone. I had to learn to use the phone after I left." But in its methods of child care, the Fairbridge Society did manage, for over a decade, to introduce orphan children to Canada in a way that avoided the lonely terrors that accompanied the childhood of so many of their earlier counterparts.

The members of the Bondfield Commission who came to Canada in 1924 and made their influential recommendation that, from that date on, only children of school-leaving age be permitted to go to Canada as child immigrants did so from motives that were humanitarian. Nevertheless, they still believed that such children—those who were fourteen years old—could be considered farm labourers whose future was in the fields. "The idea of those who apply for children," their report stated, "is no doubt that such children will be useful workers, whether in the home or on the farm. As a matter of fact, many of the farmers with whom the younger children have been placed informed us that they would have preferred an older child had one been available." Thus, it would be interesting to see if the children who came after the Bondfield Commission—presumed to be, because they were "older" more able to cope with their lot— actually fared any better than those who came earlier and younger. One such boy was Arthur Pope who was fourteen in the spring of 1930.

He was aboard the *Duchess of Richmond* when she arrived in the harbour of Saint John, New Brunswick, on March 30 of that year, carrying one of the last organized shipments of Barnardo boys to come to Canada

before the door was closed on them, not by moral or humanitarian considerations, but by the economic strictures of the Great Depression. He
came to Toronto to the distributing home on Jarvis Street, and then a
couple of days later he was placed on the train for a community called
Ivanhoe, near Stirling, Ontario. He was to work for a bachelor who lived
with his mother, but the man kept him for only a short time before writing the home and telling them he was sending the boy back—he was no
good, he was too small. Arthur was next sent to a place called Little
Bethany, near Madoc, to work, not for wages, but for his room and board
and spending money of $1.25 a month. He would always remember the
farm there for several things that had nothing to do with the long, weary-
ing hours of work. He would always remember, for example, that when
the farmer met him and took him home, he did not ask Arthur if he had
eaten that day. He simply told him to change his clothes, gave him a hoe,
and instructed him to get at the turnips. Arthur, of course, did not often
eat with the family but by himself, after they had finished. And when he
did, he was not to eat as much as the others because he was smaller. He
was always hungry, and he would eat frozen apples that he found on the
ground or he would creep into the cellar and open a sealed bottle of jam
or fruit in some furtive, desperate effort to curb the pain of his appetite.
Often, if he committed some misdemeanor or did not complete his work,
the farmer would take him to the barn and there, once a week usually,
he would beat him so severely that when Arthur was an adult the scars
would still be visible in his scalp. For the first few times he fought back,
but, like so many of the others who were treated that way he came to
realize that by fighting back he was making things worse, so he took it.
"What else could I do," he said to a friend many generations later. "I had
nowhere to go, I had nobody, not a friend in all of Canada." When the
inspector made his visit—in Arthur's case he was a benign, unsuspecting
man—he interviewed the boy and the farmer together at the kitchen
table and the farmer spoke for both of them, saying that everything was
well, and that, yes, indeed, Arthur was being sent to church. Then, in
March, when the farmer refused to pay him the pittance of spending
money he was owed, the home once again intervened and sent him to
someone else, this time to a man and his wife in another part of Ontario
near the village of Courtland. There, at last, in the care of John and
Martha Speak, he found a home that was indeed a home. He became
known—everywhere that John and Martha Speak were known—as one
of the Speak boys. There would, however, be no schooling, something he
would always regret, for he was a bright man who became, through his
own efforts, a successful dealer for Imperial Oil Limited in Waterford,

Ontario and an active member on municipal councils. But there would always be, his friends said, some deep reserve to his personality, as if he were never sure of other people, always wary lest once again he find himself beneath the raining of the fists.

He would never, of course, blame Dr. Barnardo's Home for the misfortunes of his early days in Canada. "They did the best they could," he would say, "with the funds they had and the understanding they had." In that feeling, Arthur Pope echoed the sentiments of thousands of men and women who came to this country in the same lonely and painful way, but who would never speak a word of criticism against the organizations in Britain that sent them so far from home.

Nine
The Curtain Falls

The day before Christmas, 1923.

In the village of Thornbury, on the southern shore of Georgian Bay in Ontario, the snow, which has fallen all morning, silently, steadily, now blows in gusts so strong that the trees, the farms, even the sky itself seem to vanish in a curtain of white. In the general store, men with raw hands come in from the cold to stare back at the shivering afternoon. No one is out, no one but the old man and the boy and the horse. They left the village an hour before, heading into the back country, just after the train arrived with the boy. The old man, his wild, rough beard glistening from the frost and the ice, rides high on the horse's back; the boy, clad in a light jacket, straddles the animal behind the man, his arms wrapped around him, holding on fearfully, for safety and for shelter against the raw bite of the wind. Sometimes the old man cannot see and they stop, and the man looks straight into the sky as if he is listening. Then wordlessly he nudges the horse and they trudge on through the cold and the slowly descending dark. Suddenly, as if by some unspoken command, the horse halts. He will go no further. The old man climbs down and telling the boy to stay where he is, he moves off into the snow. In a moment the boy hears him shout: "We're here, boy! We're home! In time for Christmas."

The boy is Charles Goddard, a small, frail child with a round, solemn face, made more solemn still by the events of his unhappy life. A Barnardo boy, he has been in Canada now for only five months, during which he has suffered in ways that will mark him forever. Now, on this Christmas Eve when he is eleven, he arrives once again among new strangers—two elderly spinsters and their older brother—to celebrate his first Christmas in Canada. Charles Goddard is given his supper—some potatoes, a bit of meat, and a cup of tea—and then, so silent that the women wonder if he will ever speak, he is led to the tiny room that will be his for the next ten years.

That night, as the wind comes off the water and beats against the house until it moans, the small boy sits alone in his room. He is not frightened, for, given his recent past, the tiny room is a refuge against the world. But then, softly, he hears upon the door the tap of someone knocking. The door opens and there in the bleak, gloomy hallway, the gaunt figure made starker still by large, piercing eyes, stands one of the sisters, almost eighty, and in her hand, hanging limp at her side, is a wool stocking. "Come, boy," she says, "come! We must not forget. It's Christmas." Together the old woman and the small boy descend to the cold of the front room, where in a window facing east hangs the only decoration in the entire house, a frayed wreath held by a single thread. She hangs the stocking by the empty fireplace, and then without a word she signals the boy to return to his room. The next morning—a morning on which the world beyond his window is so white it seems to sparkle like a diamond—he is awakened and ushered by his three new friends, the two sisters and the bearded old man, into the front room. There, hanging by the still cold fireplace, is the stocking, and inside, the gift that will make this the most memorable Christmas that Charles Goddard will ever know. It is a single orange.

It is not the orange, or even the exquisite joy of receiving a gift, that will give this Christmas such a special place in the scrapbook of his memory. Instead, it is the surprise, the wonderment, that he is living in a house, eating at a table, sleeping in a room, among people who do not ever beat him, kick him, or whip him. In the experience of Charles Goddard this is a discovery that marks a turning in his life.

He had come to Canada that summer, an orphan boy who had been in Dr. Barnardo's Homes almost all of his life, ever since he had been found on the streets of a village in Kent apparently abandoned, when he was only a few months old. Naturally he would never know his father or his mother. When he was about five years old, Barnardo's placed him with a man and woman—foster parents of the time—to whom, like many children in his situation, he became deeply attached. But then, one day when he was eleven, the home took him back with no explanation. He was to be prepared, along with other boys, for a new life in Australia, where Barnardo's was then sending children. But he took ill and missed the trip to Australia. So, to make up for the mistake, they put him aboard a later ship, one leaving for Canada. He arrived in Quebec on the twenty-third of June with one hundred and forty-four other boys. He was brought to Toronto and then, after just one day at the distributing home on Jarvis Street, he was put in the care of a conductor and sent to a farm near Alliston, Ontario, to begin five months of his life that, no matter how hard he would try in his old age, he could never remember without bitter tears rising behind his eyes.

They were, by any standard, deeply pious people. They prayed each morning and each evening and on Sundays they went to church three times. Charles was not invited to go to church with them, for he was too busy on Sundays cleaning the calf pen, the pig pen, the cow barn, and the horse stable, each of which was left all week so that on Sunday it could be cleaned out by Charles, who had never seen a farm in his life. He had trouble understanding some of the words used on the farm; once, when the farmer told him to run and get a whiffletree, he did run, but he did not know for what. He had never heard of a whiffletree, but when he confessed that he did not know, he received the first of many beatings. Still, it was not the work, from before dawn until after dark, or even the beatings—given him not for insolence but for shyness— that made his days on the farm beyond Alliston such a dark period of his life. It was something else.

The farmer did not give him a room in the house or even a bed. Instead, he was put in a shed outside, a dark, windowless outhouse with a floor of dirt and a pile of rags on which he would sleep at night. He shared it with the dog. Three times a day, morning, noontime, and evening, two plates of scraps would be brought to the outhouse, one for the dog and one for the boy. Sometimes Charles had a second helping, when the dog could not finish his. All that summer and into the cold of the fall he lived that way, alone most of the time, a boy bewildered by all that had taken place since that day when he was taken from his foster parents and told that, for his own good, he was being sent on his way to the bright promise of life in Canada. One day late in November, after he had been beaten badly for some reason he did not understand, he knew, even though he was eleven and had nowhere to go, that he must get away. Late that night, when the only sound was the murmur- ing of the cows, he slipped out of his hovel and ran across the yard, through the field, until he reached the pastures of a farm a mile away, where he fell panting at the foot of a huge pile of straw. For a minute he was overcome with the terror of being alone, of being discovered, of being beaten again. Driven by his fear, he burrowed into the straw and once inside, drew the pile around himself, so that he was hidden. He stayed there for over a week, peering out through his nest during the day at people searching for him, and then at nightfall coming out to eat turnips that he pulled from the field. Finally, one morning, he looked through the straw to see two men obviously looking for him, both of them dressed in city clothes, both of them, he was certain, from Dr.

Barnardo's Homes, come to find him, to rescue him, to take him away. Trembling and weeping, he crawled out of his hideaway and gave himself up. Within an hour, with only the rags he was wearing, he was on his way back to Toronto.

Thus, a few weeks later, on Christmas Day in 1923, Charles Goddard found himself on a farm beyond Thornbury, Ontario, the boy chosen by a family of two women and a man, each one of them well on in years, one of them over eighty. Life here would still be hard, beginning before dawn in the barns and ending after dark in the fields, with small rewards and smaller affections. One day, after he had been seen day after day in the middle of winter going to school in his bare feet, some neighbours complained and he was given boots though they were cast-offs from the old man and two sizes too big. But he wore them. He stayed there until he was twenty and in his last year with them he received, as his pay, seventy-five dollars for the entire year. After he became an adult and struck out on his own, he would always speak well of them. As he put it: "They were good to me in their way. They gave me enough to eat. They gave me a warm place to sleep. And they didn't beat me."

Every summer, usually in June when the countryside of Britain turns emerald green in the sun, a small band of pilgrims—grey-haired men who are all alone, or couples who have saved all their lives for this sacred journey—can be seen standing on the lawn in front of a rather conventional office building, low, grey, and rectangular, in the community of Barkingside in Essex, about half an hour by train from Piccadilly Circus in the heart of London. This is Barnardo's. They come, most of them, to find out what they can from the records—which are, naturally enough, highly confidential—about who they are and how they came to be the children of Dr. Barnardo's Homes. But always they stand awhile simply looking at the statue, pausing beside the grave, and strolling for a time across the wide, quiet green in front of the old cottages of the Girls' Village Home, refurbished several times over but still in use, the homes where hundreds of them spent their earliest days.

Today, in a modem expression of the work begun over a century ago by Thomas John Barnardo, the institution known simply as Barnardo's reaches into all of England, Scotland, and Wales, through one hundred and fifty homes and projects to give care to children who are retarded, disturbed, disabled, homeless, or just plain neglected. Each year it helps restore the spirit of some seven thousand children, providing them with everything from sports to the most complicated therapies for the mind or for the body or for both. It costs fifteen million pounds a year for Barnardo's to carry on its work, and its people are proud—as the founder would be proud—that not a cent comes from government grants, all of it being raised, as in the early days, from donations and from local authorities who help defray the costs of children they place in the care of Barnardo's. All over England, Scotland, Wales, and Northern Ireland—and in friendly neighbourhoods of faraway New Zealand and Australia—the children give their pennies and the wealthy their bequests to help Barnardo's large staff, almost three thousand in number, provide every imaginable form of child care. The days of child emigration and indeed the days of the old orphanage have long since passed, and at times the social workers who work in the hundreds of Barnardo's community programs—schools, day-care centres, family agencies—seem to grow frustrated over the antiquated impression their name inspires. "The orphan image clings to Barnardo's," one of the organization's many publications says, with a trace of complaint. "If it is inaccurate—because orphans today are fortunately rare—it at least reflects our concern for children. But you can imagine it can be maddening if everyone thinks that we gather up the six to seven thousand children, who for a variety of family reasons we help each year, and store them away in 'orphanages'. On the contrary. The majority are with their own families in their own homes, which is where every child should be, ideally."

Still, it is not merely people who do not understand who perpetuate the impression of Barnardo's as a refuge for destitute children. Often these memories are held by those who have every right to hold them, the men and women in Canada who, out of lifelong yearning, find their way back, even though it is often painful. One of them, a strong, cheerful man in his seventies, Walter Axtell of Oshawa, Ontario, who came to Canada in 1911—and who remembers Barnardo's first Canadian manager, Alfred Owen, as "a swell guy"—has been back to London, and to Barnardo's, twice, and hopes to go still again. On each of his visits, Walter Axtell, like all the others, is made to feel special by the sincerity of two people who have been with Barnardo's a long time, Ada Legg, a quiet lady with large, gentle eyes, and Albert Tucker, a sprightly man who has made so many old boys and girls feel welcome on their return to Barnardo's that he talks as if he knows every town in Ontario, though in fact he has never been to Canada. Both of them, Miss Legg and Mr. Tucker, work in a department of Barnardo's known as After Care, and their special responsibilities are for the records—massive black ledgers containing brief case histories of Barnardo children and other, smaller softer books that contain the registrations of those sent to Canada by Annie Macpherson. They answer the endless stream of inquiries from men and women who were once in the care of Barnardo's or Annie

Macpherson's Homes (or more recently, the inquiries of their children), asking for the date of a birth or the name of a parent. It is a job which, given the deepening interest in family records, grows larger every year. "In 1974," says Roy Clough, an easy-going man in his middle fifties who is now executive director of After Care, "we had sixty such inquiries. In 1978 we had two hundred and sixty. We can barely keep pace. But we do, though, of course, when the request for information comes from a descendant of someone who was in Barnardo's care, we have to be quite circumspect, for obvious reasons, in what we feel we can provide to a third party. But we do the best we can. In many cases we can offer them the date of birth, the date of entry, the date of sailing and—because of Dr. Barnardo's great interest in photography—pictures taken of them when they entered the homes, and just before they sailed for Canada."

Clough, a sensitive and committed man whose work often takes him throughout Britain to visit former Barnardo boys who in their adult years have fallen ill or into trouble, is the kind of man who has helped to achieve for modern day Barnardo's a reputation of selfless dedication. He went to work there in 1948, a long time after the emigration of children was stopped. But his opinion of it is expressed in terms that are calm and reasoned: "There were many things in that generation which, by today's standards, seem quite dreadful. But you cannot simply say that and leave it there. You must judge all of these things against the backdrop of the time in which they took place—the attitudes toward child care, the limitations of staff, the limitations of facilities, the limitations of funding. And along with that there was the almost overwhelming pressure to take more and more children into care, so you had to move more and more out of the Homes and place them elsewhere, often, in the case of Barnardo's and other such groups, in Canada. But their great concern, which we should not forget, was to give the child a better chance—a better chance than he would have if he stayed in the circumstances in which he was at the time. Quite obviously, however, when children were placed in foster homes—in Britain as well as in Canada—some of them experienced a great many pressures that were very painful. Often that was related to an economic fact—the huge number of cases one worker had to handle. That was very evident, I'm sure, in the case of the supervision and inspection system in Canada. You had not only vast numbers of children, but vast distances to cover. And only a few workers to do it all."

Once a week, usually at noon, a small group of workers can be seen leaving the office and heading toward a building off by itself, shaded by trees: the chapel, still much as it was in the days when Barnardo was alive, a dark, quiet sanctuary, with a high, vaulting roof, where they sing a hymn, bow in prayer, and hear a brief meditation. One day not long ago the service was taken by a Barnardo worker in his thirties, a scholarly looking man with glasses, a social worker, who told his fellow staff members that all that week he had been thinking of the various ways in which fear brings pain to the lives of people. The teachings of Christ, he said, do not end such fear, but they help in facing it, enduring it, coming through it. Then he repeated a verse from the Old Testament, one familiar to every child who has gone through Dr. Barnardo's Homes.

"Be not afraid," he said, "neither be thou dismayed. For the Lord thy God is with thee, whithersoever thou goest."

The suffering of orphan children in the early years of this century, in Britain as well as in Canada, was due not just to poverty and neglect, but to the strong conviction that punishment—beatings, whippings, and humiliations that broke the spirit of a child—had a high moral justification. These punishments, though not encouraged by the leaders of child immigration, people such as Annie Macpherson or Thomas John Barnardo, were commonplace in their time and carried out by people who were acting, they were certain, in the best interests of the children in their care.

One boy who was in Dr. Barnardo's Homes in the early 1900s, Harold Dodham, would never forget the times on which he and the others were made to witness the beatings of boys for minor misdemeanours. They would assemble in a large room of Barnardo's; then the boy would be paraded in, stripped naked, held down at the head and foot by two men, and beaten with a rod by a third. For all the boys who sat there, it was a spectacle that made them tremble, one they would try to forget but could never fully erase from their memories. Later, Dodham was sent to Canada, to a farm near Perth, Ontario, where he went without shoes for a whole year and once was beaten simply because he didn't walk the four miles to school fast enough. He endured his childhood by beginning, on his own, a serious study of the Bible, reading it in the nights from cover to cover, so that as an adult he became an active worker in evangelical children's work in Toronto.

Still, for hundreds and hundreds of the children, the great misfortune that would mark all their lives occurred not in the homes in Britain but in Canada, where, through some fate over which they had no control, they were placed with harsh and cruel masters and endured not just loneliness and deprivation but forms of brutality that went far beyond the ordinary punishments of the day. One boy, a slight, dark twelve-year-old named William Harris, was placed in 1925 near the peaceful little village of Waterford, Ontario, and was beaten so regularly and badly with harness straps that he also ran away. The next month, after he had been moved to another farm—where he was to become part of a fine family—the farmer was charged with assault, convicted in county court, and sentenced to three months.

Billy Andrews, a boy living in Birmingham with his desperately ill mother and two sisters in one room, was sent when he was only seven to steal food from the bakeshop down the street. When he came to Canada, to the farming lands around a Huntsville, Ontario, he had some painful experiences, but in time, in 1920, he was placed with a family in Bradford, Ontario, north of Toronto, where he learned not just farming but, out of his own creative instincts—and with the encouragement of the family with whom he would remain for over fifty years—the art of wood-carving, becoming so accomplished that today his folk art is in demand and is displayed in Ottawa, in the National Art Gallery. His work—often predatory creatures, cobras and buzzards, poised over hapless victims is, in the opinion of some who know it, a revelation of the apprehension that lurks in his spirit: "I guess I've always worried about what was going to happen next. That's in me and I guess it comes out."

If, as psychiatry has told us, the years of our childhood are the years that shape our inner lives forever, then the practice of child emigration—the act of uprooting children and sending them, alone, across the ocean to work in a strange land in a strange occupation—must be regarded as one of the most Draconian measures in the entire history of children English-speaking society. Its impact on the life of a sensitive child—even one who was placed in reasonable circumstances—is difficult to measure, sometimes difficult even to imagine.

In a small, immaculate house in Brantford, Ontario, a woman named Lillian Bradley, who is now in her early seventies, with a soft voice and a quiet manner, sat one day, along with a few photographs, very old and very treasured, saying that what affected her most in all of her life was the way in which she was taken from her foster parents in Britain, when she was only eleven and had spent almost her whole life with them, and sent to live in Canada. As she spoke she looked at a photograph, a plain snapshot in a plain frame, which she held and from time to time swept with her hand, in a gesture that went deeper than it first appeared. She has had the photo near her for over sixty years. It is of her foster parents. "I was put in Dr. Barnardo's Homes when I was barely a year old, I guess," she was saying, her voice touched with a distant and melancholy quality.

"Then the Home put me with Mom and Dad in a small English village. What wonderful people. I never heard a cross word all my childhood with them. I went to school, and after school Dad would cut the grass and pile it in a wheelbarrow and put me on top to keep it down. I went everywhere with him. And Mom. I loved her. I still remember how she would have a headache and send me to the chemist for some medicine and all the way I would be wishing I could have the headache instead of her. They so much wanted to adopt me. I remember the day that they wrote Dr. Barnardo's asking permission. Days went by and then one morning the letter came. Dad opened it and came in the house smiling and saying, "It's all right. They say she can stay." Then Mother looked at it and said no, it didn't say that, it said I had to go back." Thus, at eleven, Lillian Bradley was removed from the family in which she was so happy and sent that same month—apparently because it was the wish of her legal father—to the opportunities that awaited her in Canada. She arrived in St. Mary's, Ontario, in June 1921. Her life in this country, while never marred by the more ugly and physical forms of abuse, was nonetheless marred by some deep emptiness as if she were searching always for some sense of belonging that she would never find. "I was never abused," she has said, "not physically. But I was never again, as a child at least, in a real family."

Sometimes the wounds that bruised their spirits did not come over a period of years or even months but in one convulsive moment in which they were made to carry out an act so vulgar, or so barbaric, that it would haunt their memories forever. A boy named Charles Beer, who was sent to a man on a farm area near Belleville, Ontario, when he was thirteen, was told to go to the stony ground beyond the farm where a cow, which had been dead for four days, was lying bloated an baking in the hot summer sun. He, of course, had never seen a cow, much less dug a grave for one. He was given a crowbar as a shovel. The ground was hard. For most of the day he straggled in the heat, sometimes digging, sometimes crying, mostly vomiting, until at last he had the hole dug. Then, inch by inch, with the crowbar, he lurched the carcass toward the open grave and toppled it in. He covered it. But then to his chagrin he realized that the grave was too shallow, that the animal's legs protruded through the earth. He went to the house and explained what had happened, whereupon he was given an axe and told to go back and chop the legs off. When he was a man in his seventieth year and living in Petitcodiac, New Brunswick, someone asked Charles Beer if it bothered him as a child to have to chop the legs off an animal. He replied tersely: "You figure it out."

Or else if they were not abused or deprived or subjected to some expression of human nature that was bizarre, they could be worked, not merely hard—as were others of their time—but to a degree that would justify their feeling in the late years of their lives that they had been, in fact, slaves in their time. In July 1905, a slight nine-year-old girl with a bright, expectant smile, Ellen Keatley, was sent by train from Halifax to a farm in the famous Scottish settlement in Nova Scotia known as Pictou County to the home of a pipe major. For eight years, during which she was never visited once by an inspector from the Middlemore Home, which sent her there, she rose before everyone else and went to bed after them; she worked in the fields, the barns, the house, even the school, which was miles away and where she lit the fires for the sum of two dollars a year. When she was nine she was carrying sacks of pota-toes to the cellar, picking boulders from the fields, carrying all the water to the house and barn, and wielding a bucksaw to cut the wood. Finally, eight years later—with no winter clothes, not even a pair of mitts or gloves—she pumped up her courage and wrote the Middlemore Home in Halifax and asked to be taken away. When a man from the home arrived he found her trying to push, by hand, a horse-cart to carry manure from the chicken pen. He removed her; at last she was free.

During the same years, a boy from Dublin, George Gregory—whose father told him one day that he was taking him to see the wax-works but was in fact delivering him to Miss Smyley's Home for Boys—was trying, vainly, to accept a friendless, lonely life on a farm near Guelph, Ontario. Like all the others, he would work long, torturous hours, never going to school, never going to church, told that he would receive for his labour thirteen dollars a year. At the end of two years he was returned to the home without a cent.

And yet there were misfortunes of still other kinds, ones that were not physical or emotional but intellectual, in which some child of promise was denied, simply through neglect, the gift that was within him. One day in April 1921, a boy in London, England, named Norman McKinlay—whose father, an educated man, fell into dire poverty—was whisked into Dr. Barnardo's Homes along with his five brothers and sisters. His father, who had been a translator during the war, did his best to assure the distraught children that it would all be temporary and that once he was on his feet again, the family would be back together, living once again in the large house with the library, the conservatory, and the servants. It was not to be. His father, in the midst of his despair, gave permission for Norman to be sent to Canada, hop-ing that, unlike Barnardo children who remained in Britain to become footmen and butlers, he would have a chance to rise to a position in the professions. Thus, just a month after he was placed in the care of

Barnardo's, Norman was sent to Canada, a sensitive, intelligent boy of twelve, accustomed to an upper-class British home, suddenly thrust into the foreign life of a labourer on a farm near London, Ontario in a community called Ilderton. It was May 1921.

The shock that he endured that first year in Canada was one that he would always have difficulty describing. He was a studious boy who had spent much of his early years in his father's library, reading or listening as his father read to him from the leather-bound volumes on his shelves. Now, on the farm in Ilderton, he faced not only a strange world, but work he was not suited for, and a master who ridiculed his bewilderment and his confusion. Once, after he had been there a few months, the man shouted for him to go fetch a nail to put in a board. He went off and returned with a bag of shingle nails, whereupon the farmer yelled that he needed a two inch nail, threw the nails at him, struck him in the head, and knocked him to the ground. In time he began to fight back, and he found to his surprise that the man began to let up on him, so that for the rest of the time he spent with him they endured each other in a kind of sullen tension. But one day, after he was slow with the milking, the farmer, his eyes blazing, marched him from the barn to the pasture. There, the older man put a young farm animal to the ground, placed his knee on its side, and drew out a long, shiny knife from under his jacket. He castrated the animal. He looked up at Norman, paused a moment, and then said to him: "Sooner or later you're going to get the same thing."

School, however, was almost as painful. He wanted to go, for he was born into a studious family and he knew his father would want him there. One day in early September of that year, despite the discouragement of his employer, Norman set out for the one room school a mile away. When he arrived—a slight boy of just over eighty pounds, wearing clothes that were shabby and stained with manure—he sat alone at the back of the room for most of the day. Finally the teacher, unsure of the grade he belonged in, asked him to stand and read a passage so that she might determine his level. She handed him a book. He stood up and began to read aloud. For a moment he did not understand why, as he read, the giggles began to rise around the room. Then he caught on, and the more he read, the more the room was convulsed in laughter at the strange accent of this new boy. His face was red and his voice trembling, but he read on and finished the passage.

He went to school regularly, doing the chores before dawn and after dark, sometimes so weary in class that the teacher told him he was too weak to concentrate. A few years later, when it was time for students in that school to write exams qualifying them to enter high school, Norman was the only one in the entire school district to write the exam. He received an honours standing. But by then—old enough to be freed from his indenture and longing for a good home—he was invited to work for a family he met at the local church. In the late twenties, Norman McKinlay went to live with James and Agnes MacPherson of Ilderton, becoming in every sense but the legal one their adopted son. The MacPherson family became his family for forty years. After he left farming to become in turn a car dealer, a commercial pilot and a market analyst, he would always regard them as his parents.

Many people who knew him in the years when he was a young man wondered if he might pursue the ambition he dreamed of and become a lawyer. But in the midst of the Depression and with his personal hardships, he did not go even to high school. In the end he came back to Ilderton as if drawn by a deep sense of gratitude, to care for James and Agnes MacPherson, seeing them through their final illnesses and standing as their son beside their graves not far from the house where they made him a part of their family.

In the long history of the movement that brought children to Canada, from its beginning in 1869 to its drawn-out conclusions in the Depression thirties, no episode seemed touched with quite as much consequence as one that began very close to the end of it all, on a crisp fall evening in a room of the Broadview YMCA in a rather drab working-class neighbourhood in Toronto.

In the room that night, seated on rows of folding chairs, were some thirty young men, mostly in their late teens, obviously labourers, members of a discussion group that met weekly, often to hear a speaker. At the front of the room, seated at a plain wooden table, was the group's organizer, a man not much older than the members themselves, with straight, strong features and eyes that were blue and clear, a Y worker named Murray Ross. He welcomed the members and then in an offhand way introduced the speaker of the evening, a man from the national council of the YMCA, Richard Davis, who had just returned from a tour of Russia. Davis spoke for about thirty minutes, telling of his visits to the youth clubs in Russia and the mood he sensed in the country, and he ended by inviting questions. A few young men raised their hands and asked about wages and travel. One youth, a boy who stood out because he was so slight and so frail in appearance, began to ask, not one question but a series of them, on the theory and practice of economics in Russia, on the state of education in Russia, on the future of Russian industry. Davis, obviously struck by such a ranging intelligence in a group of boys with limited education, answered the questions and the meeting ended. Then, as the members headed toward the door, Murray Ross stopped the boy and introduced him to the speaker. His name, he told Richard Davis, was John, but everyone called him Jack.

Davis looked at him for a moment—a poorly dressed youth with a vaguely forlorn look about him—and thanked him for his questions. No, the boy said, he had not gone far in school, not even to high school. He had come to Canada as an orphan from Britain a few years earlier and worked as a farmhand and had then come to the city to do odd jobs and was, at present, working in a printing plant. Davis wished him well and turned to get his coat before leaving. Then suddenly, as if nagged by a feeling that he had not said all that he should have said, Richard Davis called out to the boy who was leaving the building and had one last word with him: "Jack, I want to tell you something. Finish school. You should go on because you're bright. If you ever want to talk about it, or take an intelligence test to see how well you might do, just let me know." The young man nodded, his expressive face curiously vague, and then he went out, alone, into the dark October night.

Six weeks later he phoned Richard Davis and asked if some day after he was finished work, he might take the test to determine if in fact he should go on to further education. The examination which was given to him a few days later by Richard Davis and Murray Ross was a standard thirty minute IQ test. He handed the test back in just over half the time allotted; every question was answered; virtually every one was correct. He was a boy of extraordinary intelligence. Ross took the test result to psychologists at the University of Toronto and was told that the boy was in the top range of the genius category, perhaps one in a million. His name was John R. Seeley; and he was to become, in the eyes of many, the most brilliant sociologist Canada ever produced.

Seeley was the son of a wealthy grain merchant in London who was away from home most of the time. His mother was a woman of personality traits best forgotten, so that his childhood was filled with great affluence and deep deprivation, an experience that would be described later in his life as a Gothic tragedy. His father, whom he loved but saw rarely, died very young, when John was only nine, and his remaining years with his mother were such that he withdrew behind the locked doors of his personality, so much so that it was felt he was retarded and suited only to work that would require little intellect. When he was fourteen, a very lonely, unhappy boy, he began to imagine that if he could only become a child of Dr. Barnardo's Homes, he would find the combination of personal freedom and emotional security for which he desperately longed. Every time he heard mention of the name Barnardo, or read of another shipload of boys heading to Canada, he dreamt of the life they were surely enjoying. But then, one day when he had just turned fifteen, he set out, walking through a London street and caught sight of a poster that was to lead him to Canada on his own. The poster showed a smiling youth, stripped to the waist, astride a load of hay and beneath, in large letters, the words: "Come to Canada, Be Your Own Boss at 21." The attraction of that promise was irresistible to Seeley. He went to Canada House, where a clerk told him that his passage would be paid, in steerage of course, provided that he accepted the farm job given him—which he knew from the shiny poster to be a ripe, golden opportunity—and stayed with farming for four years. Within a few weeks he had parted company with his mother forever, trying as much as he could to put the past behind him, and that August he landed in Quebec, not as others did, with a group of similar children destined for a common experience but by himself, alone and penniless. He was put on the train and sent to a farm in Lorneville, Ontario, a community not far from the town of Lindsay.

It may well be that no boy in the entire history of child immigration faced the depth of shock that awaited John Seeley in the summer of 1929. He who had been raised, albeit painfully, in surroundings of great wealth was met at the station by a man filthy in dress and habits, and taken to a cabin in the woods. Once it had been a serviceable log house, but now, with the cement chinking long since cracked and fallen, there were spaces between the logs, especially in the room where he would sleep, in which only tar paper separated him from the wind and the snow. He was certain at first that this man was not the farmer, that he was a hired man, and that this was not the house, that in a few days he would be taken to the large mansion where surely the gentleman to whom he had been sent would be waiting to welcome him. But after a week he realized that this shack was all there was, that this man and his mother were the people to whom he was bound. After he had been there a week, he asked as politely as he could if he might be shown the bathroom so that he might have a bath.

"Bathroom?" hooted the elderly woman. "We ain't got a bathroom. What you need a bath for? My husband lived to be an old man and he could count on the fingers of one hand the number of times he had a bath. And, son, he was a better man than you'll ever be."

His life there was filled with anguish, not because of physical cruelty, but because of its harsh contradiction: the lonely, sensitive boy writing poetry in the evening, the unthinking, illiterate farmer alternately laughing at his work and teasing him for wanting to take a bath. In time, after he had been there a few months, he went to the local Presbyterian church one Sunday morning, partly out of curiosity, partly out of a desire to escape the numbing influence of his surroundings. After the service was over, the minister, the Reverend Robert Simpson, asked him his name and spoke to him a few minutes. Quickly he saw in the boy not just the loneliness of a bereft youth, but a mind bursting with curiosity, questions, longings. He invited him to his home and they spent the afternoon talking of ethics, philosophy, and literature. John went back to Mr. Simpson's home many times and they had many conversations; he found in the older man the first adult friend he had ever had.

At the end of his first year in Lorneville, Robert Simpson helped John to move to another farm, where the family treated him well. But he was not a farmer and never would be. Late in the summer of 1930, in the deepening gloom of the Great Depression, he set out for Toronto, in the hope that there in more familiar surroundings, he might find a job, perhaps become a teacher. He found nothing. He ran out of money and was soon desperate. In September someone told him of a man living on Main Street in Toronto's east end who made doughnuts in his basement and sold them door to door, and who might give him a job. He went to the man's house and asked. "Okay," the man said, "you're on. But there's no pay. Instead, I'll give you a cot to sleep on and you can live off the doughnuts." Thus did John Seeley spend his first year in the city of Toronto. When that job ended, some people in a local congregation in east-end Toronto banded together to give him odd jobs from house to house, scrubbing floors, cleaning yards, emptying basements. Eventually he found a better job at a printing plant, but, even more important, he joined the Broadview YMCA, where, on that night in October, he was to meet Richard Davis, the man who would give his life its new and dramatic direction.

Following that day when John Seeley made his portentous score on the intelligence test, he completed high school in a matter of months working on his own. Then, with Davis's advice and support, he entered classes at the University of Chicago, where he finished his degree in only two years and began a career that was to include the famous study of suburban living based on Toronto's Forest Hill Village, Crestwood Heights, the founding of York University (where he was to be assistant to the president and head of sociology), and, in the United States, a term as dean of the Center for the Study of Democratic Institutions. He is now associate dean at a college in Los Angeles.

Sometimes, in his memory, John Seeley goes back over the experiences of his life, back through the universities and the old rooms of the YMCA, back through the east end of Toronto and out to the farm, where, in his imagination, he stands again on the hard, cold ground. More than anyone might think, he has treasured the memory of the minister who befriended him in that first year, the Reverend Robert Simpson. "I know," John Seeley has said, "that for brief times, on small scales, as far as an arm will reach, good people still do good things."

Epilogue

The funeral of Frank McLean, a farmer who lived all his life on the sweeping farmlands that spread south and west of Appin, Ontario, took place early in the afternoon on a terribly cold day in January. People had come from all over, and when the service began, there was standing room only at the Old School Baptist Church, a brown brick building located a few miles west of the village of Melbourne on Highway Number Two.

When the service in the church was at an end, the mourners came outside to stand in the churchyard until the pallbearers, his six boys, whom he had requested carry him that day, came down the steps and along the path to the open grave. His sons put the casket in its place and the family gathered round again.

Among the pallbearers that afternoon was a man who was not a son but who became one to Frank McLean. His name was Albert Wayling, and many years earlier, when his parents in Britain had died, he was placed in Dr. Barnardo's Homes and later sent to Canada. Here he was shipped from farm to farm so many times in his boyhood that he was sure he would spend the rest of his life wandering and alone. At last, in the household of Frank McLean, he found a home. Frank McLean became a father to him, and in time, to his children, a grandfather.

Now, on this day that was personal and final, he was there because he was a son. Even the affections of the McLeans, so full and sincere, were not always able to dispel his feeling that he was, at times, an outsider. Perhaps Frank McLean sensed that. For on that cold day outside the Baptist Church, standing within a family's grieving circle and sharing his own sorrow, Albert Wayling, the Barnardo boy, found himself at last where he longed to be.

Afterword

As I read these pages two decades after writing them, they raise a question that may linger permanently in my mind. It has to do with the adult lives of the men and women who are its heart. I've wondered about the cost to them in self-confidence, self-esteem and self-respect. We know now that these are not trivial things. They are essential to a healthy childhood and subsequent adult life. What did the their absence in childhood cost them?

Looking back on my meetings with many of them in the middle to late 1970s, I remember how vividly many recalled one thing: the distain they felt. Only rarely did children feel they belonged to anyone. They were foreigners. They were workers, who, on countless celebratory events, from family weddings to Christmas dinners were reminded, sometimes subtly, sometimes not, that they belonged out in the kitchen or out in the barn.

Many carried, within themselves, and reinforced by people around them, the stigma of their past. They were disdained for their background, their accent; even their dress. They provided objects for one of the least admirable traits of human beings: the need to have someone else, a lower class, to look down upon. It's all the more noteworthy that so many did so well, becoming good citizens, caring and capable parents. That is a remarkable thing.

I've been struck however, by the number of people who have written me over the years grateful as one put it, that the book is "fair to a fault to everybody." They mean, I believe, fair to the institutions that received the children in Britain and the farms they sent them to in Canada. If so, it is because I believe that both the British homes and the Canadians farmers, were expressions of ourselves, only in an earlier era. They didn't drop out of the sky. The farmers were formed by their ancestors, who are in many ways, our own ancestors. And they were shaped, at least in part, by the circumstances of the day, often hard circumstances which formed hard people.

This does not pardon the horrific forms of abuse; it does not ignore the constricted, chilly emotional world into which the children were often placed. It simply acknowledges elements that are part of the story. Too many of the families receiving children endured year-after-year failure on the land. They were often defeated by ill health, inability, or the weak, cyclical farm economy. The unfortunate children placed with them became the victims of victims.

A century after all this began, many forms of mistreatment of children, in Canada and elsewhere, still burden us. The will, perhaps the way, to protect the weakest among us from the most exploitive among us, still awaits us. In the meantime, I draw encouragement simply that the concern grows wider, stronger, year by year.

I am grateful finally for one other thing. It's my faith that the men and women whose stories you've read here, live on as do many others who are not here. They live on in the lives of those they brought into the world—children, grandchildren. Thus, through the power of memory and in other ways I cannot fully express, I deeply believe they are with us still.

Notes

1. In her Ph.D. thesis, "Dr. Barnardo and the Charity Organization Society: A Reassessment of the Arbitration Case of 1877", presented at the University of London in 1977, Gillian Wagner includes the following entry from the diary of Lord Shaftesbury, dated October 20, 1877: "Dr. Barnardo is acquitted after a fashion by the arbitrators. Is it a just acquittal? If so I rejoice. The pressure on funds is frightful. If he was guilty I lament that iniquity has triumphed. The language of the report and especially of the conclusion is like an effort of men who dare not call him innocent, and yet are zealous not to call him guilty. What will be the public response? Will he regain lost confidence? Will the money flow in? Will the reaction make him greater or less great?"

2. Mr. Watch, who began his child work in 1895, gave it up in 1901 because he was too busy as a pastor and as "social purity" editor of a publication called *The Templar*.

3. Mr. Payton, now retired in Trenton, Ontario, speaks generously of the ideals of Dr. Barnardo's Homes, but of his experience as a child immigrant on an Ontario farm he is quite restrained: "The great flaw was that most of us were denied affection entirely. There was no such thing. You were the hired boy and you were treated that way. We weren't supposed to need affection."

4. Dr. Eric Clarke, along with his distinguished father, psychiatrist C. K. Clark; participated in a study at Toronto General Hospital in 1925 which claimed that of 800 unmarried mothers studied at the psychiatric clinic, 125 were former Barnardo girls. This claim was given sensational publicity by a University of Toronto psychologist, E. D. MacPhee, who repeated it during a lecture condemning child immigration before a child welfare conference in Ottawa. But Barnardo's Canadian manager, John Hobday, and the home's honorary medical director, Albert Carless, enraged at the accusation, insisted on seeing

the list of 125 girls. They proved that fewer than 80 were former Barnardo children, that of those who were, 38 had no children at all and 22 were married women. MacPhee published a complete retraction and apology, though the harm was hard to undo.

5. Along with claiming that there was no prejudice against the children (a remark that led the *Globe* to head its report: "Children of Britain settled in Canada have fortunate lot"), the commission recommended that, in future, any youngsters emigrating to Canada be provided with long winter pants instead of "short winter pants".

Bibliography

BOOKS

Allen, Richard. *The Social Passion, Religion and Social Reform in Canada, 1914-28*. Toronto: University of Toronto Press, 1971.

Appleton, Thomas B. *Ravenscrag, The Allan Royal Mail Line*. Toronto:McClelland & Stewart, 1974.

Apramian, J. *The Georgetown Boys*. Winona, Ontario: Georgetown Armenia Boys Association, 1976.

Aries, Philippe. *Centuries of Childhood: A Social History of Family Life*. New York: Knopf, 1962.

Babcock, F. Lawrence. *Spanning the Atlantic*. New York: Alfred A. Knopf, 1931.

Barnardo, S. L., and Marchant, James. *The Memoirs of the late Dr. Barnardo*. London: Hodder and Stoughton, 1907.

Barr, James. *Fundamentalism*. London: SCM Press, 1977.

Batt, John H. *Dr. Barnardo, Foster Father of Nobody's Children*. London: S. W. Partridge, 1904.

Birt, Lilian M. *The Children's Home Finder*. London. J. Nisbet & Company, 1913.

Bready, J. Wesley. *Dr. Barnardo, Physician, Pioneer, Prophet* London: Allen and Unwin, 1930.

Cowan, Helen. *British immigration to British North America*. Toronto: University of Toronto Library, 1928.

Donovan, Frank U. *Raising Your Children, What Behavioral Scientists Have Discovered*. New York: Crowell, 1968.

Fairbridge, Kingsley. *The Autobiography of Kingsley Fairbridge*. London: Oxford University Press, 1927.

Harrison, Phyllis. *The Home Children*. Winnipeg: Watson & Dwyer Publishing, 1979.

Heasman, Kathleen. *Evangelicals in Action*. London: G. Bles, 1962.

Hodder, Edwin. *The Life and Work of the Seventh Earl of Shaftesbury*. London: Cassell & Co., 1886.

Inglis, K. S. *The Churches and the Working Class in Victorian England*. London: Routledge & Kegan Paul, 1962.

MacDonald, Norman. *Canada, Immigration and Colonization, 1841-1903*. Toronto: Macmillan of Canada, 1966.

Markham, S. F. *The Nineteen Hundreds in Stony Stratford and Wolverton*. Buckingham, England: E. N. Hillier and Sons, 1951.

Morton, W. L. *Manitoba, A History*. Toronto: University of Toronto Press, 1967.

Orr, James Edwin. *The Second Evangelical Awakening in Britain*. London: Marshall, Morgan & Scott, 1949.

Pinchbeck, Ivy, and Hewitt, Margaret. *Children in English Society*. 2 vols. London: Routledge & Kegan Paul, 1973.

Rhodes, Arnold B., ed. *The Church Faces the Isms*. New York: Abington Press, 1958.

Rose, Millicent. *The East End of London*. London: Cresset Press, 1951.

Ross, James. *The Power I Pledge (The Life of William Quarrier)*. Glasgow: The University Press, 1971.

Scholes, A. G. *Education for Empire Settlement*. London: Longmans & Company. 1932.

Splane, Richard B. *Social Welfare in Ontario, 1791-1893*. Toronto: University of Toronto Press, 1951.

Sutherland, Neil. *Children in English-Canadian Society*. Toronto: University of Toronto Press, 1976.

Tiffin, Alfred. *Loving and Sewing, The Life and Work of J. W. C. Fegan*. London: Deverell, Gibson & Hoare (undated).

Wagner, Gillian. *Barnardo* London: Weidenfeld and Nicolson, 1979.

Wallace, W. Stewart, and McKay, W. A. *The Macmillan Dictionary of Canadian Biography*. 4th ed. Toronto: Macmillan of Canada, 1978.

Webb, Sidney and Beatrice. *English Poor Law History*. London: Longmans & Company, 1910.

Williams, Gladys. *Barnardo, The Extraordinary Doctor*. London: Macmillan and Company Ltd., 1966.

Wymer, Norman. *Father of Nobody's Children*. London: Hutchinson and Co., 1954.

THESIS

Parr, Gwynth J. *The Home Children: British Juvenile Immigrants to Canada, 1868-1924* (Yale University, 1977)

NEWSPAPERS AND PERIODICALS

The value of Canadian and British newspapers and periodicals to a study of child immigration is not only as sources of fact which can be amplified by other documents, but even more as mirrors of attitudes toward the practice of certain groups of people—politicians, labour leaders, women's advocates, and so on. In this work a large number of newspapers were sampled from specific periods during which public interest in child immigration was high and could therefore be expect-ed to issue in articles and editorials. The major periods examined were 1870 to 1880, 1890 to 1910, and 1920 to 1930.

Unless otherwise noted, the Canadian publications were surveyed on microfilm held in newspaper collections in several locations: the Metropolitan Toronto Library, the Ontario Archives, the Thomas Fisher Rare Book Library at the University of Toronto, the library serv-ices of the Ontario Ministry of Community and Social Services, and the Multicultural History Society of Ontario. In addition to these, articles from the *Owen Sound Sun Times* of November and December 1894 were made available on microfilm from the Owen Sound Public Library, Owen Sound, Ontario. Other newspaper pieces from local papers in St. Thomas, Ontario, during September 1902 were provided on microfilm from the St. Thomas Public Library, St. Thomas, Ontario.

The British newspapers used in the research were studied in London at the British Library, the Barnardo Archives, or libraries at the University of London.

Canadian publications consulted: *Barrie Examiner, Belleville Sun, Brantford Expositor, Cornwall Freeholder, Glace Bay Gazette, The Globe, Guelph Daily Mercury, Halifax Evening Express* (PANS), *Hal Wax Herald* (PANS), *Hamilton Herald,* (Hamilton) *Spectator, Huntsville Forester, Kingston Whig, Lindsay Post, London Advertiser, London Free Press, The Mail and Empire, Manitoba Free Press,* (Montreal) *Gazette, Montreal Herald, Montreal Star, Niagara Falls Review, Orillia Packet,* (Ottawa) *Citizen, Ottawa Journal, Owen Sound Sun Times, Picton Times, Saskatoon Phoenix, Saturday Night, Stratford Beacon, The Telegram, Toronto Evening News, Toronto Star, Toronto World, Vancouver Sun, Walkerville Herald, Windsor Star, Winnipeg Tribune.*

British publications consulted: issues during the years 1875, 1876, and 1877 of the *East London Observer, Tower Hamlets Independent,* and *The Times.*

ARCHIVE COLLECTIONS

1. *Public Archives of Canada*

Canada, Sessional Papers, 1871-1891.

Canada, Department of Agriculture reports, 1870-1892; Department of the Interior reports, 1893-1917; Department of Immigration reports, 1918-1924.

Reports of the Proceedings of the Committee of the House of Commons on Immigration and Colonization, 1875-1885; of the Committee on Agriculture and Colonization, 1886-1889.

Court records of a trial in the county court of Grey, Ontario, in November and December 1894, following the death of George Green and the charge of manslaughter against Helen Findlay.

Report of an inquiry into the prison and reformatory system of Ontario, 1891.

Report by D. Moylan, Inspector of Penitentiaries, June 1892.

Reports in the *Manitoba Free Press*, July 1894.

Reports of Meetings of the National Council of Women, 1894-1920.

2. *Public Archives of Nova Scotia, Halifax, N.S.*

Register of children sent to Nova Scotia, 1873 to 1876, by Louisa Dirt.

Letters and reports on the life and work of J. Wimburn Laurie. *Oakfield and Its Founder*, a monograph by Margaret Laurie.

Biographies of the Masonic Grand Masters of the Jurisdiction of Nova Scotia, 1738-1965.

Halifax Herald, May 11, 1900.

Correspondence between the Honourable Edgar Rhodes, Premier of Nova Scotia, 1925-1930, and Paul
Cadbury, Birmingham, England.

Clippings and letters related to the work of the Middlemore Home, Fairview, N.S.

3. *Public Archives of New Brunswick*

Certain minutes of the Executive Council of New Brunswick, 1880-1910.

Cabinet papers, especially correspondence in 1907 and 1908 between Canada's emigration branch in

London and the Honourable C. W. Robinson and the Honourable L. J. Tweedie, Fredericton, N.B.

4. *Ontario Archives*

Annual Reports, 1893 to 1918, 1923 to 1930, by the Superintendent of Neglected and Dependent Children of Ontario.

An article, "Miss Rye's Children and the Ontario Press, 1875", by Wesley Turner, in *Ontario History*, a publication of the Ontario Historical Society, September 1976.

Several criminal indictment files dealing with charges laid in connection with immigrant children and their employers.

5. *Peterborough (Ont.) Centennial Museum Archives*

Clippings and records dealing with Hazelbrae, the distributing home in Peterborough for Dr. Barnardo's Homes.

6. *Provincial Archives, Manitoba*

Articles, letters, documents, and photographs dealing with the establishment of Dr. Barnardo's Farm, Russell, Manitoba, and his later distributing home in Winnipeg.

7. *Archives of British Columbia*

"The community of the Prince of Wales Fairbridge Farm School", a study (about 1945) by Barbara Logan, daughter of the school's first principal, H. T. Logan.

8. *British Library, London*

Report by Andrew Doyle to the President of the Local Government

Board on emigration of pauper children to Canada, Parliamentary Papers, 1875.

Letter from Maria Rye to the Local Government Board in reply to Andrew Doyle's report, Parliamentary Papers, August 1877.

Rebuttal by Andrew Doyle to Maria Rye's criticism of his report, Parliamentary Papers, 1877.

Report of the British Overseas Settlement Delegation to Canada, 1924, Parliamentary Papers, 1924.

9. *Goldsmith's Library, University of London*

"Dr.Barnardo's Homes, Startling Revelations", a pamphlet by George Reynolds.

Charity Organization Reporter, 1872-1884.

"TheBarnardo Investigation", a report of the final two days of the arbitration hearing on Dr. Barnardo's Homes September 5 and 6, 1877.

TheTimes, October 19 and 20, 1877, dealing with the award of the arbitrators in the Barnardo case.

10. *Barnardo's Archives*

Annual Reports of Dr. Barnardo's Homes, 1882 to 1905.

Night and Day, a publication edited by Thomas Barnardo, 1877 to 1905.

Ups and Downs, a publication edited by Barnardo's Canadian representatives and distributed to Barnardo boys and girls as children and adults until the mid-1940s.

Rescue the Perishing, a detailed report of Barnardo's early work at the East End Mission, London.

Something Attempted, Something Done, a major assessment of his work, including a chapter on emigration, by Thomas Barnardo, 1890.

On Our Defense, a vigorous argument on behalf of Barnardo's work by Canadian superintendent Alfred Owen (undated).

T.J. Barnardo, an adaptation from a larger work by J. Wesley Bready (undated).

"Dr.T. J. Barnardo", a brief life sketch in *Night and Day*, October 1905.

Focus on Canadian Emigration, a monograph on the work of Dr. Barnardo's Homes in Canada by the modern-day staff of Barnardo's in the publication *The Guild Messenger*.

11. *Private collections*

Articles from the library of Bert McKay, Moosomin, Saskatchewan, dealing with Dr. Barnardo's Farm, Russell, Manitoba.

Family memoirs of Reta Hind-Smith, Bexhill-on-Sea, East Sussex, England, dealing with work of Dr. Barnardo's Homes in the early 1900s, during the time her father was a member of Barnardo's council.

Hudson Taylor Papers, specifically letters dealing with Thomas Barnardo's plans to become a missionary to China, made available through Dr. A. J. Broomhall, East Sussex, England.

Materials, including *The Widow's Importunity* by J. W. C. Fegan, from the offices of Mr. Fegan's Homes, Kent, England.

Registers, records, and correspondence on Mr. Fegan's Homes, Toronto, in the possession of Victor Fry, Toronto.

A book such as this one depends heavily upon written historical sources, but in the end it draws its life from people who know the subject it treats from personal experience. All of them— those whose names appear here and those whose names are mainly in my memory— have helped to inform my attitudes and influence my judgments on the many aspects of child immigration. A number of those with whom I have talked at special length are mentioned here with my deep gratitude: William Andrews, Walter Axtell, Charles Beer, Lillian Bradley,

Mabel Carlton, William Coe, Margaret Crooks, Harold Dodham, John Dove, Eva Drain, Flora Durnin, Charles Elliott, Winnifred Frost, Victor Fry, Charles Goddard, Roy Grant, George Gregory. William Harris, Ellen Higgins, Kathleen Hobday, Emily Leader, Norman McKinlay, William Maclaren, Cant Major, Katherine Major, Nellie Merry, John Mileham, Phyllis Owen, Harry Patience, James Payton, Arthur Pope, Annie Smith, Ann Louise Stuart, Richard Todd, Alice Tomison, Horace Weir, Cyril White, Ernest Willerton, Lily Wilson, Margaret Wilson.

Index

AGMV Marquis

MEMBER OF SCABRINI MEDIA

Quebec, Canada
2001